3674

FROM THE LIBRARY OF
DONN STARRY

HEADQUARTERS, 1ST CAVALRY DIVISION
Fort Hood, Texas

July 30, 1992

The last two years have been momentous ones for the 1st Cavalry Division. They have been years of farewell and deployment, campaign and victory, training and growth. They have been years of opportunity to prove our value to the Nation. They have been years worth remembering.

Together, we have done great things. We have gone to the defense of freedom and have emerged from the crucible a stronger Army and Nation. Through the dedication and sacrifice of our families, our communities, and our soldiers, we have rekindled the flame of patriotism.

These pages will take you through a significant period in the history of our Army and Nation. You will see not just the story of an event in history, but America's sons and daughters making good the timeless pledge of President John F. Kennedy, "[W]e shall pay any price, bear any burden, meet any hardship, support any friend, oppose any foe to assure the survival and the success of liberty."

On behalf of the soldiers and families of the 1st Cavalry Division, past and present, I welcome you to our First Team.

Sincerely,

John H. Tilelli, Jr.
Major General, U.S. Army
Commanding

Cover: Modern heirs to a cavalry heritage, the 1st Cavalry Division Color Guard bears the colors of the United States, Saudi Arabia, the division and the Division Support Command during the October 28 DISCOM change of command in Assembly Area Horse. DAVE MARTIN, ASSOCIATED PRESS

Below: A 1st Brigade M1A1 races across the table top desert of the Wadi al Batin's western plain. STEVE ELFERS, ARMY TIMES

Page 4: In the soft glow of dawn, a military policeman of the 545th MP Company guards the division main command post entrance in Assembly Area Horse. J.E. PHILLIPS

Page 7: To the traditional symbols of the fallen, the inverted rifle with helmet and boots, comrades of Pfc. David M. Wieczorek have added his desert issue sunglasses, ukelele and Game Boy for a memorial ceremony on the battalion's position in Iraq, March 2. Pfc. Wieczorek, Charlie Company, TF 1-5 Cav, was mortally wounded on the morning of the ceasefire. CURTIS HOCOM

Copyright © 1992 by Taylor Publishing Company. All Rights Reserved.

Unless stated otherwise, all photos are property of the United States Army.

Published by the Taylor Publishing Company, Dallas, Texas

Jeffrey E. Phillips and Robyn M. Gregory, Authors
Jeanne T. Warren, Editor
Anita Stumbo, Typography and Layout Consultant
W. Jay Love, Coordinator

Library of Congress Cataloging in Publication Data:92-062930
Phillips, Jeffrey.
    America's First Team in the Gulf
    ISBN 0-87833-037-2 Standard Edition
    ISBN 0-87833-041-0 Limited Edition

AMERICA'S FIRST TEAM IN THE GULF

By
Jeffrey E. Phillips
Robyn M. Gregory

This book is dedicated to the soldiers and families of America's First Team, past and present.

For over seventy years these patriots have answered the challenge to safeguard liberty and democracy. With selfless devotion, they have bought justice and freedom with their own blood, the price paid as the vanguard of our Nation's principles.

Today's First Team, heir to their heritage, continues its enrichment. This is their story. It is about their call to defend freedom 10,000 miles from home in the deserts of Saudi Arabia, Iraq and Kuwait.

With all its uncertainty, sacrifice, and danger, it was a life with purpose and mission, hope and accomplishment. It was a life of comrades moving forward together, individuals bound into teams and tempered in the heat of war, as so many before them.

And as before, we remember those among us who did not return, who made the very highest sacrifice. To them, we especially dedicate this book. These fine troopers, our comrades, will live in our memory and in the legacy of the Cavalry.

The Authors

IN MEMORY

Specialist Steven D. Clark
HHC, 3-32 Armor

Private First Class Ardon B. Cooper
Co. A, 1-5 Cav

Private II Michael L. Fitz
Co. D, 27th MSB

Staff Sergeant Jimmy D. Haws
Btry. C, 4-5 ADA

Specialist James P. Heyden
Co. E, 27th MSB

Specialist David C. Hollenbeck
Co. E, 27th MSB

Corporal William Palmer
502nd MP Co.

Sergeant Ronald M. Randazzo
Co. A, 1-5 Cav

Private First Class Roger E. Valentine
Btry A, 3-82 FA

Private First Class David M. Wieczorek
Co. C, 1-5 Cav

Sergeant Scott L. Wittenburg
Co. D, 27th MSB

Sergeant First Class Harold P. Witzke III
HHC, 3-67 Armor

The loss of these gallant warriors tears at our hearts; yet we can all take great pride in their valiant stand against injustice and tyranny. Our thoughts and prayers are with the families of these true American heroes.

—H. Norman Schwarzkopf
General, U.S. Army Ret.

AMERICA'S FIRST TEAM
IN THE GULF

THE LEGACY	10
EVE OF WAR	18
INTO THE DESERT	30
RACE TO THE DEFENSE	78
DECEPTION IN THE WADI	94
TO THE EUPHRATES	126
COMING TO AMERICA	152
CONTINGENCY FORCE	164
APPENDIX	170

Garryowen I, the home of 1st Squadron, 7th Cavalry Regiment, in Assembly Area Horse, November 1990. STEVE RAYMER, NATIONAL GEOGRAPHIC SOCIETY

1 "No greater record has emerged from the War than that of the 1st Cavalry Division — swift and sure in attack, tenacious and durable in defense, and loyal and cheerful under hardship. It has written its own noble history. My personal connection with it in many moments of crisis has especially endeared it to me."

— General Douglas MacArthur

Living link to history, the division's Horse Cavalry Detachment at full gallop. With the alert in August 1990, the detachment was temporarily disbanded. Its members — regular soldiers — went to units, trading horses for armor and a charge across Texas for a race across Iraq. KILLEEN CHAMBER OF COMMERCE

THE LEGACY

The 1st Cavalry Division, in the Army's table of organization, is an armored division, the Army's heaviest. Fully modernized, the "1st Cav" can deploy quickly to crisis worldwide with over 16,500 of America's finest soldiers and the world's most deadly, state-of-the-art, land combat weapon systems. Today it is cavalry in spirit only, but that spirit runs deep.

The division was activated at Fort Bliss, in El Paso, Texas on September 13, 1921, under the National Defense Act of 1920. This Act provided for a Regular Army, a National Guard, and Army Reserves, a structure essentially unchanged today. The original organization included the 1st, 7th, 8th, and 10th Cavalry Regiments, 82nd Field Artillery Battalion (Horse), the 8th Engineer Battalion (Mounted), the 13th Signal Troop, the 27th Ordnance Company, the 1st Cavalry Division Quartermaster train, and Division Headquarters. In 1922 the 5th Cavalry Regiment replaced the 10th Cavalry Regiment and in 1933 the 12th Cavalry Regiment replaced the 1st Cavalry Regiment.

In its cavalry regiments, the new division inherited a rich tradition. Under their guidons, American cavalry fought in the Civil War and against the Arapaho, Apache, Cheyenne, and Sioux as the American West was settled. Gladys Fitch "Mother" Dorsey, the wife of the 7th Cav Commander, designed the new division's patch to reflect the cavalry heritage. On a Norman shield, in gold, the color of cavalry, is a diagonal stripe symbolizing a medieval scaling ladder and the "baldric" from which hung a sword. A horse's head, symbolizing the heart of cavalry, completed the design. It was, and remains, the Army's largest patch,

Recruits practice cross-country riding ca 1937. The riders lack sabers, which were dropped in the early '30s.

"Large enough to be seen through the dust and sand of Fort Bliss," Mother Dorsey said. "and…worn by big men who do big things."

The division's early history was largely spent in west Texas, where they patrolled against bandits, guarded the railroads, and constantly trained. These were lean years for the Army. The cavalry was the only force capable of piercing the harsh desert quickly and checking the elusive gangs that operated along the Mexican border.

During the Great Depression, the division's 3,300 troopers provided training and leadership for 62,500 members of the Civilian Conservation Corps in the Arizona-New Mexico District. Later, as many of these young men entered the armed forces, the discipline learned from the 1st Cav served them well.

By the start of the Second World War, progress had rendered the horse obsolete, evidenced by the German Blitzkrieg and Pearl Harbor. The division was equipped with some motorized transport, armored cars, a tank company and even a squadron of observation biplanes; however it continued to train as horse cavalry and impatiently awaited the summons to war. In February 1943, the division was ordered to turn in its horses and prepare for combat in the Pacific — as infantry.

In February 1944, after final training in Australia, the 1st Cav stormed the beaches of the Admiralty Islands, at the tip of the strategic Bismarck Archipelago. In fierce combat that lasted through May, the division's troopers earned a reputation for determination, skill, and courage.

In October 1944, the division went ashore at Leyte, making good Gen. MacArthur's pledge to return. They met little resistance on the beaches, but fighting stiffened as they went further inland. The enemy had orders to hold the Philippines at all costs. On Leyte and adjacent Samar, fighting remained heavy throughout 1944. As the year closed, with over 6,000 dead, the enemy capitulated to the 1st Cav.

1945 brought new orders for the battle-weary division. MacArthur directed them to "Get to Manila!" One hundred miles of rough terrain, obstacles, and enemy lay before them. Three mobile "serials" leapt forward, to be followed by the rest of the division. Called the "flying column" by Division Commander Maj. Gen. Verne D. Mudge, the serials actually averaged 15-20 mph over a difficult route, but made Manila, securing it after house to house fighting. The 1st Cav was the first U.S. unit into the capital. There, they freed 3,700 half-starved American internees at the Santo Tomas University. It was

The First Team enters Tokyo in September 1945.

As his buddy crouches, ready with another round, a cavalryman fires his M79 grenade launcher at the enemy in Vietnam.

in the Philippines that the hard-driving division earned its nickname, "The First Team."

Following the war, the division served in the occupation of Japan. Its soldiers, the first U.S. troops into Tokyo, raised over the American Embassy the flag that had flown over the Capitol Building in Washington on the day Pearl Harbor was bombed. The division stayed in Japan until 1950, and the outbreak of fighting in Korea.

Reinforcing an Army barely holding on, the 1st Cav went ashore at Pohang-dong in July in the first major amphibious operation of the war. The landing helped halt the enemy on the Pusan Perimeter, which became a virtual fortress in the vicinity north of Taegu, South Korea. On Sept. 15, MacArthur unleashed an invasion at Inchon, far behind the enemy's front. Soon after, the 1st Cav attacked from the Pusan Perimeter, fighting north to take the enemy capital of Pyongyang in October, the first Allied troops to enter the city.

It seemed the war was about over, but in October, Chinese Communist troops flooded into North Korea. Strung out by their rapid advance, American forces fell back in the paralyzing cold of a Korean winter. In the see-saw fighting that characterized the rest of the war, the 1st Cav fought tenaciously, successfully defending Seoul, recaptured by the Allies after falling in January 1951.

In December 1951, 549 days of fighting ended with the division's transfer to Hokkaido, Japan. The war dragged on until 1953 when a border on the 38th Parallel finally was established. The 1st Cav had done its part, and its troopers left proud of their role.

Duty in Japan ended abruptly in 1965, with the 1st Cav returning to Fort Benning, Georgia to be trained and equipped as an airmobile division. The concept blended the technical advance of the helicopter with the traditional mobility of cavalry. Embracing the concept, the division raced through conversion and headed for Vietnam.

The 1st Cavalry Division (Airmobile) arrived in Southeast Asia in 1965 and was in combat almost immediately as the enemy tested their new arrivals. Its first major action occurred in November when it struck an enemy stronghold in the highlands of Pleiku Province. Fierce combat ensued. Attacking into the Ia Drang valley, the 1st Battalion, 7th Cavalry landed squarely in the midst of two North Vietnamese regiments. In desperate fighting, with the 1st Cav taking heavy losses, the enemy was decisively beaten and the 1st Cav blooded and proven. The heroic, successful campaign earned the division the Presidential Unit Citation, the first awarded for action in Vietnam.

Taking the high ground, Skytroopers make a combat air assault on terrain overlooking the A Shau Valley.

From Pleiku, the division's "Skytroopers" continued their war of lightning movement into Vietnam's most inaccessible reaches to fight an enemy that quickly grew to fear the approaching chop of helicopter blades. Once located, the enemy was rocketed and shelled, while "Air Cav" gunship helicopters enveloped him, cutting off escape routes. Meanwhile, airmobile infantry landed to clean him out, supported by gunships firing from above.

The division continued fighting. It helped defeat the Tet '68 offensive, then broke the siege of the Marines at Khe Sanh Airbase and cleared the A Shau Valley stronghold. In May 1970, the division attacked into Cambodia, destroying enemy sanctuaries there, another First Team first. This was the division's final major action before returning home. In March 1971, the 1st Cav stood down from combat (less its 3rd Brigade, which remained another year), its record a proud one: the first division into Vietnam and one of the last to leave.

After 28 years, the First Team returned to Texas, its birthplace. Located at Fort Hood in central Texas, the division was reorganized as the Army's first "triple capability" (TRICAP) division. Comprising an armor brigade (1st Brigade), an air cavalry brigade (2nd Brigade), and an air mobile brigade (3rd Brigade), the division tested combined arms operations. The test resulted in the formation of the separate 6th Cavalry Brigade (Air Combat) at Fort Hood in 1975. That year, the end of TRICAP brought

King of the road, First Team armor in northern Germany during REFORGER '83.

the 1st Cav a new identity: reorganization as an armored division, essentially the configuration it retains.

In the opening chapter of a story which climaxed on the battlefields of Kuwait and Iraq, the division was chosen to field test the new XM-1 tank in 1980. At the same time, the division shed its weary M551 Sheridan armored reconnaissance airborne assault vehicles for M60 tanks.

In the fall of 1983, the division deployed to Europe for the 15th annual Return of Forces to Germany (REFORGER) exercise. No stranger to Germany, the division had contingency plans for its reinforcement as part of NATO and twice before had sent elements of the 2nd "Blackjack" Brigade on the wargames; however, REFORGER '83 was the division's greatest deployment since Vietnam. A real test of equipment war stocks, it also marked the first REFORGER led by the Dutch, the First Team being the first U.S. division deployed to Holland since WWII. It was, therefore, an opportunity to show not just warfighting prowess, but international goodwill and cooperation, all skills the First Team would use in war within a decade.

The exercises were successful. Four years later, the 1st Cav deployed on REFORGER '87 with the 2nd Armored Division and other units sharing Fort Hood, nearly emptying the post's military community for six weeks. With the Warsaw Pact's decline, the size of REFORGER troop deployments was reduced, but command and control elements continue to "recon" war stocks, develop plans, and maintain contact with their opposite numbers, ensuring readiness should deployment be necessary.

The division thrived at Fort Hood. There it gradually assumed the organization it would take to the Gulf: two maneuver brigades, the 1st "Ironhorse" and 2nd "Blackjack;" the Aviation Brigade of reconnaissance troops and helicopters, and attack and utility helicopters; the Division Artillery (DIVARTY) with self-propelled 155mm howitzers, rockets, and counter-battery radar; the Division Support Command (DISCOM), with the division's logistic support; and the separate battalions and companies — the 8th Engineers; 13th Signal; 4th Battalion, 5th Air Defense Artillery; 312th Military Intelligence; 68th Chemical Company; 545th Military Police Company; and a band second to none. The First Team, jealous of its roots, kept a ceremonial horse cavalry detachment, officially equipped in authentic frontier uniforms and equipment, and drilled to the 1885 Army Cavalry Manual.

The new XM-1 tank was accepted, named the M1 Abrams, and issued throughout the division. It was followed by the Bradley M2 infantry and M3 cavalry fighting vehicles (BFV and CFV). The division fielded the multiple launch rocket system (MLRS) and the AH-64 Apache with its Hellfire guided missile. The old unreliable "GOER" and beloved, but obsolete "jeep," bowed to the Heavy Expanded Multi-purpose Tactical Truck (HEMTT), and the High Mobility Multi-purpose Wheeled Vehicle (HMMWV) — the "Humvee" — both trucks proving invaluable in the Gulf.

Systems for command and control of the First Team made quantum leaps. Falling in step with technology, the division fielded Mobile Subscriber

The legacy of cavalry — Mirror image of his 1885 counterpart, the Horse Cavalry Detachment bugler awaits the charge.

Equipment, essentially cellular phones both for "fixed" sites and for vehicle use. MSE complemented FM radio, the traditional means of communications.

All of this equipment saw hard use in training at Fort Hood and in rotations to the National Training Center (NTC) at Fort Irwin in California's Mojave Desert. By the late '80s the NTC was the Army's pre-eminent training arena. There maneuver brigades faced a "Warsaw Pact" enemy, portrayed by soldiers who fought better than those they mimicked! The division made the most of the NTC, in 1989 and 1990 deploying its Apaches and MSE systems for an integrated workout with its Abrams and Bradleys. The lessons they brought home could not have come at a more propitious moment.

2 "The Security Council...condemns the Iraqi invasion of Kuwait; demands that Iraq withdraw immediately and unconditionally all its forces to the positions in which they were located on 1 August 1990; calls upon Iraq and Kuwait to begin immediately intensive negotiations for the resolution of their differences and supports all efforts in this regard and especially those of the League of Arab States..."

— United Nations Resolution 660

Loading around the clock at the Barbours Cut Terminal, the Port of Houston in September, the USNS Capella as seen from the upper deck of the Saudi-registered Saudi Abha, itself taking on 1st Cavalry Division cargo. BRITT TOALSON

EVE OF WAR

In late July 1990, the 1st Cavalry Division was conducting business as usual at Fort Hood and was well into its customarily heavy summer schedule. Training on the post's 217,000 acres always seemed to be busiest between May and October, when the mercury topped 90 and, except for the occasional violence of an evening thunderstorm, rain ceased. The summer of 1990 was shaping up to be typical.

Since 1974, after its return from Vietnam, the 1st Cav had focused on the reinforcement of NATO in Europe. Like much of the Army, the division's vehicles were dark green to blend with Germany's forests and fields. Over time spanning two generations of soldiers, the Army had developed intricate plans: If war threatened, U.S.-based troops — Fort Hood's among them — would fly into Europe, draw pre-positioned equipment and face off against the legendary Warsaw Pact. Most headquarters knew down to the barn and gasthaus where they would set up shop, down to the field and woodline where their tanks would first meet the enemy.

As summer deepened, the division staff was busy planning a routine commanders' reconnaissance in West Germany near the eastern border, unaware that in days their orientation would change profoundly.

While the division staff planned, the 2nd "Blackjack" Brigade prepared for its deployment to the National Training Center (NTC) in the Mojave Desert of Fort Irwin, CA, one of three scheduled month-long rotations for the division each year. The 1st "Ironhorse" Brigade had trained there in May 1990. Perhaps the Army's finest maneuver training resource, with its vast area and Warsaw Pact look-alike Opposing Force, the NTC challenged units as no other training could. Non-stop battles drove them into numbing round-the-clock operations. The slightest tactical error could cost an entire battalion. It was a crucible. Commanders called it the pinnacle of their tour; soldiers declared it the closest thing to combat without bullets. Fort Irwin was considered the Army's greatest classroom, and while its desert bore little surface resemblance to Europe, its lessons were considered wholly applicable to combat there.

The division's intelligence staffs watched the Conventional Forces Europe agreements and the dazzling convulsions of Eastern Europe with a world lulled by peace and an end to the 45-year-old Cold War. Though events in the Middle East were being tracked, with history unfolding in Europe they did not command a high priority…

Across Fort Hood, victim of a shrinking budget and a faltering enemy, the 2nd Armored Division had inactivated one armored brigade; its remaining brigade, the 1st "Tiger" Brigade would — after 45 years of peace — quietly disappear in September. The loss depressed morale. Many could not understand why the historic "Hell on Wheels" division — Patton's own — was chosen for inactivation. Local communities deeply feared the effect of 12,000 fewer soldiers (and their families) on their economies.

At 2:00 a.m. local time on August 2, with the world looking the other way, Saddam Hussein moved. Within 48 hours his tanks penetrated to Kuwait's southern border. His troops began sacking the capital unopposed. The Kuwaiti armed forces had melted before the heat of his lightning assault.

President George Bush responded immediately. The day of the invasion, he authorized the freezing of all Iraqi assets held in the U.S. On August 6, the United Nations, in U.N. Resolution 661, imposed economic sanctions against Iraq. That day, at the request of King Fahd, Bush ordered U.S. armed forces into the Gulf to help defend Saudi sovereignty.

At 12:50 a.m. Greenwich Mean Time, August 7, Gen. Edwin Burba, Commander-in-Chief, Forces Command, controlling all forces in the continental U.S., issued a deployment order for Southwest Asia operations. Immediately, Lt. Gen. Richard Graves, Commander, III Corps and Fort Hood, alerted the 1st Cavalry Division and, three days later, the Tiger Brigade for deployment. The summer of 1990 changed irrevocably.

Brigadier General John H. Tilelli Jr. learned of the alert just before leaving for the annual 1st Cavalry Division Association Reunion, held in Columbus, GA. That morning, at 5:00 a.m., Division Chief of Staff Col. Leon LaPorte briefed him on the staff's proposal for a training program. Tilelli approved.

To the 1,000 veterans gathered at Columbus, the scent of war was familiar. Rumors flew. Tilelli, in command of the division since July 20, felt the close scrutiny of veterans of three wars and 70 years. He could say nothing. At 10:00 a.m. on the 7th, he was scheduled to deliver the annual "State of the Division Address," a review of the past year and synopsis of what lay in store for the division. The address was typically the reunion's climax. This year the atmosphere was electric. Calmly, Tilelli faced a packed hall. To the dramatic accompaniment of slides and stirring music, he made his presentation, omitting mention of the alert. As the program ended to the last notes of Lee Greenwood's "God Bless the USA," Tilelli thanked the audience, now standing in emotional applause. Then with Command Sergeant Major Robert Wilson, he strode out to a waiting airplane and a division already in motion. Behind him, still on their feet, some in quiet tears, 600 veterans knew that once again history had grasped their First Team.

Plans called for the division to deploy within 40 days, by September 15. The work day was extended to 14, 16, and even 24 hours. Light bathed Fort Hood's motorpools, banishing the night. The work week lengthened to seven seamless days. Bound by security, soldiers could tell their families little, but could not hide emotion from each other: one captain, caught up in the drama, exclaimed his hopes for a combat patch to Lt. Col. David Neyses, division deputy chief of staff. He referred to the Army practice of wearing on the right shoulder the patch of the unit one had gone into combat with. Neyses, a veteran of combat in Vietnam, replied in a voice edged with foreboding that he might just get his combat patch.

The division was to deploy after the 3rd Armored Cavalry Regiment (ACR), stationed at Fort Bliss near El Paso. The 3rd ACR was now enroute, along with the 24th Infantry Division, preparing to load at Savannah, GA. That allowed the 1st Cav 12 precious days for a final training surge. On August 13, the train-up began. Directed by the division commander, each soldier zeroed and qualified with his individual weapon and solemnly underwent training in nuclear/biological/chemical (NBC) warfare. Emerging from the gas chamber, soldiers realized the next chemicals they encountered might not cause mere tears.

Day and night, the pop of small arms fire and the crump of big guns erupted from over 30 ranges ringing Fort Hood. With the exception of the Multiple Launch Rocket System, which would prove chillingly effective nonetheless, every weapon system in the division was fired. Every tank and Bradley crew went through a series of engagements designed to test their skill as an individual crew and as part of a platoon of four coordinated weapons. Some engagements approached 2,500 meters; few could have predicted the near-4,000 meter kills that some crews would make in Kuwait and Iraq.

For two weeks, the thud of heavy artillery rattled windows through the night for miles in every direction. A year later, after the division had returned and resumed gunnery training, a local politician was asked if the gunfire bothered residents. "No," he replied. "What bothered us was the *lack* of it for so long!"

If soldiers were busy training, the division's logisticians were busier. They too were faced with readying themselves for deployment; they also had the mission of supporting the training everywhere around them and preparing the division for sustained operations in the desert. Ten thousand pieces of equipment had to be painted desert sand — and some repainted, as one shipment of paint turned out to be decidedly pink when it dried. To complicate matters, the paint carried a toxic compound making it resistant to chemical weapons. Soldiers applying it wore elaborate respirators and were constantly monitored. The assembly line operation was highly organized, with combat vehicles the first to be painted. But even with vehicles rolling out of six booths 24 hours a day for six weeks, a few still went to the desert wearing European forest green.

As each unit concluded its training surge, a feverish binge of maintenance began. Every piece of equipment had to be operational before it was shipped. Vehicle track with fewer than 300 miles useful life was replaced, as were tank guns with a service life of fewer than 150 rounds. Blurring lines of responsibility, mechanics and crewmen worked together, replacing all lubricants and filters, and checking, tightening, and retightening every nut and bolt. Tank crewmen accustomed to regarding their 60-ton M1 Abrams as simply the vehicle they took to the range, now realized the sober reality: they might well go to war in this machine; their survival depended on it working.

Following the alert, soldiers pitched into intense training, making the most of the weeks left before departure. Every soldier fired his personal weapon, tested his protective mask, and attended classes on subjects from personal finance to Arab etiquette and enemy order of battle.
1st Cav PAO

Since Vietnam, the Army had relied on a recruiting strategy that emphasized the educational benefits of service. The financial gains, travel, and work experience were touted in an effort to get solid recruits. Many young men and women had somehow missed the fundamental point that soldiering meant the possibility of one day going to war — real, perhaps deadly, war. As America reached the last decade of the 20th century, that just didn't strike a lot of folks as possible. Only it was. And for more than one young soldier the stark truth was horrifying.

In the midst of training, painting, and maintaining, the division's soldiers drew a special issue of desert clothing and equipment. It included two sets of desert camouflage uniforms ("DCUs"), a desert pattern helmet cover and soft "boonie" cap; rucksack cover (frequently used to cover the M16A2 rifle); flak jacket and desert pattern cover; neckerchief; goggles; sunglasses; two pair of Vietnam-era jungle boots (the tan suede models got to the division in March — in time for the flight home); a two-quart canteen; poncho-liner; and a night desert parka and trousers in a bizarre light and dark green grid pattern. All this was stuffed into duffle bags to be packed deliberately later (and repacked as packing lists changed). Finally, each soldier drew two green foil packs the size of small pillows: chemical suits, with gloves and boots. These they handled with great care…

With all its equipment, the Army is people-intensive. Each soldier sat through hours of classes

(Above right) Having completed a mask confidence exercise, reassured soldiers emerge into Fort Hood's August sun. Aware of Iraq's past use of chemicals, soldiers took chemical defensive training earnestly.

(Right) A convoy of 27th Main Support Battalion 5,000 gallon fuel tankers assemble before moving to Fort Hood's railhead for the trip to Houston and the port.

One of 10,000 pieces of equipment painted, a HMMWV gets a coat of sand color paint. The paint was made to withstand the corrosive effect of chemical agents and decontaminants. Amusing some soldiers and horrifying others, one batch of paint had a distinctly pinkish hue.

Departure imminent, soldiers tie down vehicles on railcars at Fort Hood's railhead.

(Below) Soldiers replace dog tags, make out wills and update records and vaccinations in preparation for overseas movement.

Equipment loaded on the USNS Mercury, at Houston.

on desert survival, and customs and courtesies in the Gulf (never, NEVER show the sole of your boot to an Arab; an insult of awesome dimensions). Each soldier's personal affairs must be handled individually. Wills, powers of attorney, pay allotments, insurance, new ID "dog" tags, and — inevitably — vaccinations are brought up to date one soldier at a time. Desert Shield's deployment was no different. In crowded, stifling gyms across post, soldiers, some buoyant with bravado, some somber, assembled to prepare for overseas movement. While dog tags were meant to be worn around the neck, each soldier wore one threaded onto a boot lace; no one had to ask why.

There was little bravado among the families who were destined for the toughest challenge: to wait at home. With quiet courage and determination, they coalesced into support groups. Made frighteningly clear by the media, the potential casualty rates were appalling; support was critical. Sponsored by the division's commanders, each unit had its chain of concern, a less formal parallel to the unit chain of command. Commanders, most with their own families, knew that the last concern a soldier entering combat needed was one for his family's welfare. Volunteer spouses in each unit's chain served to speed information to the unit's spouses and get help to families in need.

Weeks before the first flight left, support groups began coaxing information through the networks of spouses. For the entire deployment, the division's rear detachment, staffed with officers and sergeants, functioned as an information center. It was a place for families to go for support of every conceivable type, whether they needed medical care or merely to dispel a rumor (one had the soldiers under enemy fire as they tried to offload ships at the Saudi port, another maintained that the instant a soldier's mouth opened to speak, it was mobbed by flies).

In early September, it was obvious that the First Team wasn't going to be deployed by September 15. Still ferrying the 3rd ACR and the 24th Infantry Division, the ships just weren't available. Anxiously watching the news for signs of an Iraqi assault into Saudi Arabia, a push that must succeed against the desperately light 82nd Airborne Division, the division waited its turn.

In mid-September, it came. Over 800 heavy vehicles loaded at Fort Hood made the trip to Houston and Beaumont by rail. Over 4,200 wheeled vehicles rolled in interminable convoys that left every few hours around the clock. As the convoys, headlights blazing, made their 10-hour journey to the ports, they passed crowds all along the way, on roadsides and overpasses, cheering and waving flags. They could not know that six months later, their

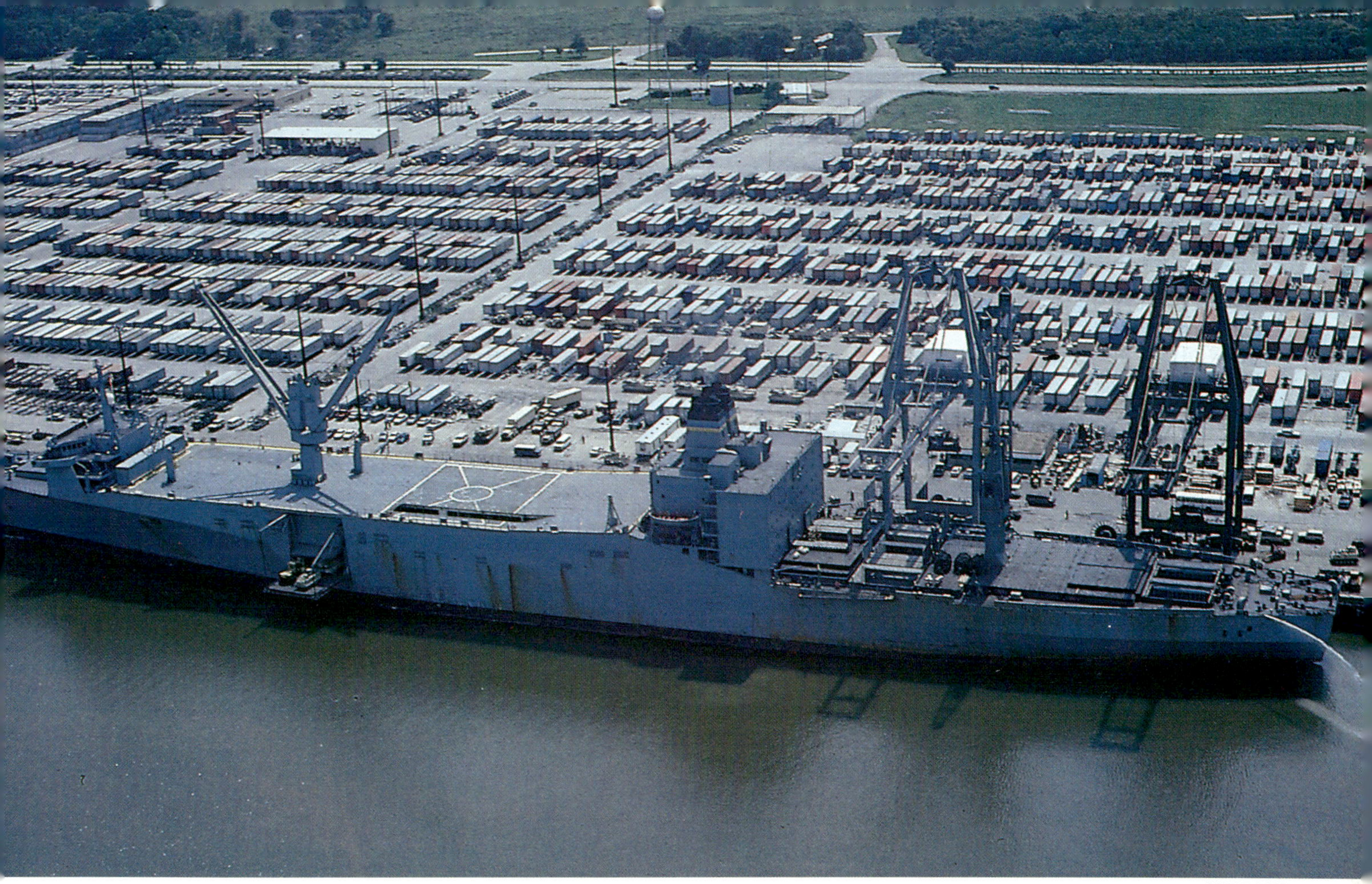

BRITT TOALSON

The USNS Capella, a fast sealift ship capable of 33 knots, prepares to load. A roll-on, roll-off (RORO) vessel, it could be quickly loaded with over 700 vehicles and represented the Navy's most modern sealift.

(Below) Nearing its destination, a convoy passes by Houston on the way to the port, where a ship taking it to the Saudi port of ad Dammam, on the kingdom's eastern coast, waits.

BRITT TOALSON

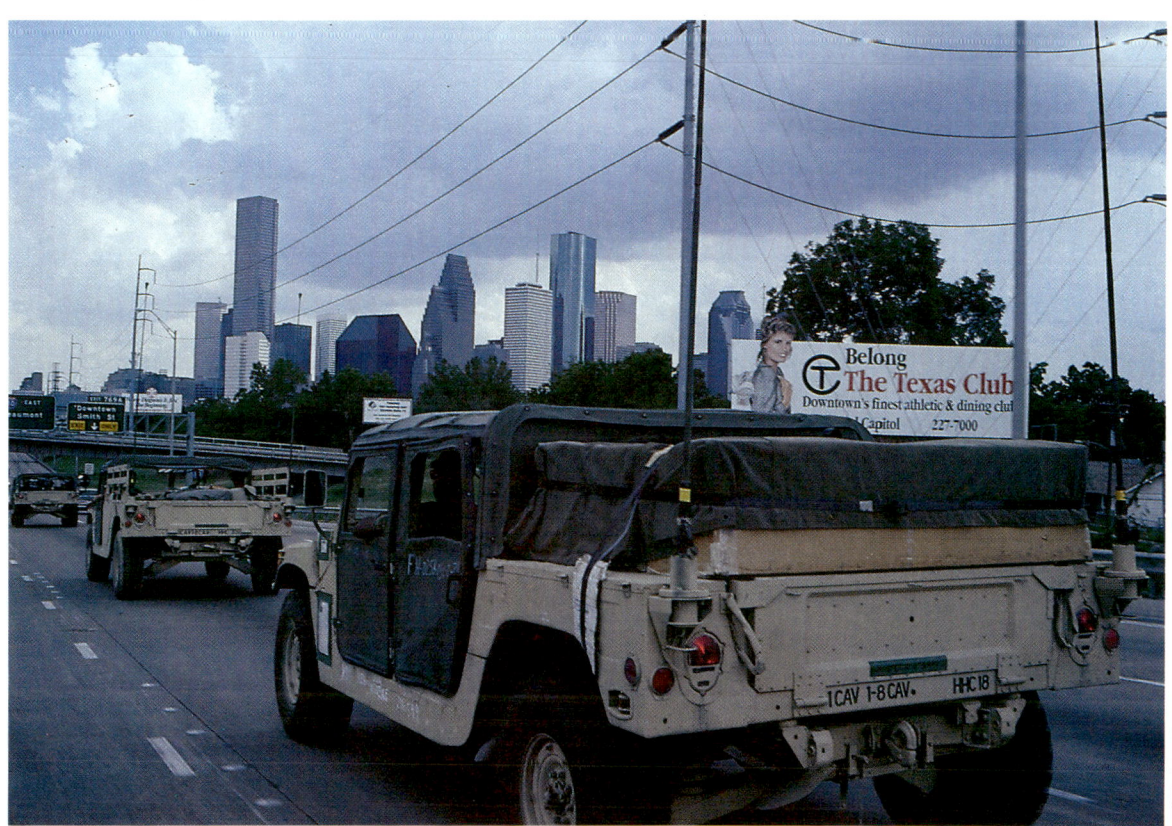

A display of confidence at Robert Gray Army Airfield.

welcome home would eclipse this heartwarming farewell.

At the port, civilian stevedores took over, driving tanks and trucks onto the great ships. Entire battalions disappeared into the cavernous holds. Packed inches apart, the armored vehicles that would soon subdue the world's fourth largest army looked puny. It took 17 vessels, among them the Navy's Fast Sealift Ships, each carrying 700 vehicles, to get the First Team's equipment through the Suez Canal into Saudi Arabia's eastern port of ad Dammam. The voyage averaged 11 days. On each ship a small contingent of soldiers along for the journey, called "supercargo," accounted for the cargo checking for bad batteries, leaks, and damage. Treated to shipboard comforts and a fairly leisurely passage, their deployment was a far cry from the airlift that had begun at Fort Hood.

The tranquility of Fort Hood's Robert Gray Army Airfield, aside from the ceaseless darting of dragonfly Apache attack helicopters and occasional visits from Air Force C-141 transports, belies the presence of a 10,000 foot runway and state-of-the-art air traffic control systems. On September 16, all tranquility vanished with the first departing flight. Curving east, an impossibly big Air Force C5A Galaxy carried the division's advance headquarters and assistant division commander for maneuver, Brig. Gen. Tommy Franks. Franks and his team were to set up at the port of Dammam, establish contact with

Media deluged Fort Hood during the deployment. Largely supportive throughout the crisis, they welcomed soldiers returning from the war, one radio station airing arrival updates from crowd-lined "Victory Corner," where soldier-filled busses passed enroute to anxiously waiting families. Here, the author on camera at Robert Gray Army Airfield as troops depart.

Getting in a little summer reading, a soldier waits for the bus to the airfield, sitting against some of the 26,000 personal hygiene comfort packs provided by local communities and given to each departing Fort Hood soldier.

XVIII Airborne Corps, and receive the 17,000 cavalry soldiers soon to follow on 51 flights through mid-October.

In the final drama played out before departure, soldiers assembled for manifest roll call in the division's gyms — where they'd played basketball, worked out, and only days before, sworn out wills and winced through injections of gamma globulin. Families accompanied them and waited outside along a cordon. Some tried to manage noisy uncomprehending children, some wept quietly, others were dumb with shock. As the roll was called, soldiers emerged, sweating in their stiff new DCUs. Here they said goodbye; busses would carry them from the gyms to Robert Gray. There, they would walk past the 1st Cav's band and TV cameras, straight to a waiting jumbo jet. The families could drive 10 minutes to a low knoll overlooking the runway to wave them off. Some did. Others couldn't bear it.

Outside the gyms, families gathered in knots, offering final whispered promises, little gestures of confidence, and then the moment had come. The busses pulled up, the plane was in; a last embrace and the time for nurtured memories had begun.

Soldiers board a B747 activated as part of the Civil Reserve Air Fleet, one of 117 civil aircraft that served the CRAF airlift in its first-ever use.

Farewell.

3 "Dear soldiers,
I hope you don't dei (sic). When are you going to come back. I hope you guys come back soon. I am in the thied (sic) grade. try to win the war. I am doing fine. How are you guys doing. fight Iraq good. I hope you guys have fun."

— Brittney Ingersol
Downey Elementary School
Downey, Idaho

Pulling guard duty in 3-82 Field Artillery. J.E. PHILLIPS

INTO THE DESERT

As the autumn of 1990 wore on, economic sanctions and threats of military action appeared to have little effect on Saddam Hussein. He remained in Kuwait, steadily increasing his forces and spoiling for a fight. Prefabricated bunkers, over 400, were shipped into Kuwait by mid-October. The Iraqis deepened their front, typically stacking two light infantry divisions behind a highly mobile armored or mechanized infantry division. Between these divisions, extensive obstacle belts of mines and earthen ridges called "berms" developed. In front of all this, it appeared the Iraqis were digging trenches and filling them with oil.

In the blistering desert, anxious troops of the XVIIIth Airborne Corps prepared for the nightmare of an attack into their desperately thin line. Their defense of Saudi Arabia seemed little more than a speedbump on the road to Riyadh.

Forty-thousand feet below their wings, the Red Sea gave way to land and 1st Cav soldiers peered out at the unbroken moonscape passing beneath them. Saudi Arabia, even from seven miles up, looked forbidding and it looked big.

Jumbo jets, drawn from U.S. airlines on the activation of the Civil Reserve Air Fleet in August, brought the soldiers over Europe and on to the Middle East. Their crews were volunteers who lavished attention on their passengers. In exchange for good cheer, access to the cockpit, and a ceaseless flow of food, they won unit emblems, crests, and rank insignia, all immediately and proudly pinned on. As the descent into Dhahran International Airport began, it was unclear whose anxiety was greater — the soldiers about to disembark, or the crews who would leave hoping to return soon, and bring them home.

LINDA CHRIST

"A few days after I got to the port (of ad Dammam) we had an inspection and a sergeant measured the distance between cots with a 12-inch ruler," one soldier recalled of Pegasus warehouse complex. In early October, troops pouring in pushed the port's facilities to their limits — and beyond, necessitating a nearby "tent city." The desert was a relief by comparison.

When the cabin door opened, whether it was night or day, the heat slammed in. Reflecting later, a soldier said, "I don't think I ever got used to the heat, so much as I got used to being miserable in it." As they emerged into the heat, they were flooded with sensations: the first sight of an Arab in red and white checked headdress; from nowhere, a band playing (the division's, split into a group playing for departures and a group for arrivals); the first drop of sweat trickling down the small of their backs… After a quick stop at a dusty tent to collect a one-liter blue plastic bottle of water, busses whisked the arrivals off to a place called ad Dammam and a home called "the warehouse." Inside the dusty busses, soldiers opened their water and took their first pull. The water was warm. They'd have to get used to that, too.

Pegasus Complex, eight metal warehouses on the water's edge in the port of ad Dammam, housed the 1st Cav's billets and headquarters. Even with 1,000 cots shoehorned into each warehouse, 12 inches apart, eight were not enough. Nearby, in "Ironhorse City" — aptly renamed "Tent City" — 3,000 more cavalrymen lived under canvas.

Troops arriving at Pegasus spent two days, essentially work-free, acclimatizing to the time difference, the stifling heat, and the humidity. That

An M2A1 Bradley fighting vehicle is hoisted gently off the USNS Pollux in the Port of Dammam (ad Dammam).

While morale remained high in the 1st Cav, anxiety rooted in uncertainty peaked in November. The announcement of VII Corps' deployment ended doubts and stiffened resolve; the Army would go home when the job was done. Here, Army Chief of Staff Gen. Carl E. Vuono visits the 1st Cav at ad Dammam in October.

done, leaders were off to the desert to inspect their slice of the division's assembly area. Soldiers began training with their rifles, protective masks, and whatever other equipment had accompanied them on the plane. Blindfolded weapons assembly was a favorite challenge. Choruses of chanting broke the dawn each morning as units took up physical training. Maps went out. Areas for which no maps existed were represented by blank paper overdrawn with the military grid system. It mattered little; few features stood out in this desert.

Living at Pegasus required a certain amount of technique. Here in the sauna of ad Dammam sprouted the adaptability that would blossom in the wastes of the desert. With privacy nonexistent in

The arrival of the German-made Fox nuclear/biological/chemical agent detection vehicle brought rejoicing in the 68th Chemical Company. Six Foxes, capable of detecting chemical agents with the crew safely inside, were sent from the 3rd Armored Division in Germany.

these huge coed "dorms," dressing took place under one's poncho liner. An emptied case of Meals, Ready to Eat (MRE) could be fashioned into a functional drawer, placed under the cot. Empty water bottle cases, when stacked, became company orderly "room" walls. The band even performed concerts. None of this changed the fact that from the moment a soldier arose, to the final relief of sleep, he was bathed in sweat, orbited by flies or mosquitoes (or both), and tormented by boredom and the hell of too-fresh memories of home.

Time spent at Pegasus was mercifully short. Units saw their ships arrive within two weeks. Once completely off-loaded, they headed west with antici-pation for a place said to be blessed with dry air and space to stretch out: It was called Assembly Area Horse, over 150 kilometers into the desert.

Getting to AA Horse was not to be easy. Equipment was loaded onto flatbed trucks, called heavy equipment transports (HETs), not all military. The heavy transport requirement had overtaxed the Army's transportation capabilities and it had contracted locally, much as it might have in a European war.

The HETs were formed into great convoys, led by well-briefed officers holding manifests, schedules, and maps — identical to the convoys that snaked from Fort Hood to Houston only weeks before.

Identical except for one detail: in the cabs of these trucks were locally contracted drivers wholly unconcerned with the protocol of an Army convoy. They saw no need to conform to rules that kept them from stopping to pray when they felt called, eating at a favored roadside stop, or taking a shortcut. Within miles — sometimes yards — of the port, many convoys were stricken with maverick departures to the horror of the young officers leading them. Inevitably, the errant trucks were found and shepherded home, or just turned up according to their own schedule.

By October 29, the last units left Pegasus for their new home. Assembly Area Horse was a patch of naked desert broken by rolling hills and dunes, wadis and jagged ravines, and isolated buttes standing sentinel. It also was a bustling frontier community of 17,000 souls, divided horizontally into brigade sections. The 1st Brigade occupied the north, 2nd Brigade the center, and Tiger Brigade the south. The Division Support Command (DISCOM), with the division's logistic support, occupied the southeast corner with the Aviation Brigade. Artillery battalions stayed near the brigades they habitually supported. On the northern border, the 1st Squadron, 7th Cavalry Regiment screened against incursion: in October, Saudi Arabia was not a secure place. The mission was to defend the Kingdom; talk of an Allied offensive was virtually nonexistent. Should the Iraqis attack, the First Team was to counterattack through

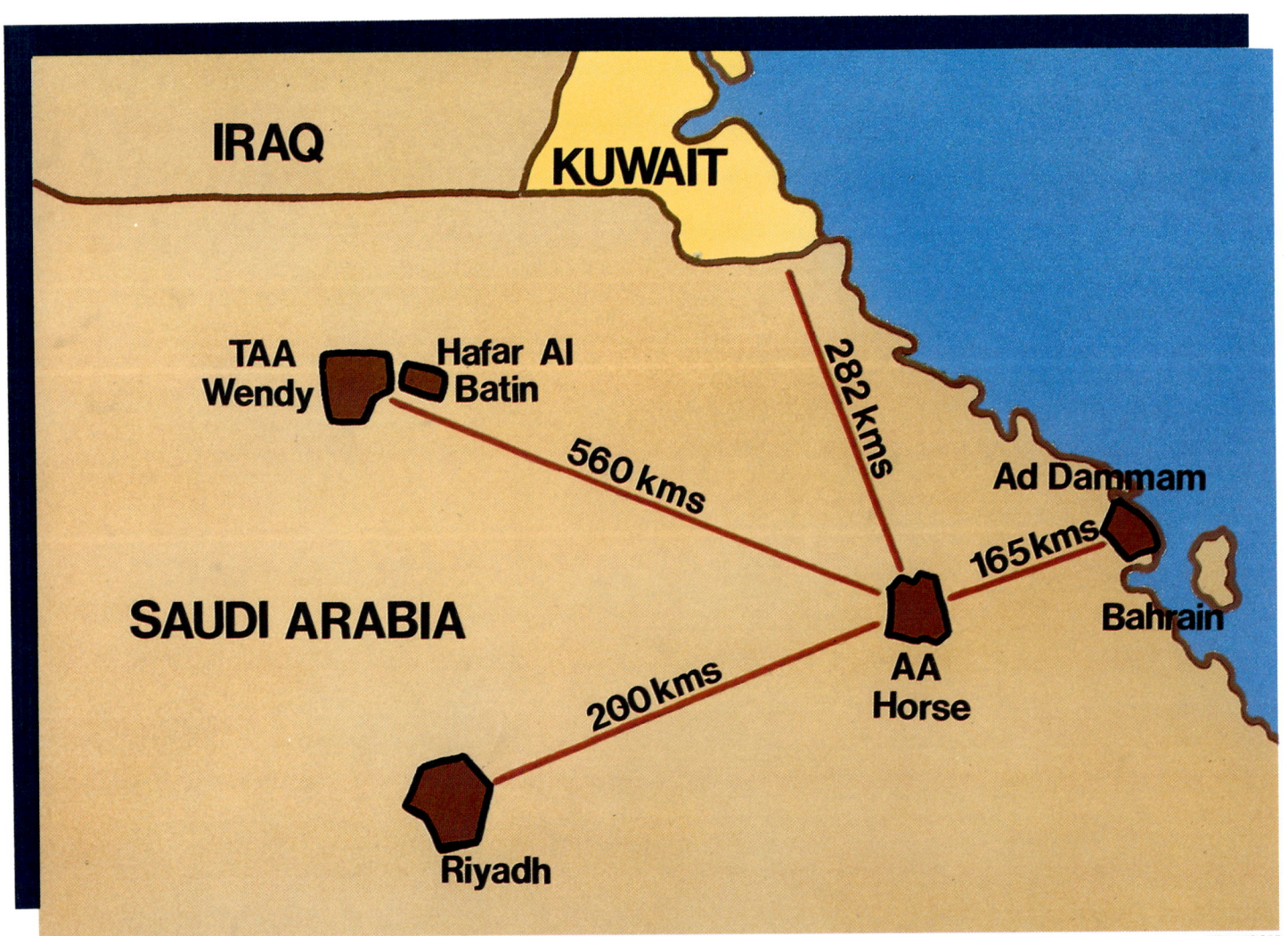

DESERT HOME: First Team's Area of Operations.

DON MOORE

Eyeing his driver, an escort soldier prepares for an adventure — riding into the desert in a convoy manned by locally contracted labor. Virtually fearless, the drivers delighted in passing on congested, crumbling roads at breakneck speed, while carrying the division's heaviest armored vehicles.

Over anything but relatively short, tactical movements, tracked vehicles moved by heavy equipment transports. Here, new M1A1s roll from the port to AA Horse on Army transports.

the defending American 24th Infantry Division into the heavily armored Republican Guard. In October 1990, with 27 enemy divisions identified in Kuwait, that alone seemed ambitious enough.

Scattered in olive and tan clusters throughout AA Horse, the battalions, companies, and platoons settled in. Each battalion formed a nearly self-contained community. It was connected to the rest of the division by invisible microwave communications links, commanders scuttling back and forth to meetings, and the daily supply convoys carrying food, fuel, spare parts, and mail — at first an agonizing trickle; by December, an overwhelming torrent. Each unit cluster mounted guards, primarily against terrorists, but scorpions and venomous desert vipers turned out to be a more serious threat. Everyone seemed to have a story about a snake materializing at his feet, or a scorpion climbing into his cot. The good news about the viper was that it preferred solitude and once provoked, allegedly had to "chew" its venom in, however, the scorpion offered no such solace.

Sand, an enemy more insidious than an occasional scorpion, proved the real threat. Desert Shield was literally awash in it. From the moment soldiers stepped onto Saudi soil, they sank into its dust. For the first — but not last — time, they watched the talcum powder explosion around their ankles.

The desert of AA Horse was loose sand. It could whip up in a good breeze, turning the air a grey, gritty fog. Sand and dust got everywhere. Soldiers learned quickly to roll sleeping bags up each morning, cover radios, and put away anything valuable — if they didn't, by evening, it was coated.

Far from a mere nuisance, grit chewed away at equipment. Helicopter turbine engines, normally flushed with cleansing water every 50 hours, were cleaned after each flight. Computers, totally out of their element, choked on grit. The grease on weapons

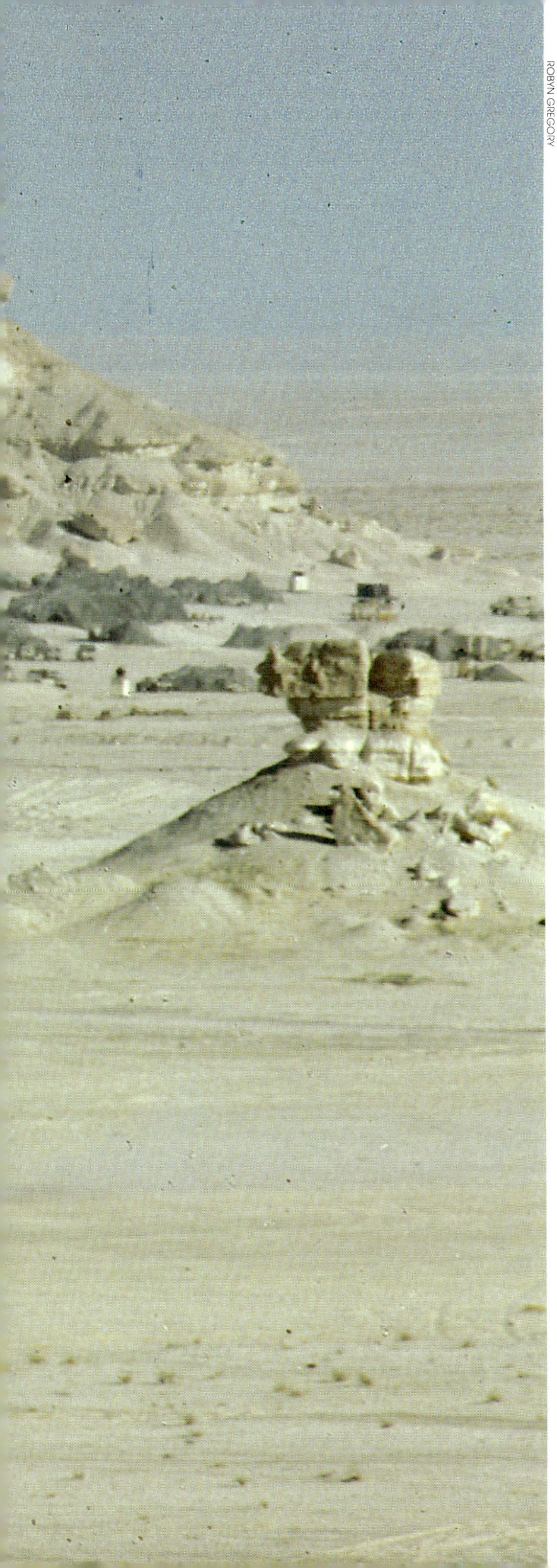

ROBYN GREGORY

1st Cav PAO

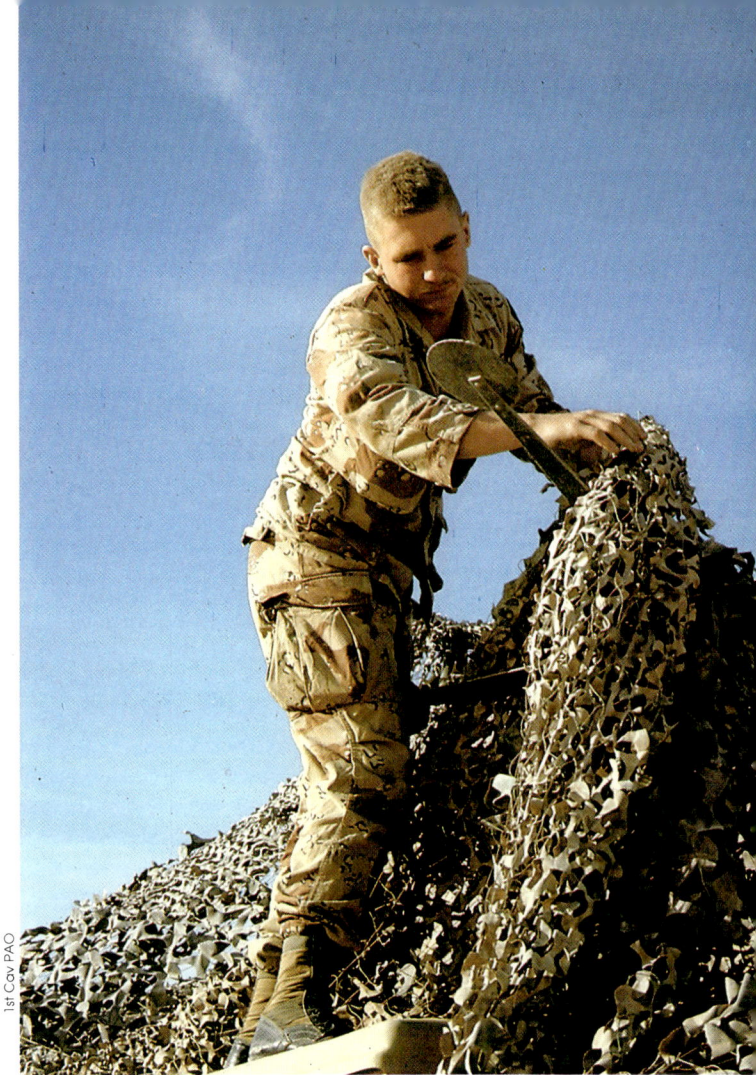

Camouflage netting, although far from invisible, did effectively conceal the type and amount of equipment and was used extensively. It also offered a veil of shade, a more practical benefit to sun-weary soldiers like this DISCOM trooper.

ROBYN GREGORY

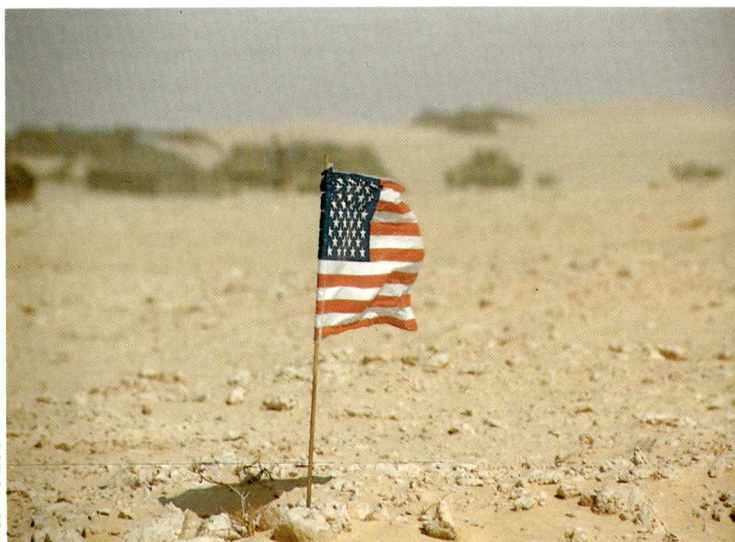

The ubiquitous, revered symbol of pride — and hope.

(Left) Desert sentinel, a butte named Jabal Farhah and known as "the rock," marks the home of the Tiger Brigade's 502nd Forward Support Battalion, whose vehicles and tents crouch, dwarfed, at its foot.

Providing showers, washstands, and latrines was among the Army's highest priorities as troops flooded into Saudi Arabia. Fashioned locally, the makeshift facilities were everywhere and accompanied units when they moved to the border in January.

and suspensions attracted it like a magnet, then held it like sandpaper. And when it swirled into the evening chili — as tedious as chili got — well, that could be plain irritating.

In the desert, each small community, usually a battalion of 500-700 soldiers, established a motor-pool for equipment and a life support area (LSA) where they would eat, sleep, and spend leisure time. The LSA was a city of tents grouped by company and platoon and pitched in neat rows. The uniformity was challenged only by the presence of airy, white, squarish "Bedouin tents" bought locally by the Army to solve a tent shortage. They were lined with red cotton in an Arabic pattern; on entering, one half-expected to meet a sheikh. Close by, a sand volleyball court or football field quickly was marked out. A short walk away was the latrine area, with its steel-mirrored washstand, screened in four-holer toilets, and gravity-fed shower, all made locally. Refusing to submit to a cold dousing, soldiers painted the water tanks on their shower stalls black in a partially successful bid to harness solar heat. They also refused to accept the austerity of the desert. Inside the tents, they installed MRE-case chests of drawers and waterbottle-case tables. Emptied by chain-drinking soldiers, water bottles became the common denominator of improvisation: two bottle tops, cut off to form two cones, with the earpieces of a Walkman inserted in the spout, became acceptable stereo speakers; half buried water bottles marked sports fields, pathways, and motorpools; cut to form a cone, the spout inserted into a length of white PVC pipe stuck in the sand, they served as urinals. Water bottles even wound up in the hands of medics, who used them as jury-rigged splints.

Each morning, a soldier hoisted Old Glory, bathed in the pastel glow of a desert dawn, to the top of an antenna-mast pole at the 2nd Brigade headquarters on "Blackjack Hill." The ritual included a recording of Reveille. Soldiers reluctantly stirring in their sleeping bags knew what followed: the voice of singer Lee Greenwood and the familiar strains of "God Bless the USA," a sort of Desert Shield theme song. It was 0600, 6:00 a.m., and across the brigade, and much of the division, the day's routine had begun.

An hour of PT kicked off the day: push-ups, sit-ups, a run in the sand, or perhaps a game of soccer or football. Then an hour or so to wash up and eat breakfast. Two meals a day consisted of tray rations, or "T-rats," the Army's version of a TV dinner. Invariably, it seemed, breakfast was chili with rice or chicken cacciatore, and supper scrambled eggs. Lunch was an MRE, the Army's version of trail food. The MREs which included a tiny bottle of Tabasco sauce were preferable. Savvy chowhounds learned to carry a bottle with them. Some MREs even included M&Ms. Less than palatable cold, MREs improved with heat; 15 minutes in the sun on a tent roof or vehicle fender was enough. Tankers heated chow by wedging an MRE packet in the exhaust grill against the scorching blast of their turbine engine.

Following breakfast and the morning formation, the day was spent training. The searing heat of midday brought many units to a siesta-like halt. At 5:00 p.m. most units, troops by now ravenous, stopped for supper.

If chow was inhaled, mail was devoured. Usually held by platoon sergeants surrounded by soldiers

In his chapel made of MRE cases, 1-7 Cav Chaplain (Capt.) Scott Borderud tends his flock of forward-based "Garryowen" troopers.

Detached from their battery, a Vulcan crew lives on their position.

Most hated of details, the daily refuse burning ritual takes place in Alpha Battery, 333d Field Artillery (FA).

41

(Right) Main Street, DIVARTY. Rows of "bedouin" tents mark the living area of an artillery battalion in AA Horse. In the foreground, water bottle tops mounted on PVC pipe mark the men's room.

In a world with few distractions from work, soldiers needed a release. Sports filled the bill, taking the form of football, baseball, soccer, or volleyball as shown here. Even weights and horseshoe pits appeared in the desert gyms.

(Right) Each soldier had only two desert uniforms. Tuesday and Thursday were "BDU days," or "green days," reserved for the green battle dress uniform — soldiers could launder their wardrobes, yet units looked uniform. Theoretically sound, the policy was observed unevenly in the face of practicality. While local laundering was available, the results were often switched or missing garments. Many soldiers preferred the washtub approach.

For soldiers away from the life support area, the Kevlar helmet was de rigueur, for personal safety and as conditioning for combat. The rule gave rise to several tongue-in-cheek jibes.

Anticipating the stifling heat of the Army's heavy canvas tents, some soldiers brought along their own tents, as did this Bradley crewman cum barber.

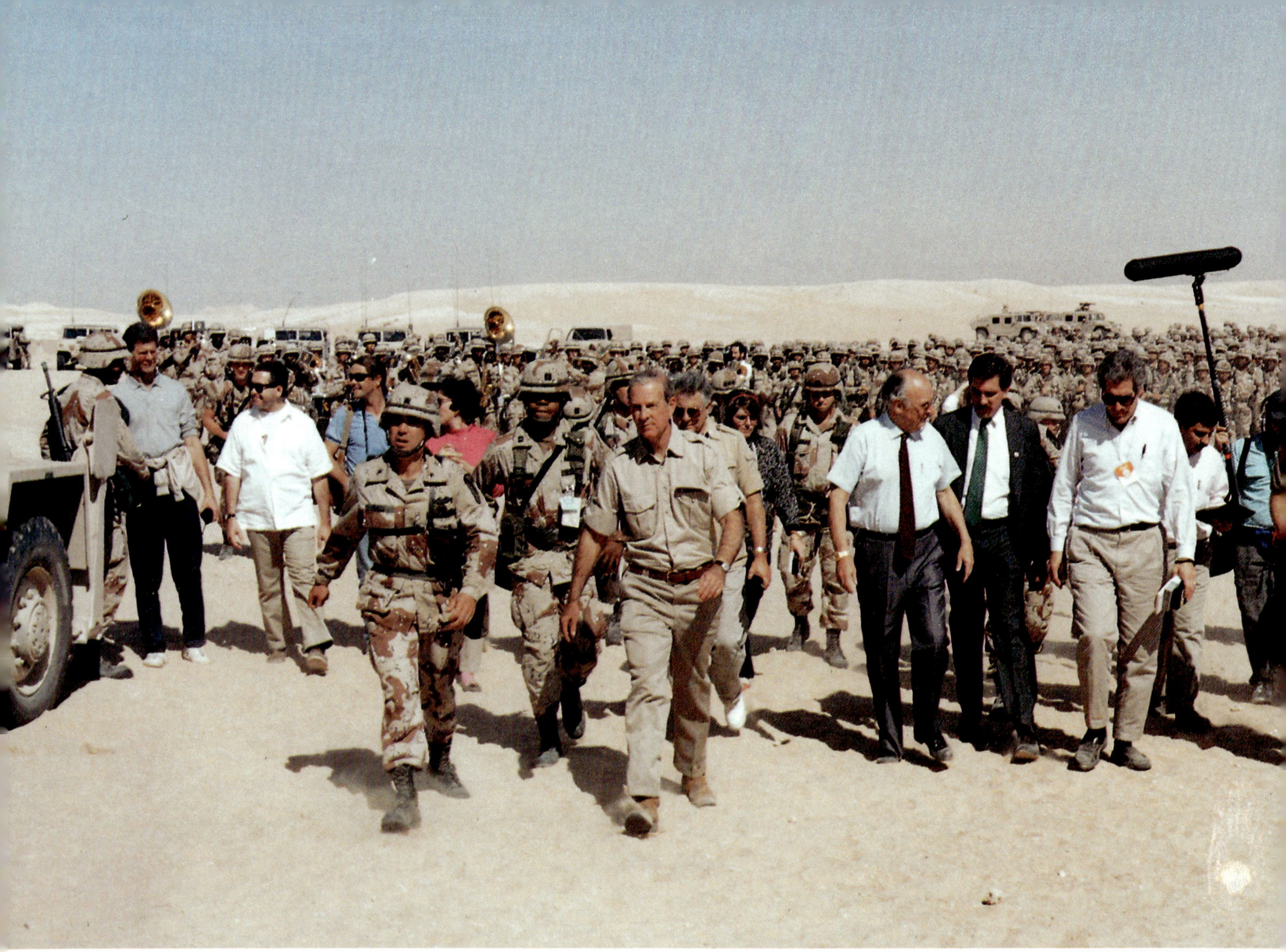

49TH PUBLIC AFFAIRS DETACHMENT

(Then) Brig. Gen. Tilelli (L) escorts Secretary of State James Baker (C) to speak with soldiers following his Nov. 4 visit.

ROBYN GREGORY

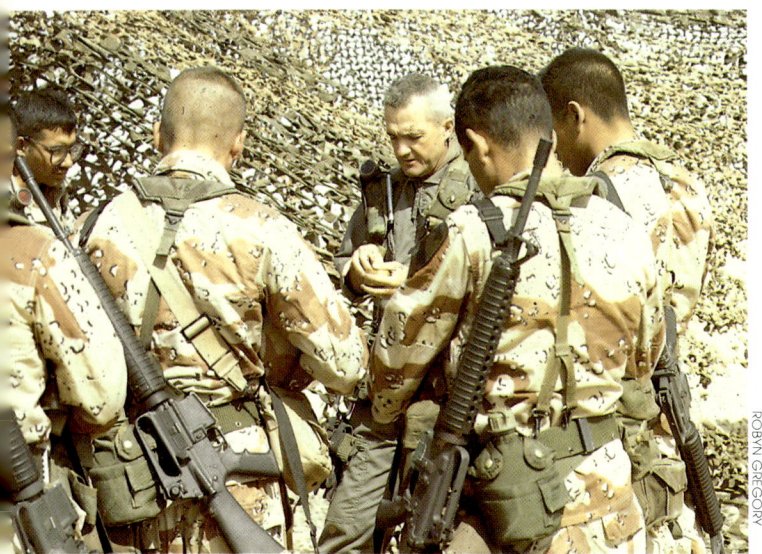

Chaplain (Maj.) Richard Santree holds communion in the Aviation Brigade.

J.E. PHILLIPS

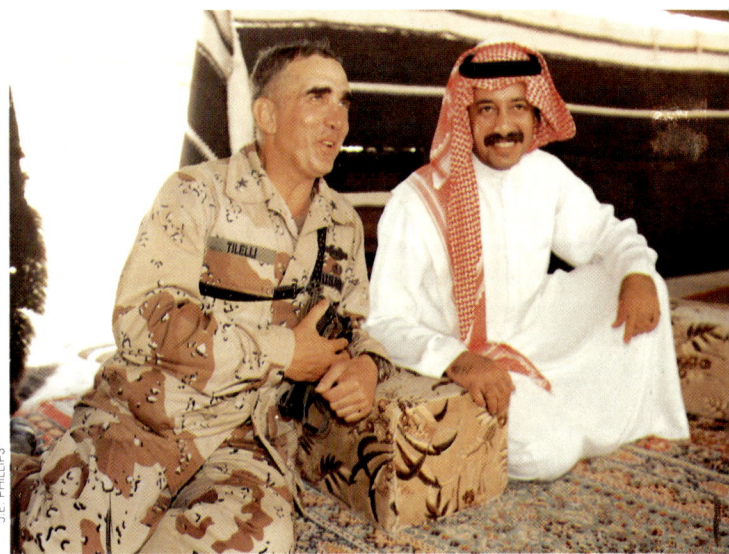

The division used over 120,000 gallons of water daily, much from local wells. The good will and cooperation of area authorities opened access to wells. Brig. Gen. Tilelli accepts the hospitality of the emir of Haneedh in his Bedouin tent.

At Fort Hood, 1st Cav leaders customarily review parade-ground formations on horseback. Preserving the tradition with a uniquely Arab approach, Col. Harold Burch reviewed his troops from a camel during his change of command on Oct. 28, as he turned over the reins of DISCOM to Col. Richard Fousek.

Royal guests, Maj. Charles Aycock, division civil-military officer (C), and Lt. Col. Lawrence Schneider, division intelligence officer, enjoy the local emir's cuisine, sans utensils. The display of the lamb's head on the platter signified a freshly killed animal.

Long the traditional desert mount, now increasingly supplanted by subcompact pick-up trucks, camels remain a Bedouin symbol of wealth, power and freedom. Division Command Sgt. Maj. Robert Wilson climbs aboard one of the emir's camels for a canter through the desert.

Inspection.

J.E. PHILLIPS

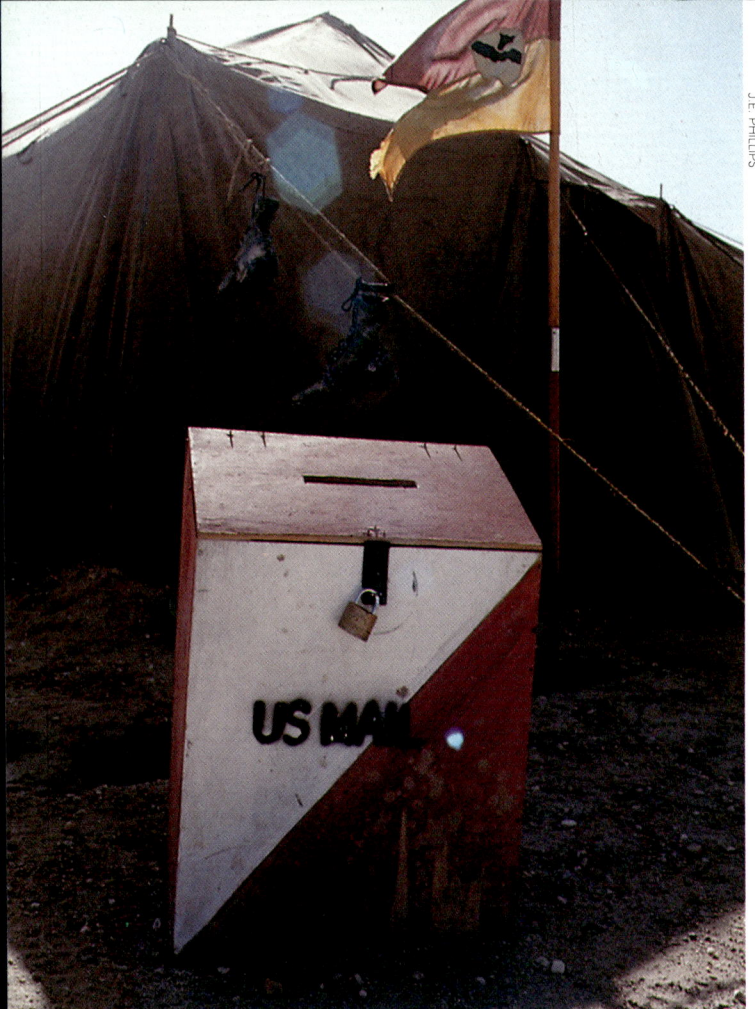

U.S. Post Office, APO NY 09306-1001 — Headquarters Company, 1st Cavalry Division.

1ST CAV PAO

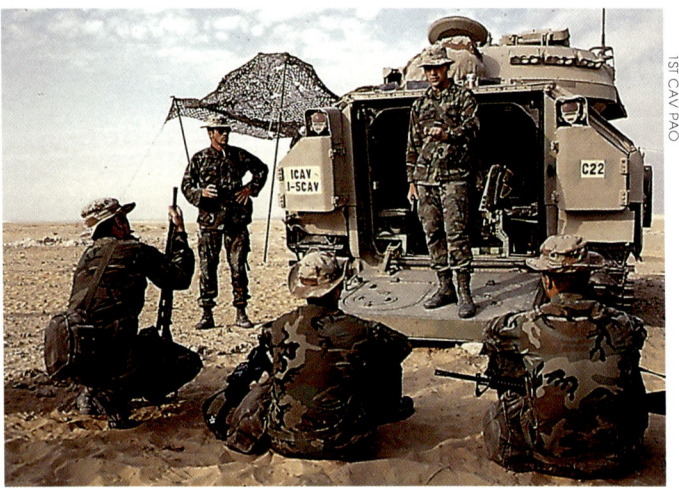

Dismounted infantrymen of Charlie Company, TF 1-5 Cav "in class," by their M2A1 Bradley. This company would suffer its first combat loss on Feb. 28 — hours after the ceasefire.

(Right) Air defense for the division's main command post, a 4-5 Air Defense Artillery (ADA) crew keeps watch from their M163 Vulcan. During Desert Shield, the Vulcan's 20mm gatling gun guarded against terrorists. Later it was used against ground targets with devastating effect.

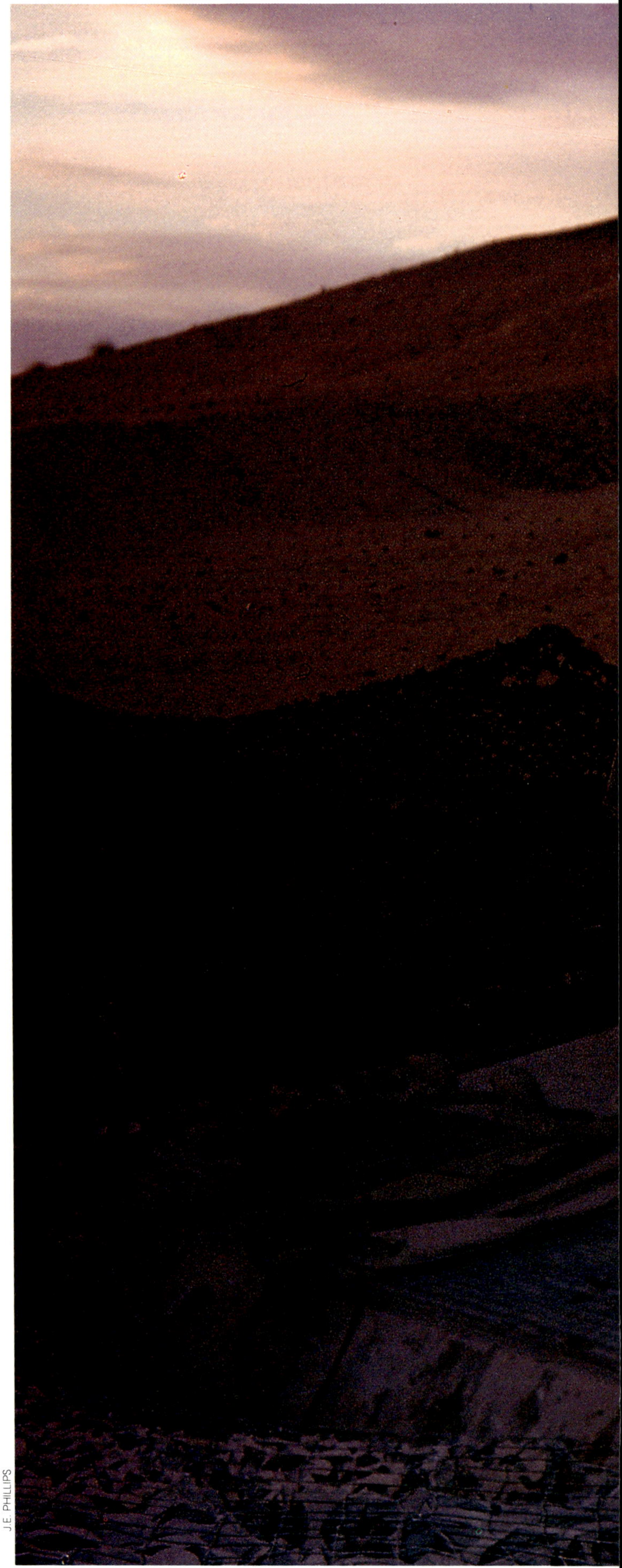

J.E. PHILLIPS

New Sikorsky UH-60 "Blackhawk" helicopters, scheduled to replace the venerable UH-1 "Huey" helicopters of Vietnam vintage, had not been completely introduced when the division deployed. Silhouetted by dawn, "Pegasus Six," Brig. Gen. Tilelli's UH-60, awaits its next mission.

J.E. PHILLIPS

An M109A3 Howitzer silhouetted by the desert sunset.

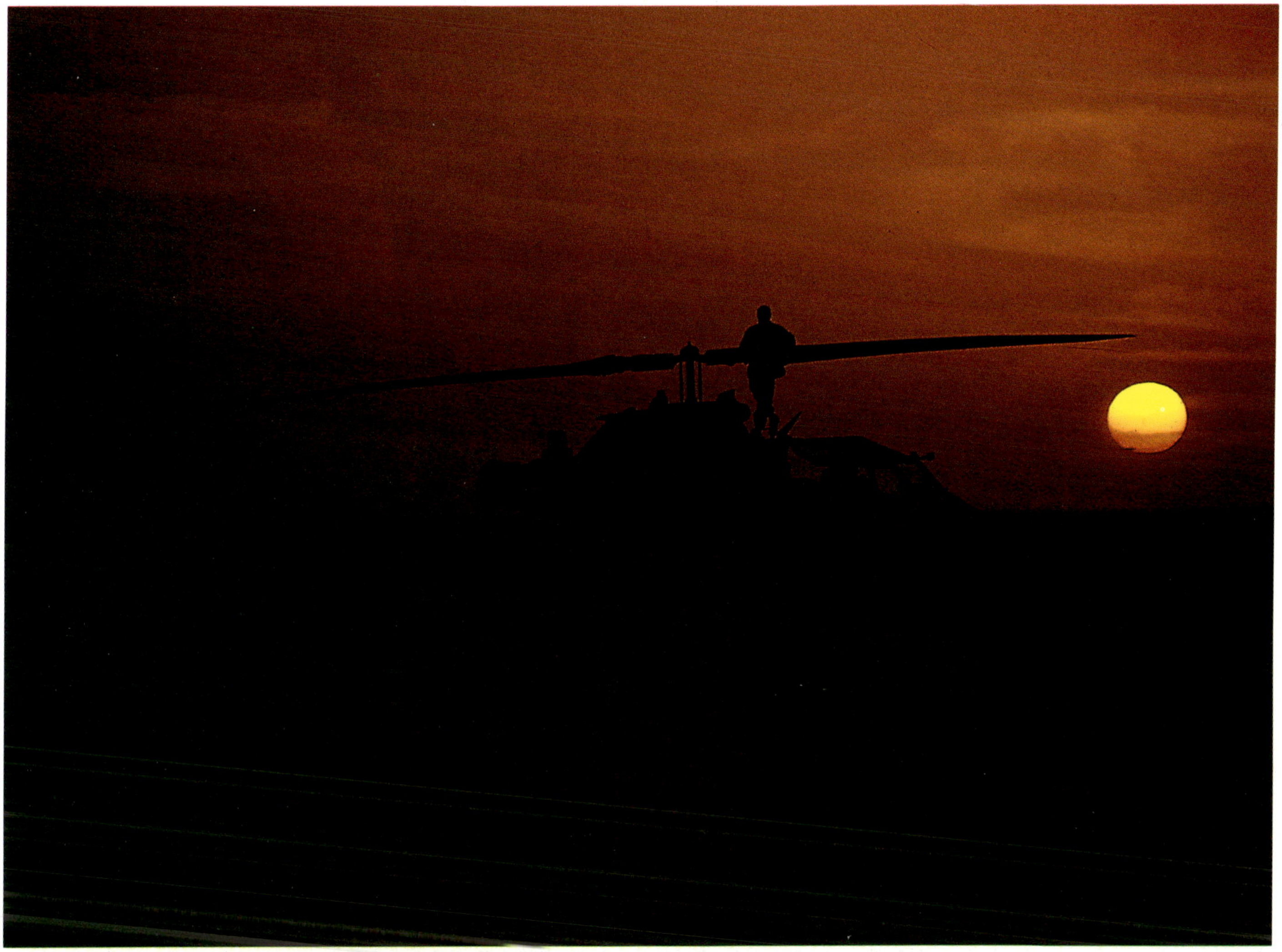

J.E. PHILLIPS

Evening's tender touch; a 1-7 Cav crewchief secures his AH-1F Cobra gunship. Tomorrow, another mission.

J.E. PHILLIPS

BRITT TOALSON

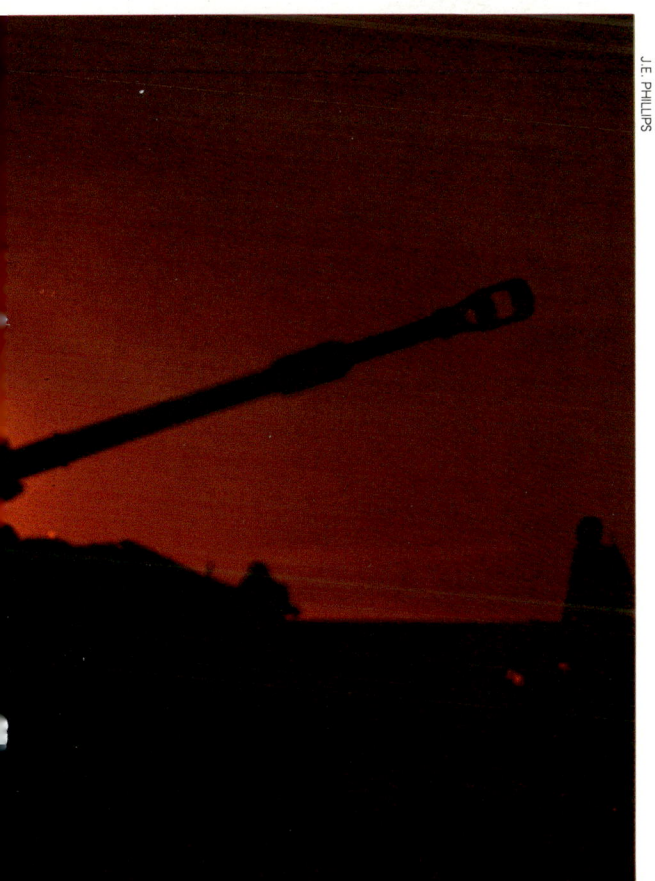

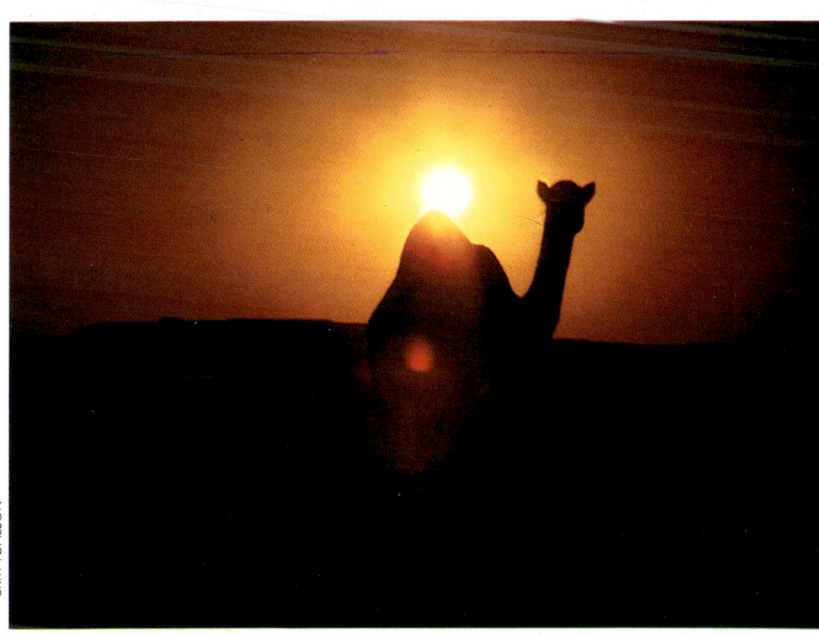

Desert vision.

barely able to contain their anxiety, mail call occurred in the evening or whenever the supply run brought mail. It was a daily drama; a tragedy to those who left empty-handed, a triumph to those who left with something, anything. Slow at first, by the holidays over 100,000 pounds of mail arrived in the division daily. Schools, churches, offices, even entire sororities and dorm floors sent mail. For several soldiers, letters developed into romance and for some, wedding vows.

It was not unusual to see a soldier — perhaps an infantry sergeant, tired and dust-coated from a day's training, sitting on the ramp of his Bradley — intently reading a letter from a 3rd grader he'd never met.

The evening brought free time to read, catch up on letter writing, play a game of volleyball, fall prey to boredom born of routine and isolation, or think of those waiting behind or what lay ahead — rumors had the deployment becoming a six or 12-month rotation and Saudi Arabia evolving into a regular overseas assignment. A six-month rotation was tolerable (The average 1st Cav soldier's deployment in fact lasted six months), but thoughts of a year in the desert, or worse yet, a return in the near future, were abhorrent.

By 9:00 p.m. or 10:00 p.m., exhausted, most soldiers were dead asleep. Only soldiers in night training and the guards walking the perimeter were awake to see the slow march of a million stars across the black night's vault; more stars even than the Iraqi Army had men...

Every morning, it fell to enlisted soldiers to wash the pots and clean the latrines. The pots were easy as long as everyone was eating T-rations and MREs. The latrine detail, while absolutely necessary, was disgusting. Every morning, the waste had to be burned. Unlucky pairs of soldiers would mix it with diesel, ignite the slop, and trying desperately to stay upwind of the greasy black smoke, stir it occasionally.

Then the ashes — and any unburned sediment — were buried. A soldier said that after this most hated of duties, she would go to the shower and stand under the cold water until the tank ran dry.

Separated from the world by the desert's vastness, the lack of news isolated soldiers. Not until mid-November did Armed Forces Network (AFN) radio broadcasts reach AA Horse; limited by short range, FM radio required relays to reach the 1st Cav's antennas. Relay sets, many weakened by lengthy storage, repeatedly failed. Eventually the signal made it. Known as Wizard 106 to the division's troops, AFN brought varied music, armed forces and broadcast news, and even occasional ball games. The Stars and Stripes newspaper, and two English-language Arab papers began filtering in,

Minding the store, a Tiger Brigade First Sergeant tends the "Company Store" he has provisioned from local shops. Some company stores were elaborate affairs featuring counters and, as DISCOM started delivering ice, coolers of frosty drinks.

(Left) Infantrymen of Alpha Company, TF 1-8 Cav take a break from training at Assembly Area Horse in December.

along with the XVIII Airborne Corps newspaper, "Desert Dragon," and the division's "Cav Country," both printed weekly by the respective public affairs offices. Eventually, Baghdad Betty signed onto the airwaves and along with a tolerable playlist, came up with some laughably incompetent propaganda. Visitors coursed through AA Horse. Secretary of State James Baker visited on November 4, addressing over 4,000 assembled troops. "I want you to know that you are constantly on the minds of the leadership of the United States," he said. On November 8, President Bush announced that U.S. troop strength would increase by 200,000. In AA Horse, and Fort Hood, hopes of a short rotation vanished: this was going to be for the duration — whatever that was…

A division must train constantly to keep its edge. If it does not, its performance plummets. The First Team's mission was to defend the Kingdom against an enemy army, the world's fourth in size and at the moment, first in voracity. It began to train immediately. Even before the last Bedouin tent was up, armored vehicles charged back and forth through the desert. Dismounted infantry dashed from the compartments of their Bradley fighting vehicles, then leap-frogged across the sand under cover of the Bradley's guns. Artillerymen drilled the placement of their guns in a noisy, excited scramble of running and gesturing men. Everyone learned how to live by the desert's rules and practiced land navigation in a land virtually without terrain features. Everyone refreshed their first aid skills and drilled with their chemical defensive gear over and over again; the mask had to be on within nine seconds of the alarm, the rubberized hood in another six. No corner of AA Horse was too remote for questing armor, no corner was beyond the staccato chop of helicopter blades.

Like much of the division, The Tiger Brigade

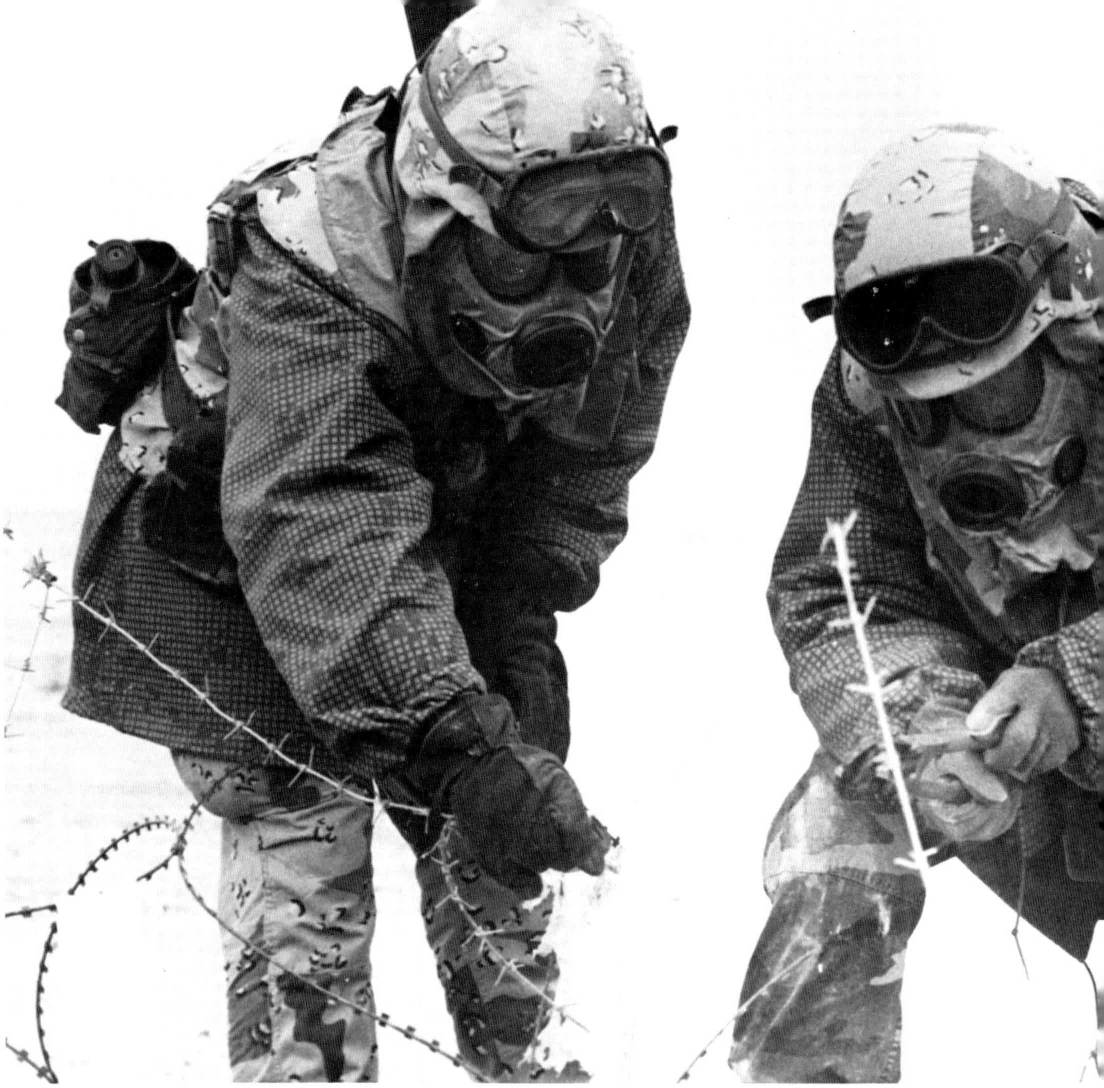

Soldiers wearing protective masks reduce a concertina and barbed wire obstacle during training in AA Horse in early January.

1ST CAV PAO

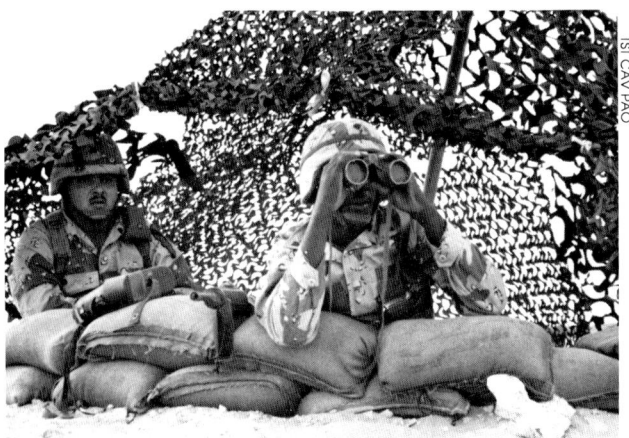

Even in the remote desert, terrorists presented a threat. Here, Sgt. Hector Galindo (L) and Spec. Eddie Truit (R) guarding TF 1-32 Armor's perimeter in AA Horse.

ROBYN GREGORY

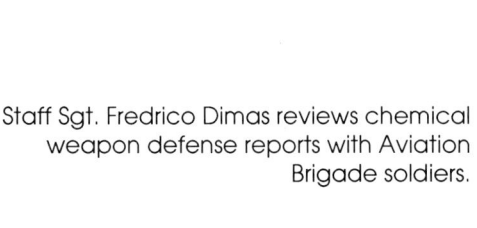

Staff Sgt. Fredrico Dimas reviews chemical weapon defense reports with Aviation Brigade soldiers.

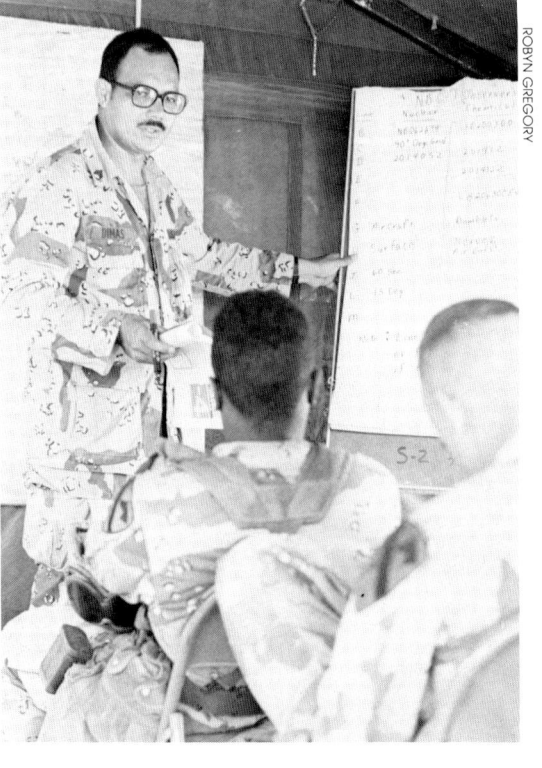

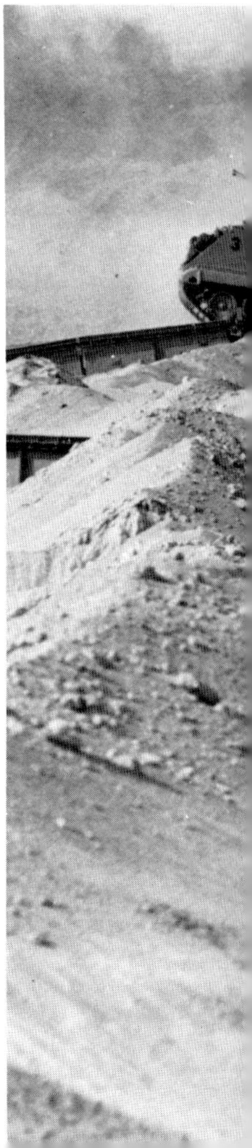

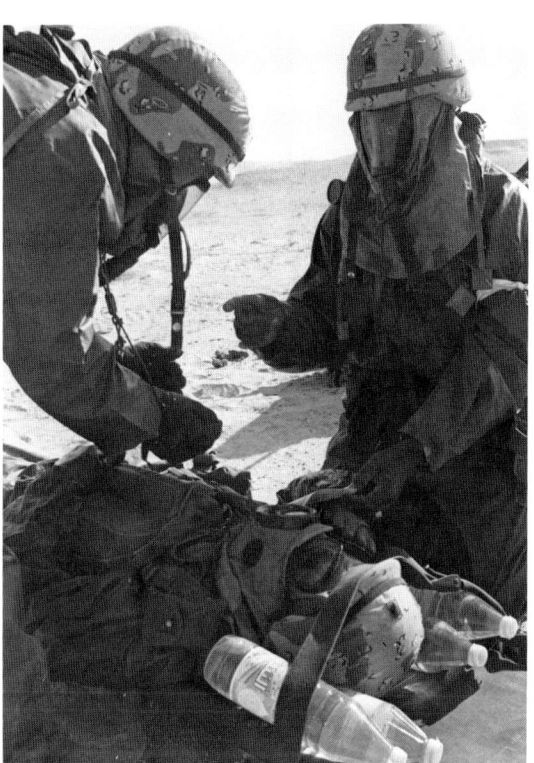

(Left) Making due. Combat medics use water bottles to immobilize a soldier's head during medic training at AA Horse. The photographer would himself go into combat as a medic (see pg. 112).

(Below) Out of the sand, much of the aircraft maintenance was done inside a capacious, tent-like portable hangar called a "clamshell." Within one, Spec. Katherine Speer, Foxtrot Company, 227th Aviation Regiment checks the rotor system of an OH-58 helicopter.

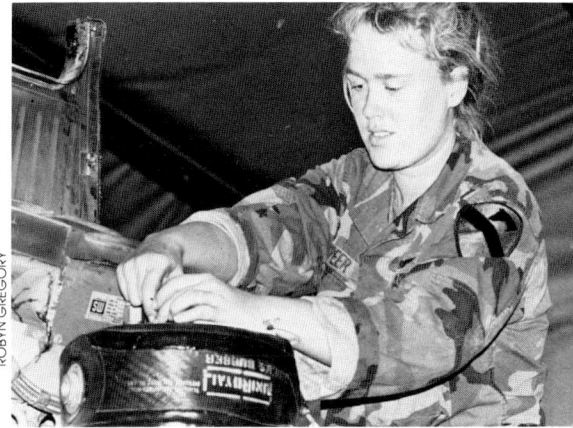

For a January obstacle breaching exercise in AA Horse, enemy trenches were recreated down to the burning oil that would greet troops in the Wadi al Batin weeks later. A 2nd Brigade fire support team vehicle crosses these trenches as Bravo Company, 8th Engineers overwatch.

Inching forward, 2nd Brigade dismounted infantry practice marking lanes through minefields under the covering guns of their Bradleys in January, bare weeks before they would penetrate the enemy's obstacles in combat.

Squinting behind his goggles, a 2nd Brigade infantryman fights the desert's worst enemy: flying sand. By December, winds whipped up grayish brown clouds of it, driving the fine grit into everything for endless hours. Hoping to spare his rifle's bore, the soldier has capped its muzzle.

That the enemy would use chemical weapons was a foregone conclusion. Chemical defensive training permeated the division's preparations in AA Horse.

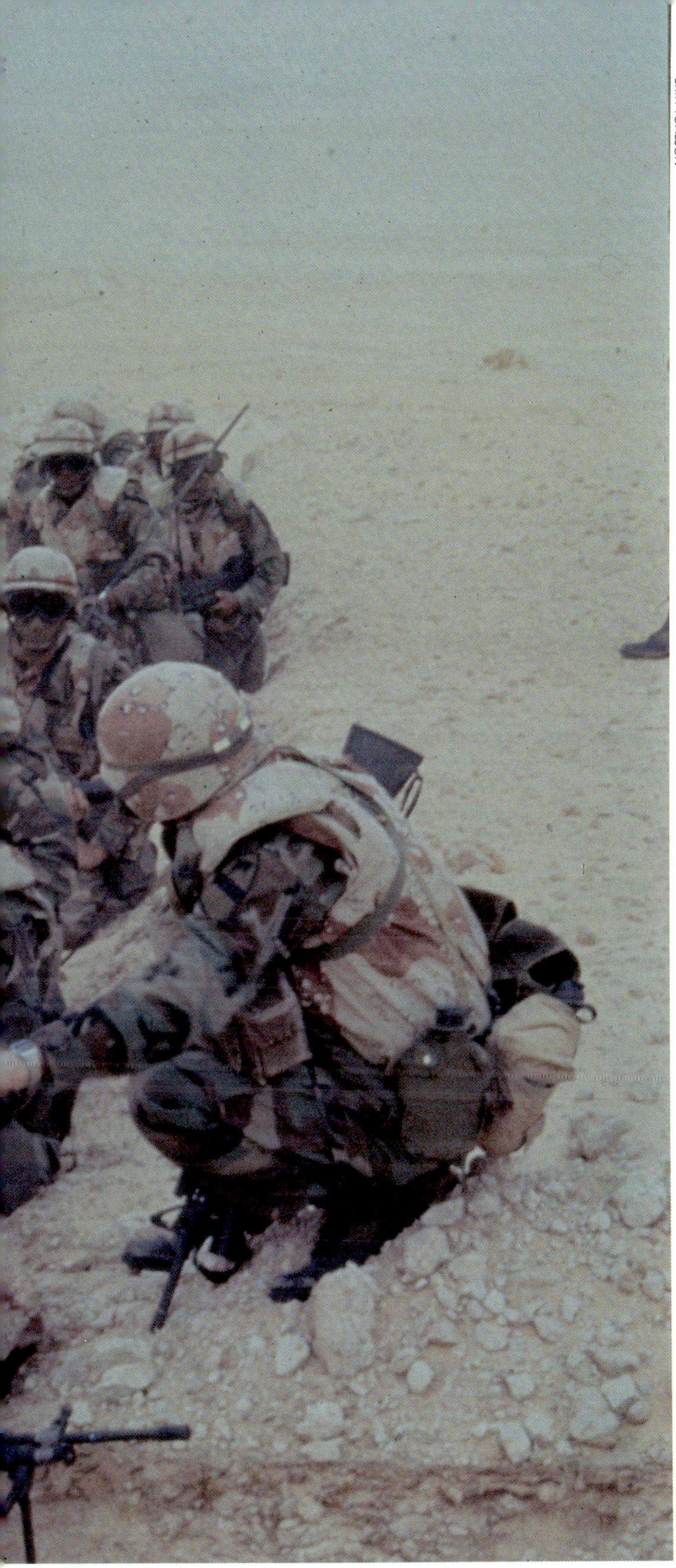

BRITT TOALSON

An infantry squad, crouching in a low ditch as the squad leader gives final directions, prepares to move out under the covering fire of its Bradley in an exercise at AA Horse.

Like tank and Bradley crews, dismounted infantry learned to move by bounds, in a leapfrog fashion. With one element covering, others moved forward. A squad leader from TF 1-5 Cavalry motions for his men to begin covering infantry moving up alongside them.

CURTIS HOCOM

THOMAS FULLER

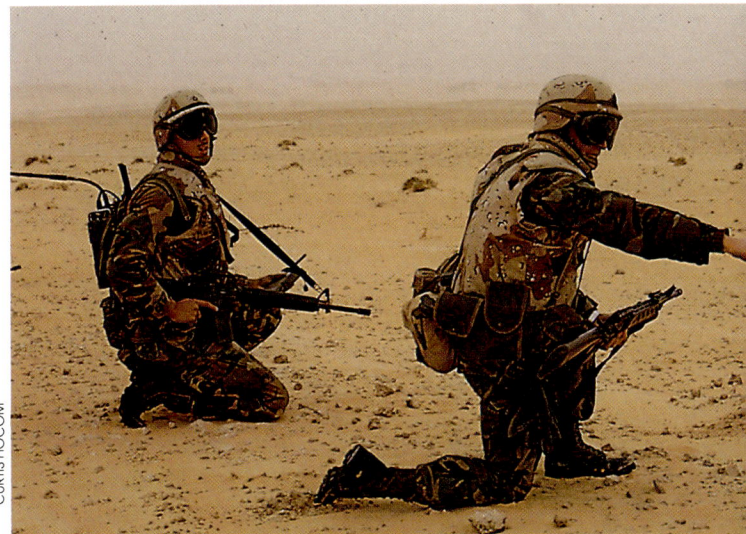

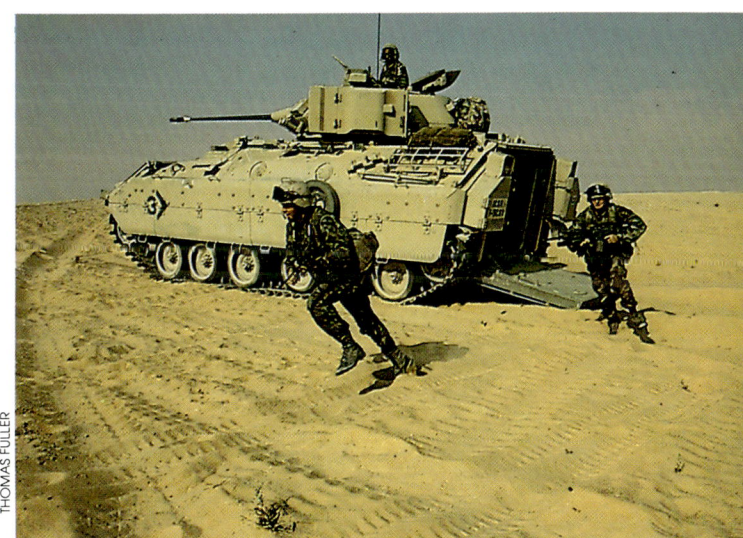

An infantry squad dismounting from the dark cocoon of their Bradley had to instantly overcome disorientation and deploy to fight on the proper course. Squads drilled incessantly, the Bradley crew staying mounted to provide overwatching fire and a ready escape — or ride forward.

started training with the individual soldier and crew. Then platoons and companies came together, working on battle drills and maneuver techniques. By November, units moved in the desert wedge, a steel arrowhead of moving armor. Developed for fast movement in open terrain, the wedge became the standard formation in the division, and eventually throughout U.S. armored forces.

In early January, just before departing to reinforce the Marines below Kuwait, the brigade maneuvered as a whole. There was plenty of room. For an army used to making do with shrinking maneuver spaces at home and overseas, the Saudi desert was training gone to heaven. If only a GI could get a beer after a day's work…

Desert Storm had to be the first war fought without the services of the oldest profession or even liquor. But most units took a stab at providing their soldiers something more than just T-rations, MREs, and warm water. The company first sergeant would saddle up his "Humvee" and head for the nearest shop, universally called "Bedouin Bob's." There he'd load up sodas and anything packaged; the cakes and pastries were safe enough. Several units opened "company stores" in their mess or recreation tents. While the inventory usually sold at cost, the capitalistic urge needed little coaxing. TV correspondent Peter Jennings, visiting 3-82 Field Artillery in November, stopped by the battalion's company store and accepted a Saudi near-beer. He took a pull on the

Sand, whipped into a fog by a helicopter's rotor-wash, enveloped pilots in "brownouts" until they learned to dispense with gradual approaches and land while moving forward. Here, as an AH-64 Apache comes in, the grit's already flying.

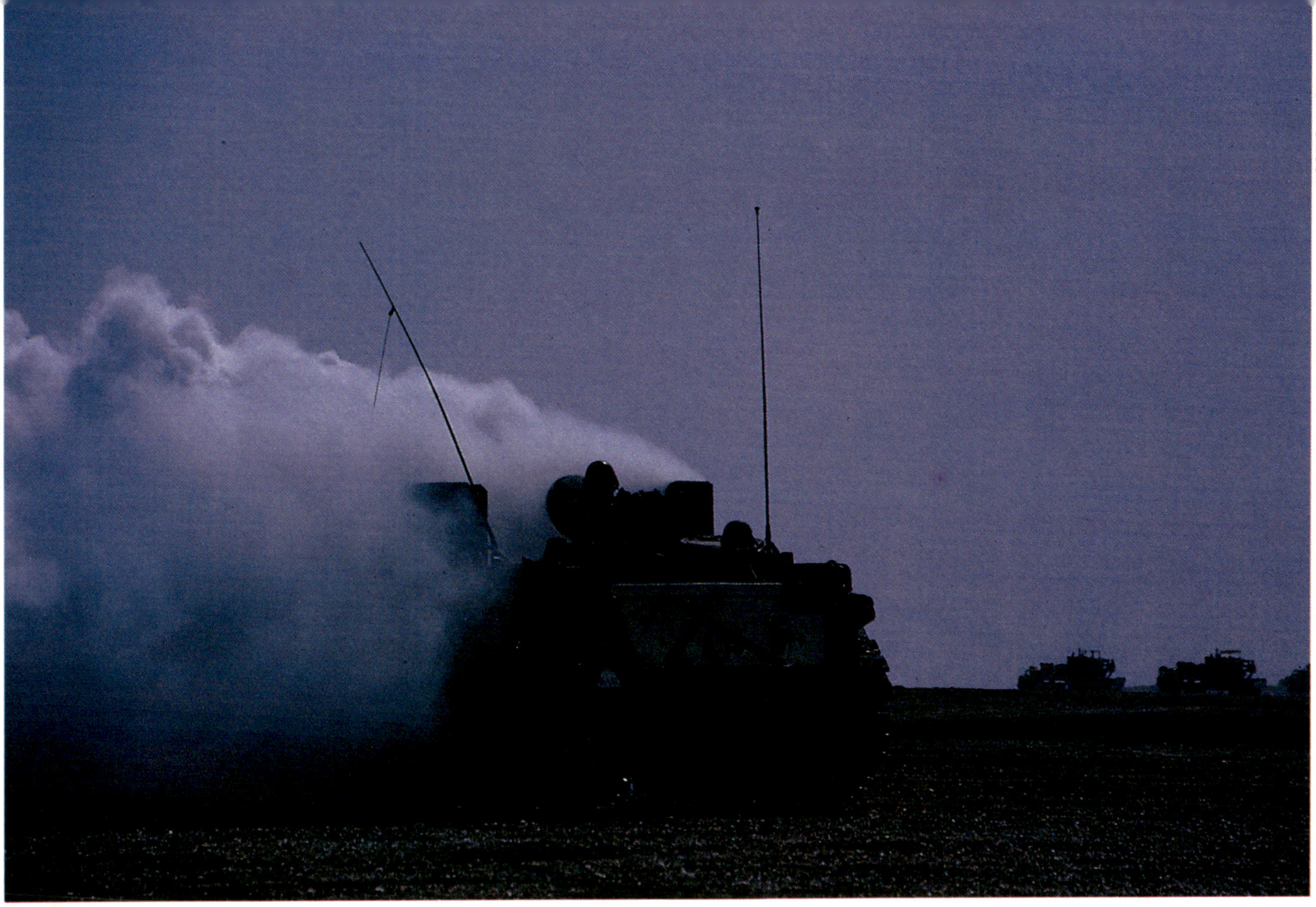

ROBYN GREGORY

A smoke discharger-equipped personnel carrier from the 68th Chemical Company practices laying a smoke screen.

BRITT TOALSON

BRITT TOALSON

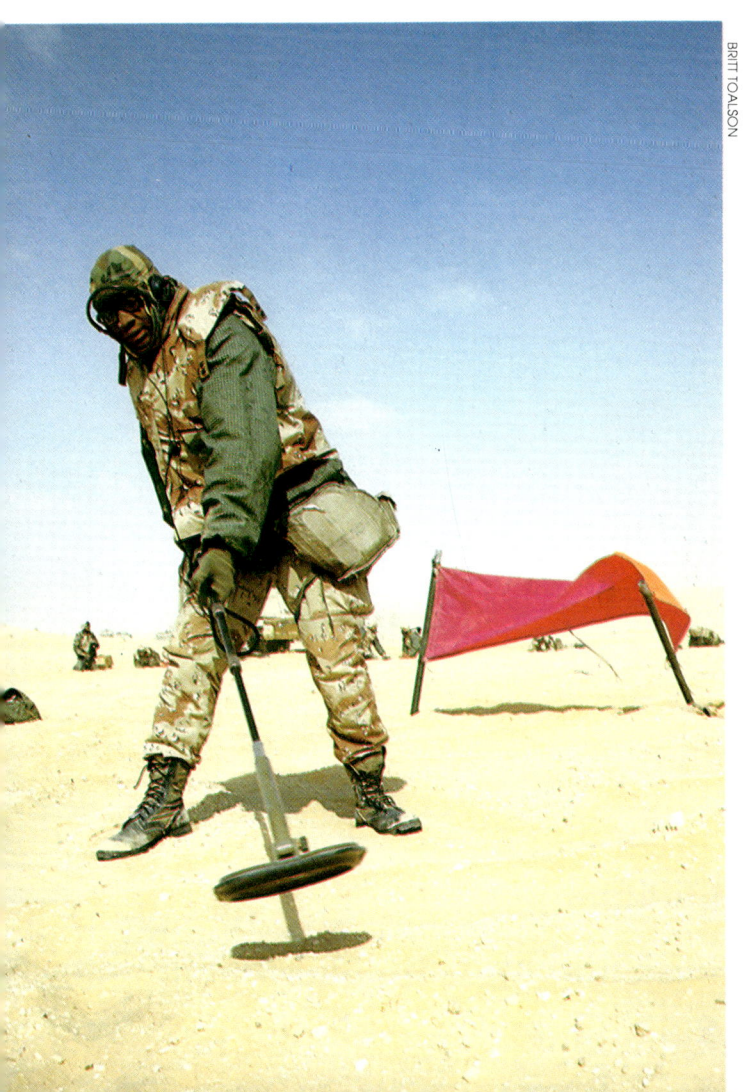

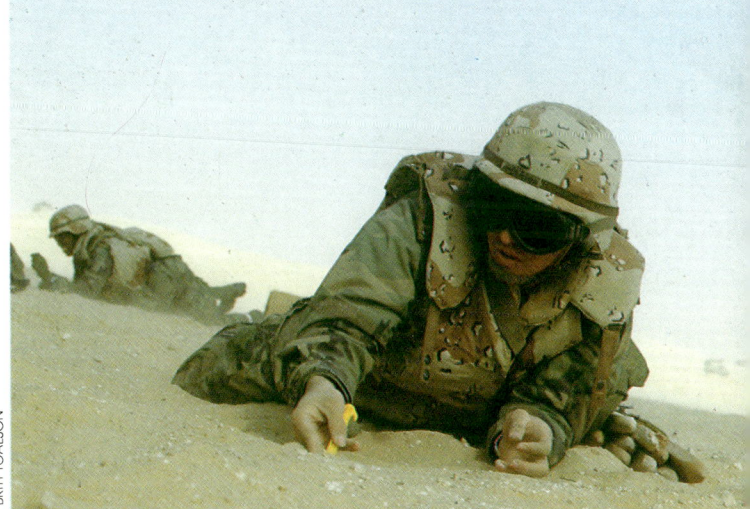

With all the high-tech trappings of modern warfare, the "human touch" still counts. Here, a 2nd Brigade infantryman practices probing for mines using a plastic tentpeg, a precaution against magnetically sensitive mines.

(Left) That the Iraqis had emplaced heavy belts of mines was common knowledge. Before tank-mounted mineplows were issued in February, 8th Engineer soldiers practiced the painstaking, dangerous craft of magnetic mine detection.

JOSE ZUNIGA

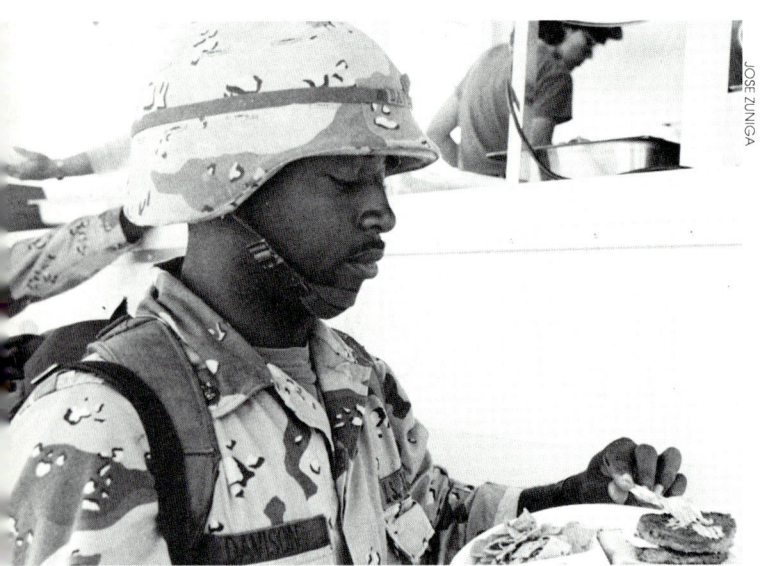

All American meal. The division's logistics office ran Chuck's Wagon, a mobile grill, at the soldier's mall phone tent in the division rear. Chuck's served free burgers and chips to soldiers visiting the mall.

CURTIS HOCOM

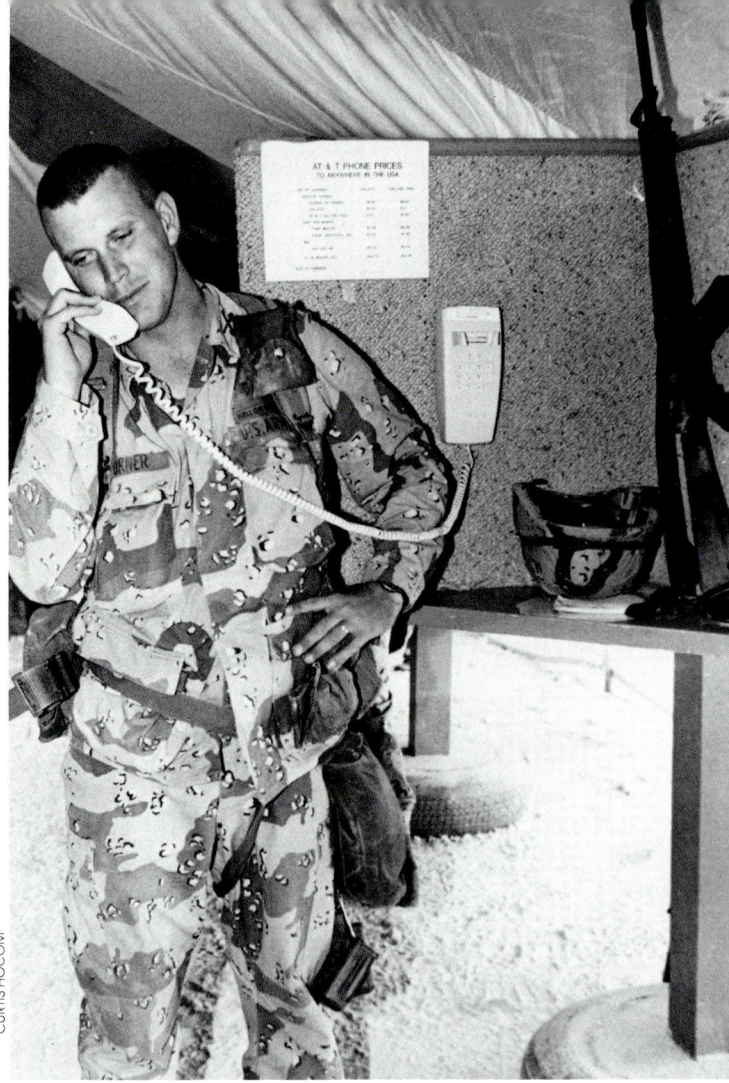

First call home, Thanksgiving day. Courtesy of AT&T, each soldier got a free 15-minute "USA Direct" call.

(Below) While at AA Horse, the band performed in talent shows and concerts for units throughout the division. During Desert Storm, musicians put down their instruments and picked up rifles as guards for the division's main command post. Here, the band plays at a holiday talent show in AA Horse, led by Bandmaster Chief Warrant Officer Freddie Vincent.

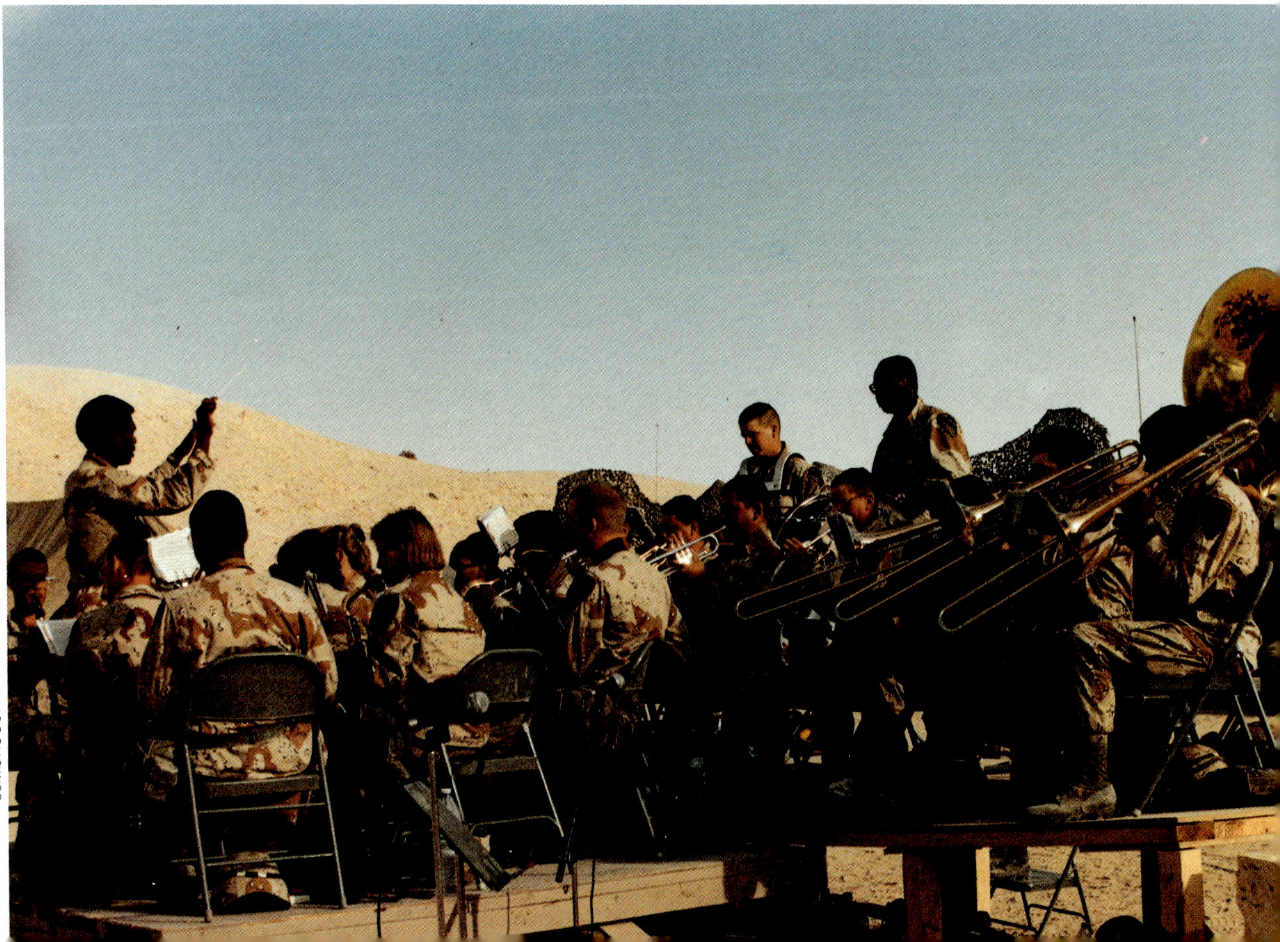

CURTIS HOCOM

bottle, and like many soldiers, never took a second. One sergeant, seeing his opportunity, had Jennings autograph the bottle for auction. Whether anyone finished the contents remains a mystery.

AA Horse was developing nicely. It featured nearly unrestricted maneuver space, and even a "soldier's mall" boasting a mail tent, PX van, satellite phones, and a Baskin Robbins ice cream truck. It had company stores and 17,000 soldiers training to a froth. But AA Horse had no range.

When Brig. Gen. Franks' team initially scouted AA Horse, they found a perfect site for a gunnery range. A valley 30 kilometers long and 7 wide, every weapon system in the division could use it, several units could fire simultaneously. But not until November was the plan approved by XVIII Airborne Corps, which had its own "Ali Range" nearby. The division trained there through the fall, but Tilelli was concerned over Ali's adequacy for the December upgrade to M1A1 Abrams tanks, M2A2 Bradley fighting vehicles (BFV), and M3A2 cavalry fighting vehicles (CFV). While Tilelli waited for approval, Division Master Gunners Sgt's. First Class Dennis Heim and William Davis worked furiously over plans for the facility they called Pegasus Range, designed to outclass anything in the desert. Tilelli, on inspecting their plans, asked how long construction would take. "Twenty-one days," Heim answered. "Good, go with it. You're now on day 12," Tilelli said.

Heim collected his labor; combat engineers from the division's 8th Engineer Battalion and the Tiger Brigade's Alpha Company, 17th Engineers, trained to destroy enemy obstacles, but now ready to build. Tankers from Charlie Company, TF 1-8 Cav came to haul thousands of plywood targets, but the electric target lifting devices that would raise them had not arrived from the States. On Thanksgiving day, as if by signal, they arrived. After a break for the much-

Comparison shopping in the desert, a soldier prices goods in the soldier's mall PX van.

anticipated holiday meal, the work resumed. Directing construction with an architect's care, the two watched their range develop — and December approach.

Near the docks at ad Dammam, Alpha Company, TF 2-8 Cav was busy turning in its old M1 tanks for new M1A1s. The first division unit to go through transition, TF 2-8 Cav began a process that tank and Bradley units would repeat through December. The battalion's mechanics arrived for classes, followed by tankers and the M1s, transported on HETs. They inventoried the old tanks and turned them in, complete with ammunition. Parked there, the M1s would spend the war, ready for use as combat loss replacements.

The next day, crews accepted their new tanks. In

CURTIS HOCOM

ROBYN GREGORY

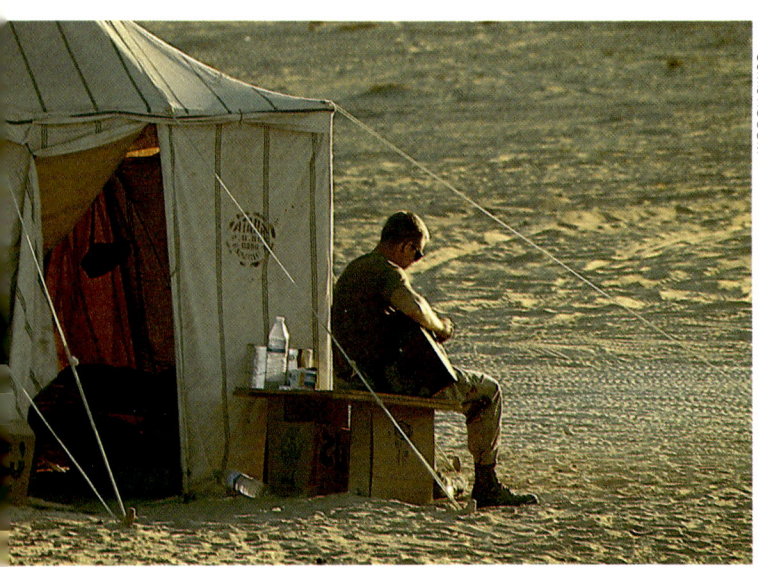

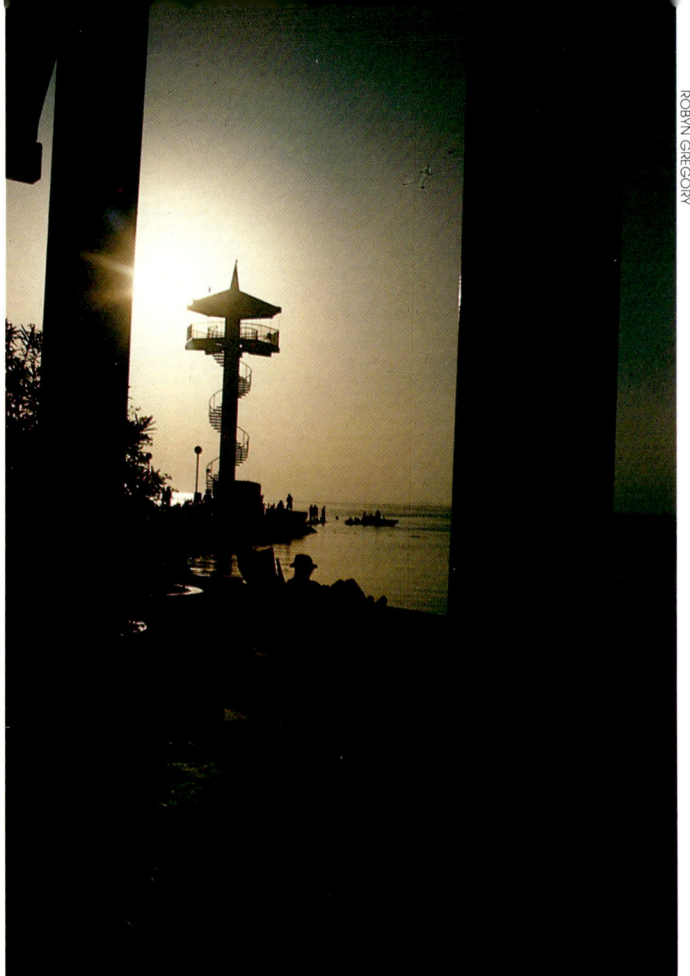

Even with the demands of Desert Shield's frenetic buildup, soldiers needed time away from the swirl of sand and training, whether spent in precious solitude (above), on the QE2 anchored off Bahrain, or at the rest and recreation center called "Half Moon Bay," (right) on the Saudi coast.

(Below) But the training continued relentlessly. In the blast of its 120mm main gun, a TF 2-8 Cav Abrams crew destroys an "enemy" T-72 from 2,000 meters at Pegasus Range. The M1A1 replaced the division's decade-old M1s, which sat out the war in ad Dammam as combat replacements.

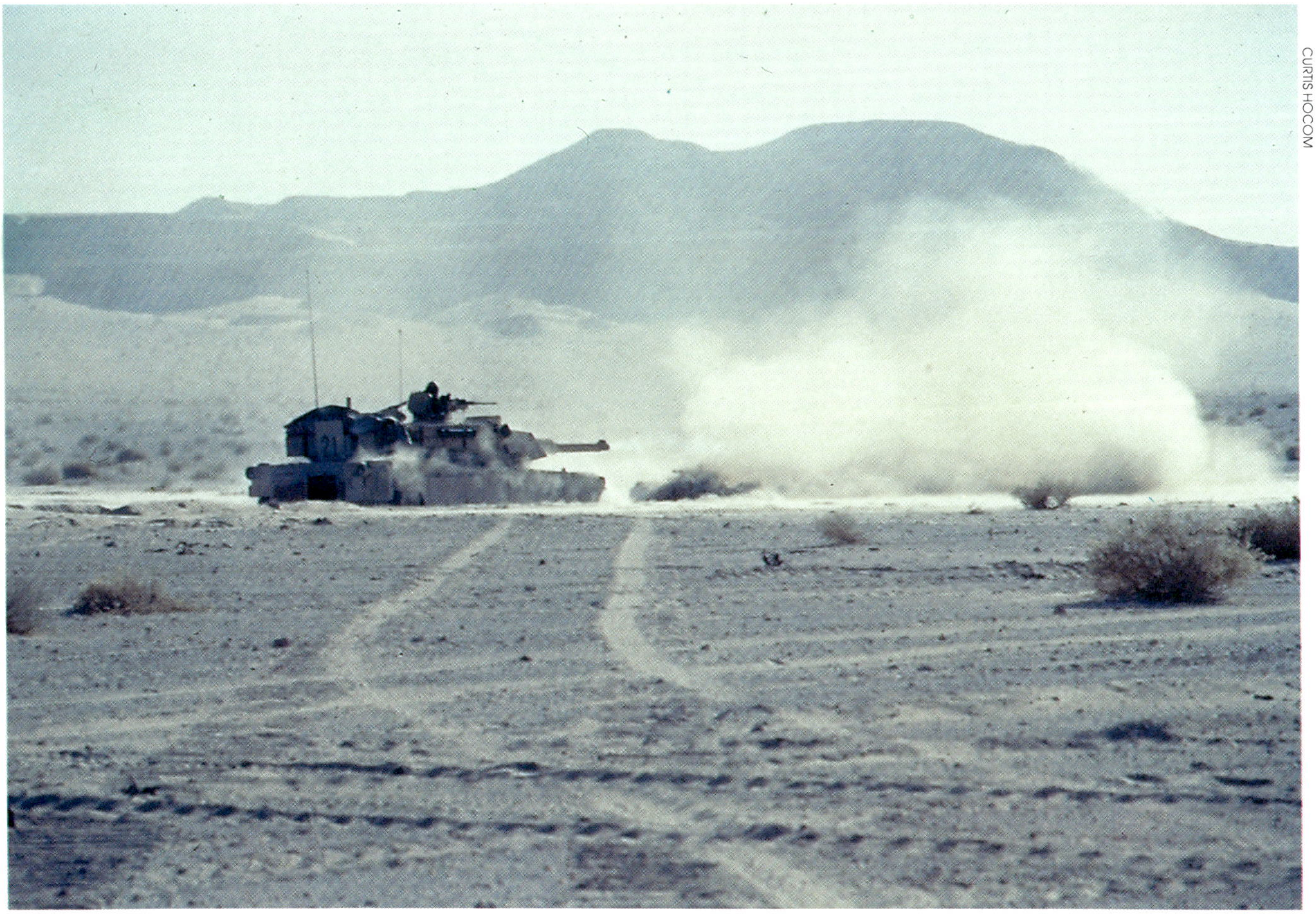

CURTIS HOCOM

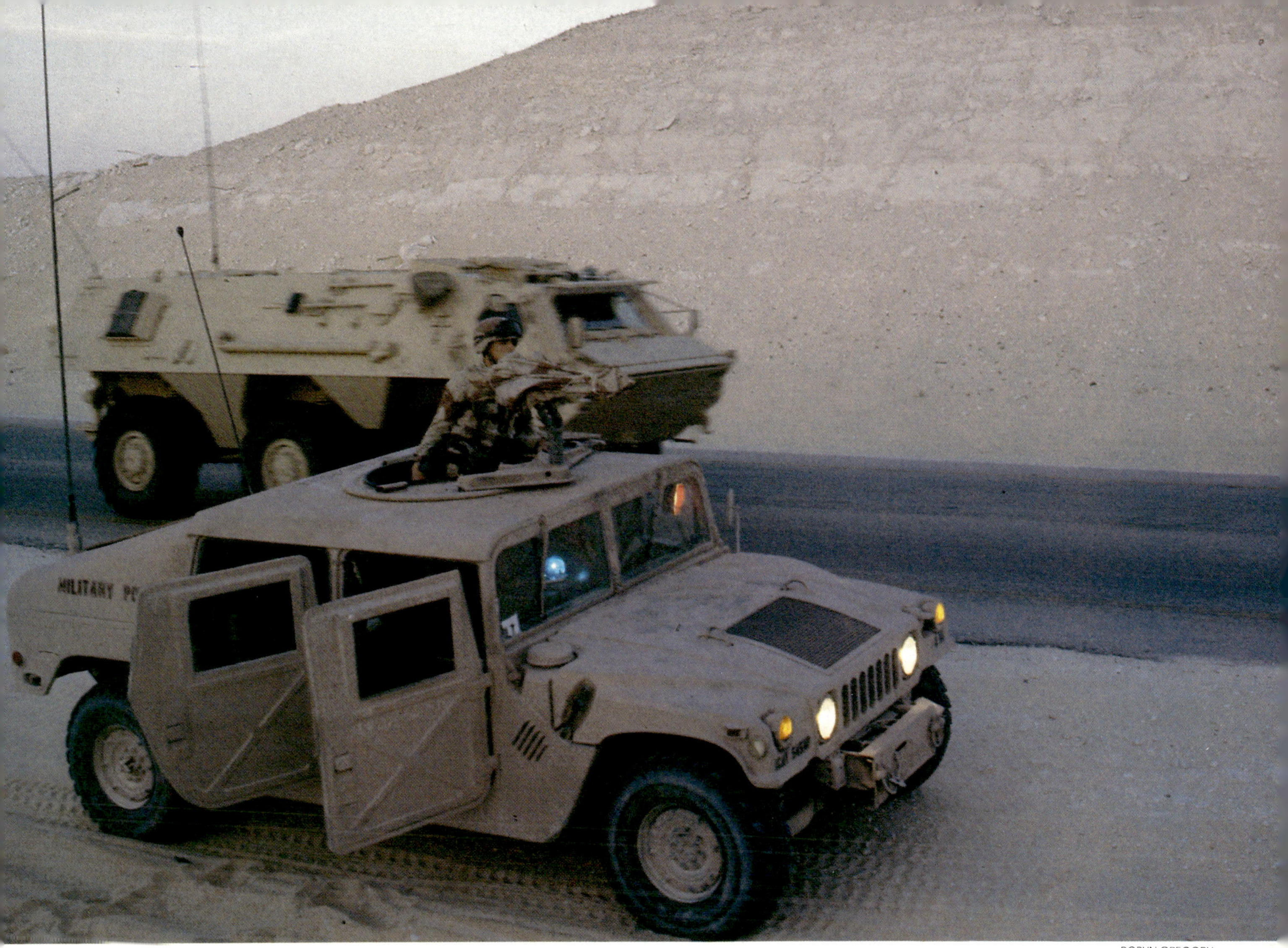

ROBYN GREGORY

1ST CAV PAO

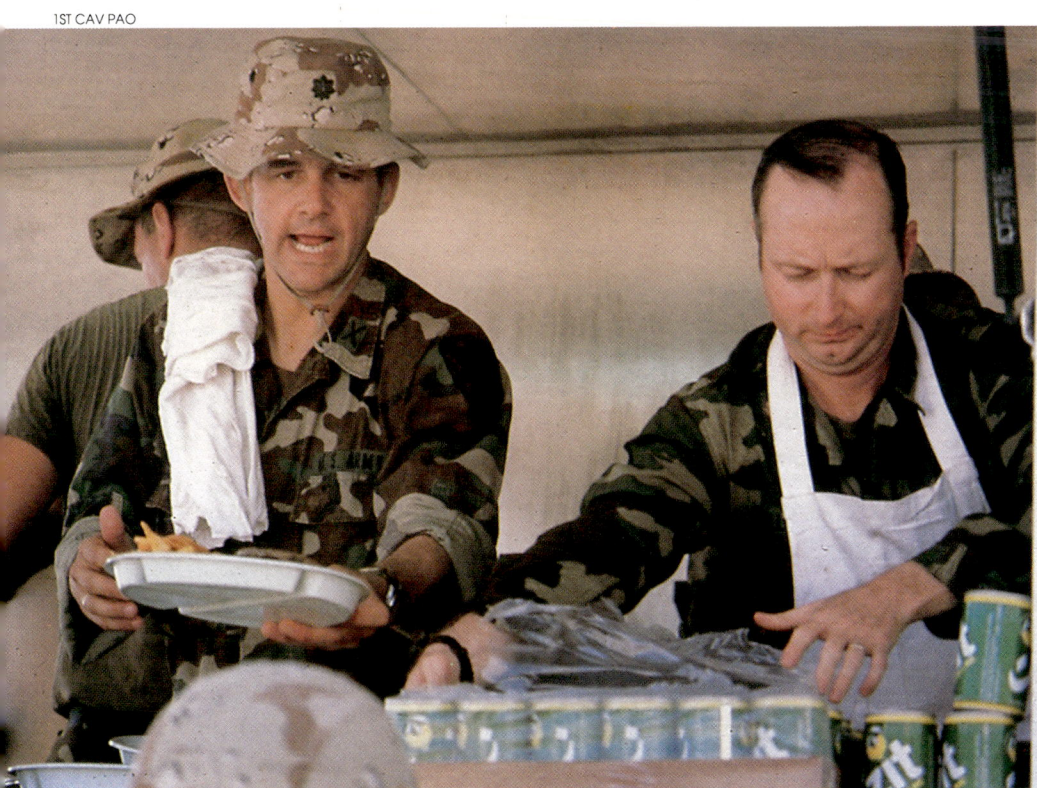

(Above) The paved roads connecting desert towns were surprisingly good, until pummelled by the endless, heavy traffic of deploying armies. A 68th Chemical Company "Fox" chemical detection vehicle passes by a traffic control HMMWV of the 545th Military Police Company.

(Left) Serving his soldiers from behind the counter of Chuck's Wagon at the soldier's mall, Lt. Col. Michael Starry (L), DIVARTY executive officer, dishes up burgers and chips to troopers in from the desert for a phone call home.

a christening ceremony, a TF 2-8 Cav tanker shattered a bottle of sparkling water against the first tank accepted. After two more days of instruction in the port, crews loaded their freshly painted war horses onto the diabolical HETs and headed west to AA Horse — and Pegasus Range.

December 2 dawned a glorious morning of relief for Heim. Working 20-hour days, his teams had completed the range with hours to spare. The Tiger Brigade's engineers had surveyed and dug vehicle fighting positions and target pits. Using their tanks like 60-ton pick-up trucks, tankers had hauled the targets cut by the engineers to the pits and installed them on the lifting machines. Meanwhile, the 8th Engineers had built two range towers, complete with radios and verandas for VIPs. Built to stay, the towers were supported by telephone poles sunk into rock. Tilelli said it symbolized "a relative training permanence."

For the sake of a flock of golden sheep, Pegasus Range nearly didn't happen. The amiable Heim, crisscrossing the valley in his dusty tan pick-up, had persuaded every Bedouin but one to take their camels and sheep and move away. One old Bedouin refused Heim's pleas to move. Desert Shield, whipping a world into marshal frenzy, had failed to reach this shepherd and his flock. He refused the exhortations of the Saudi liaison officer. He refused to budge. The huge flock made use of the valley impossible. In an inspired move, the local prince was informed; the sheep it turned out, were his. The old shepherd was no fool. The prince sent an officer of his militia to convey his approval, the Bedouin nodded, and the royal sheep trotted from the valley and Heim's harried life.

The gunnery "course" included three engagements against full-size plywood silhouettes by day, three more at night. In each engagement, the crew had to identify and shoot their targets as they rose from the sand at distances up to 2,500 meters. The engagements forced crews to fire on the move, using the tank's stabilized gun, and to fire while in their gas masks. Every command was evaluated by remote radio, everything was timed; a 120mm tank round, a 25″ depleted uranium arrow 1″ in diameter, flew 1,700 meters a second, but only if the crew survived to fire it.

Finally, Charlie Company, TF 1-8 Cav took their old M1s "downrange" a last time to proof the shooting gallery they had helped build. They returned with their thumbs up.

"Initially, Iraqi gunners responded to our artillery raids. However, our...counterfire engaged the enemy with devastating effect. The message was unequivocally received..." (1st Cav Div Command Review). A 333rd FA counterfire radar crewman prepares his Q37 radar for a training mission. Later, the radar would track enemy shell trajectories back to their guns, targeting them for friendly strikes.

First Team commanders at AA Horse, from left (standing): Col. George Harmeyer, 1st Bde; Col. Randolph House, 2nd Bde; Col. John Sylvester, 1st "Tiger" Brigade; Brig. Gen. Tommy Franks, Asst. Div. Cdr. — Maneuver; Brig. Gen. John H. Tilelli Jr., Commanding General; Brig. Gen. Josue Robles Jr., Asst. Div. Cdr. — Support; Col. Leon LaPorte, Chief of Staff; Col. William McGill, Aviation Brigade; Col. Richard Fousek, DISCOM; Col. Richard Cadorette, 43rd Corps Support Group; (Kneeling): Capt. Marshall Townsend II, HHC Cdr; Lt. Col. Hans Van Winkle, 8th Engineer Bn; Lt. Col. Walter Sharp, 1-7 Cav; Lt. Col. Randall Harris, 4-5 Air Defense Artillery Bn; Lt. Col. Richard Armstrong, 312th Military Intelligence Bn; Lt. Col. Edgar Steele, 13th Signal Bn; not shown: Col. James M. Gass, Division Artillery.

Not missing the opportunity for a ceremony, the last TF 1-8 Cav crew to fire an M1 and the first TF 2-8 Cav crew to fire an M1A1 presented the spent shells to the commanding general. Pegasus Range was in business.

During the ceremony, Iraq fired a symbolic shot of its own, sending a Scud towards Israel. The missile fell inside Iraq's border, but its use raised anxiety for several days.

On Thanksgiving, when Heim had released his crews to return for dinner to their units, he had stayed with Davis and five drivers. Before driving out a load of targets, they too had paused for a repast brought out to them. Later, the commanding general stopped at the tower. Tilelli had come expressly to ensure they were eating right that special day.

Thanksgiving was symbolic. Along with Christmas, it had always meant home to soldiers away. In 1990, it also stood for America's support of her troops in the desert. The President decreed that all soldiers would eat as they would at home. To soldiers used to field rations, beholding tables bent under platters heaped with turkey and ham, stuffing and potatoes, squash and breads, and all those pies —

T.J. WILCOX

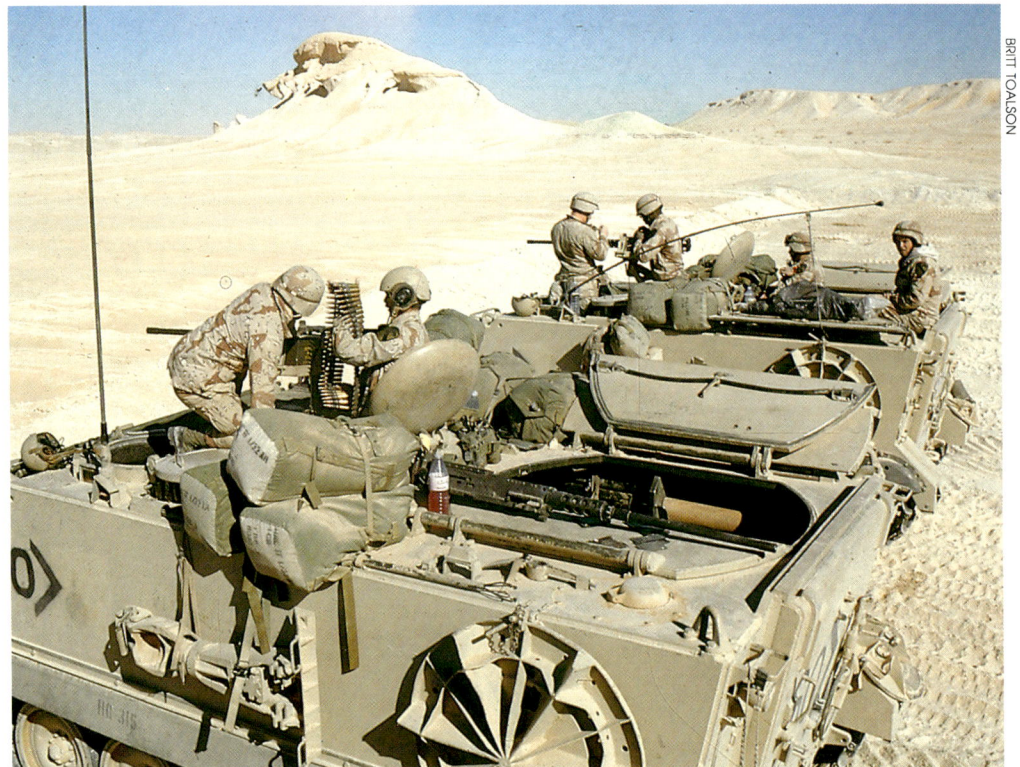

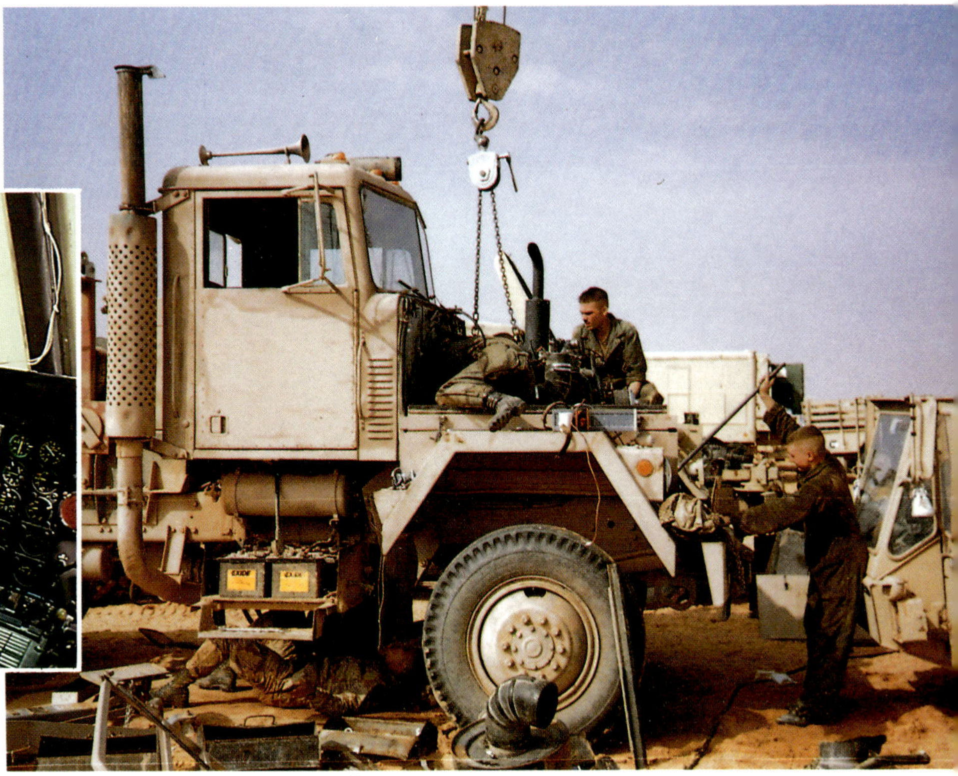

J.E. PHILLIPS

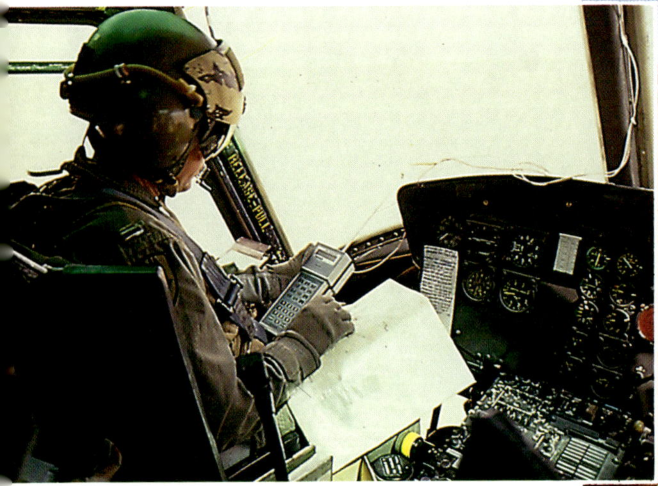

Navigation in a featureless desert was greatly eased by navigation aids such as loran and global positioning systems (GPS). Here, UH-1 pilot Chief Warrant Officer Ken Weust navigates with his loran.

Heavy use and the ravages of sand made vehicle maintenance critical. In the untidy world of field maintenance, 115th FSB mechanics at work on an 8th Engineer 5-ton tractor.

BRITT TOALSON

Each mechanized infantry and tank battalion had its own armored mortar platoon of six 4.2" mortars. Affectionately called "hip pocket artillery," mortars were especially responsive and heavily relied on, and normally led by the best officers and sergeants. Here, mortar crews prepare for gunnery at Pegasus Range in January.

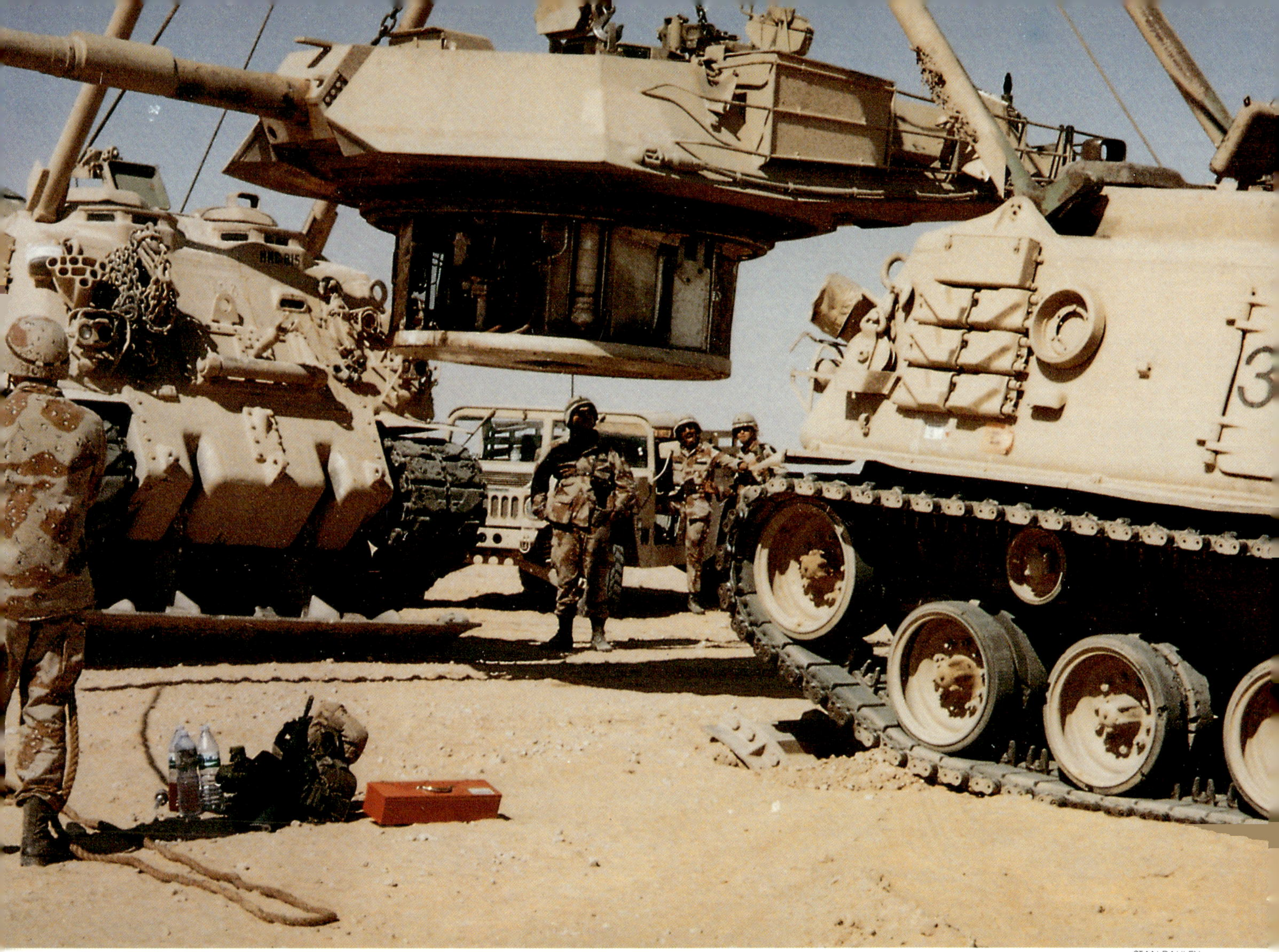

STAN PAULEY

1ST CAV PAO

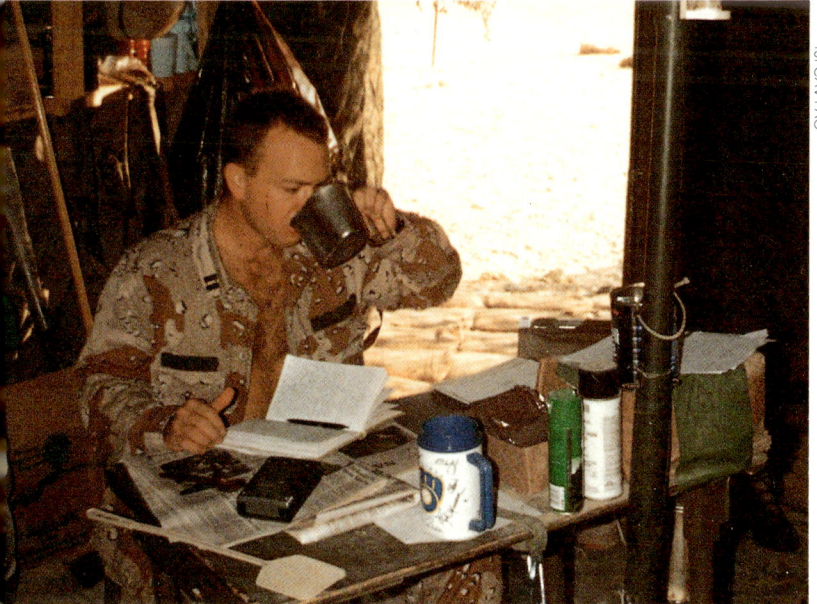

(Above) An M1 turret, suspended by two M88A1 armored recovery vehicles at the 115th FSB, about to be set into its chassis following heavy maintenance.

(Left) In the desert, only the necessities counted. Capt. David Lemelin commands Headquarters Company, TF 1-32 Armor from a field table in his tent, with a flyswatter close at hand, a flytrap overhead and Baghdad Betty on the radio.

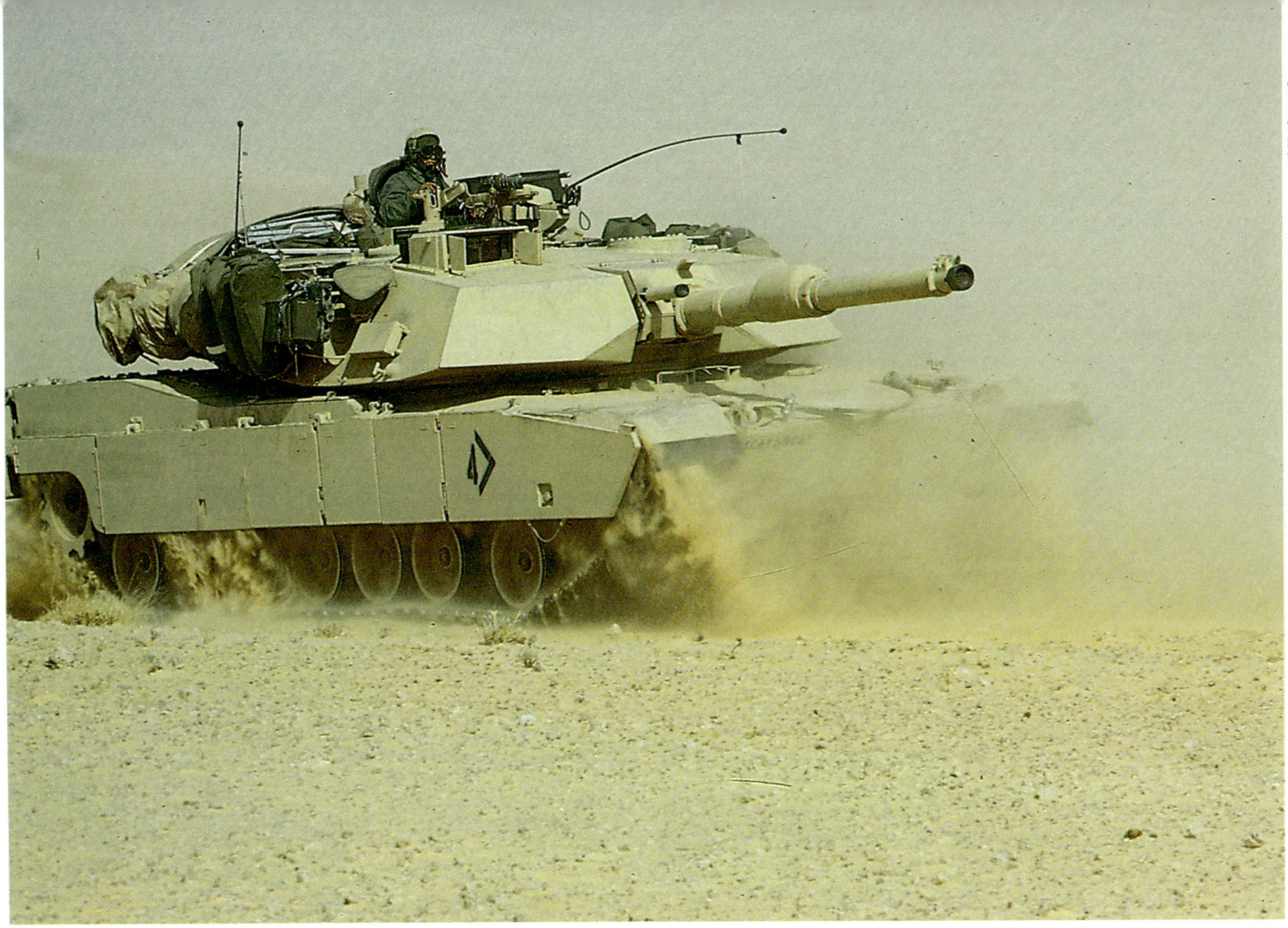

BRITT TOALSON

Taking their new mount for a ride, a TF 1-5 Cav crew races over the desert in their M1A1 Abrams. Like their infantry brothers, maneuvering tank crews kept muzzles capped against the sand.

1ST CAV PAO

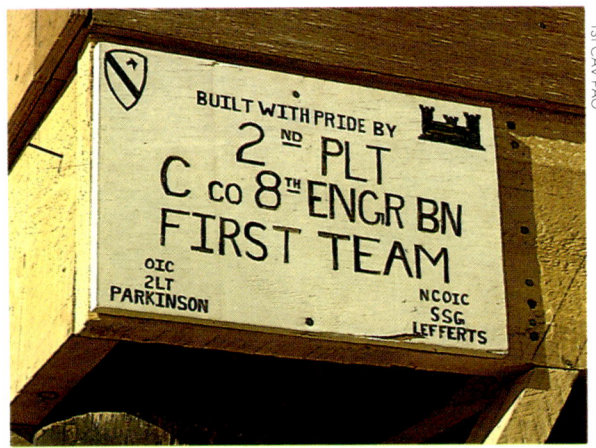

The 8th Engineers, who in February would show their skill at combat demolitions along the border, spent the fall in construction. From native claylike "marl," they paved roads through the division's high traffic areas, from imported lumber, built the control towers of Pegasus Range, proudly proclaiming their solid work.

CURTIS HOCOM

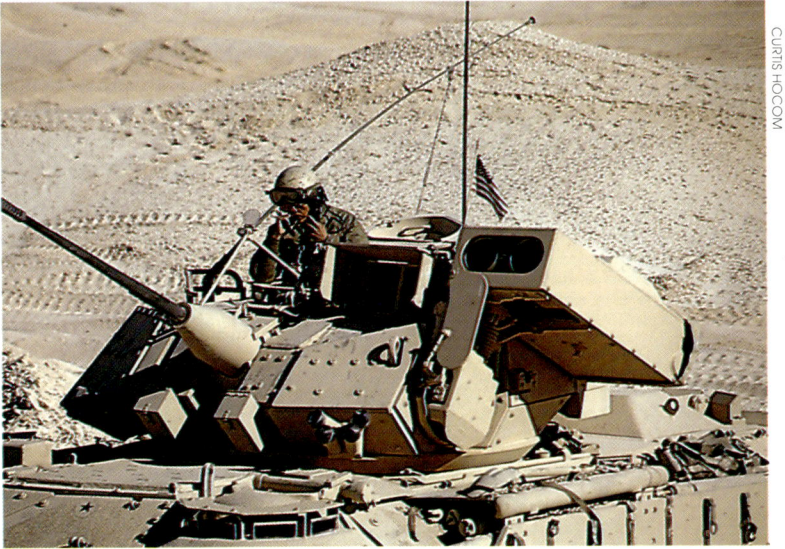

With Old Glory waving, a Bradley commander prepares for his first engagement at Pegasus Range.

(Right) Before engaging full-size, pop-up enemy tank targets, new M1A1 main guns were test-fired and gunsights aligned on the Pegasus Range screening line, preparing the system for the main course. 1st Brigade M1A1s fire their first rounds. CURTIS HOCOM

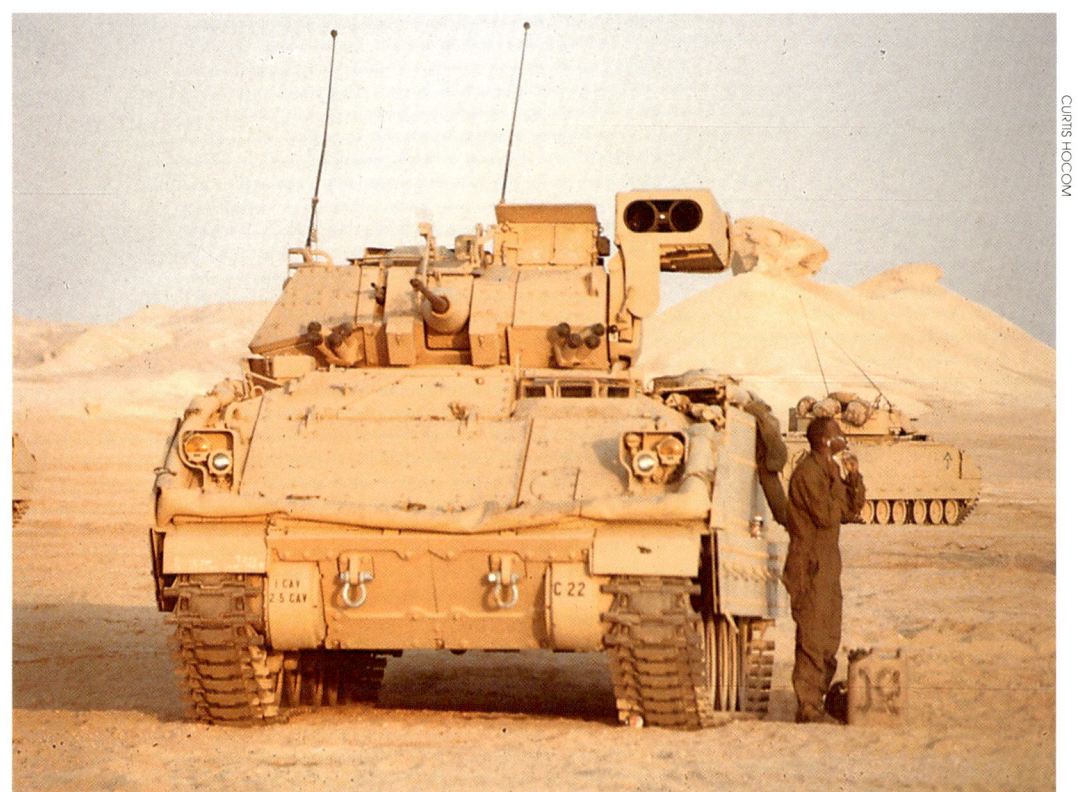

(Right) As the day begins at Pegasus Range, Sgt. Dwayne Crutchfield gets in a quick pre-gunnery shave.

(Below) Gunnery at Pegasus Range was an around-the-clock affair, each crew firing night – as well as daytime engagements. In a brilliant lance, the tracer of an Abrams 120mm round streaks to the target, a mile away.

CURTIS HOCCOM

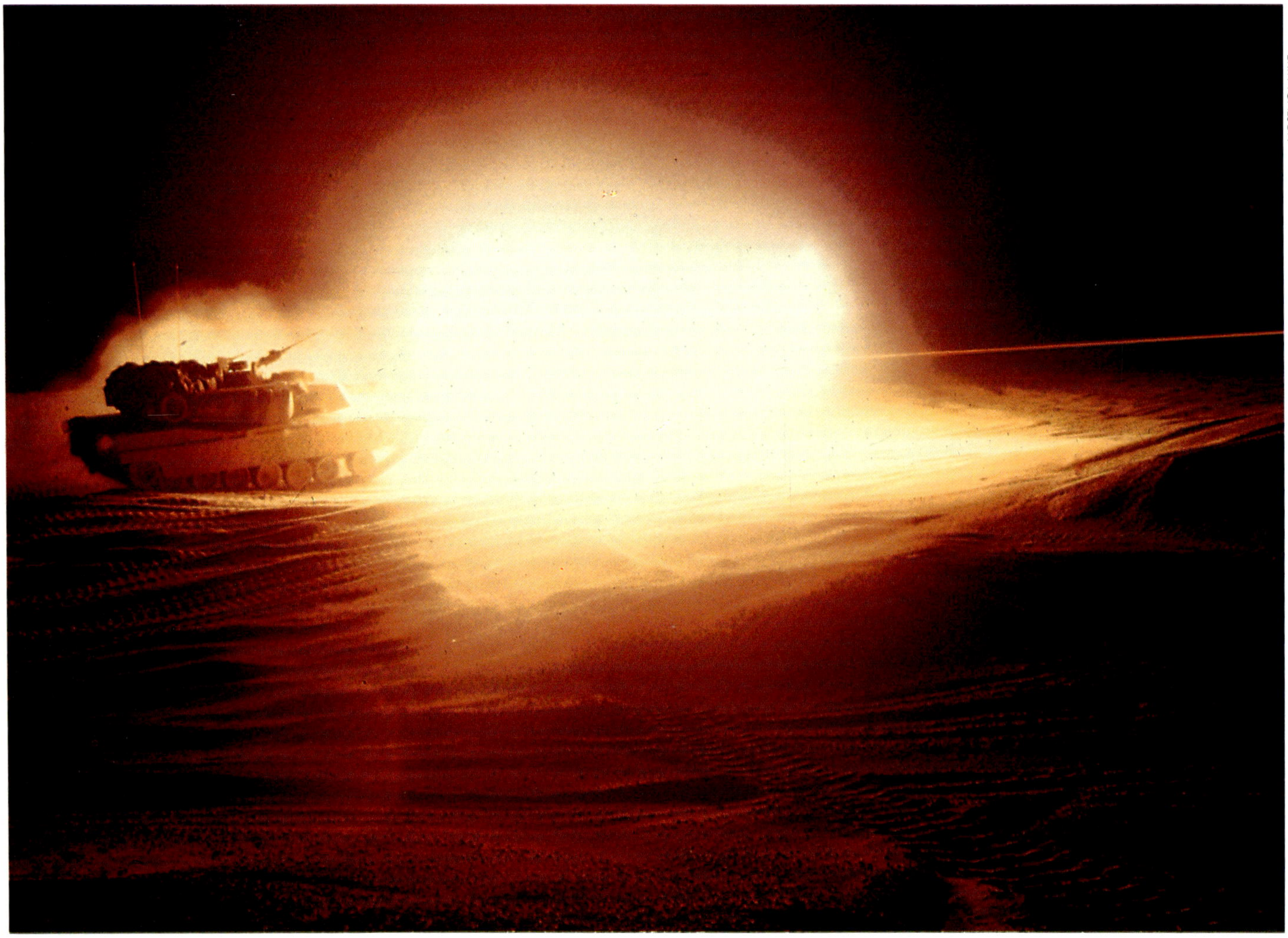

BRITT TOALSON

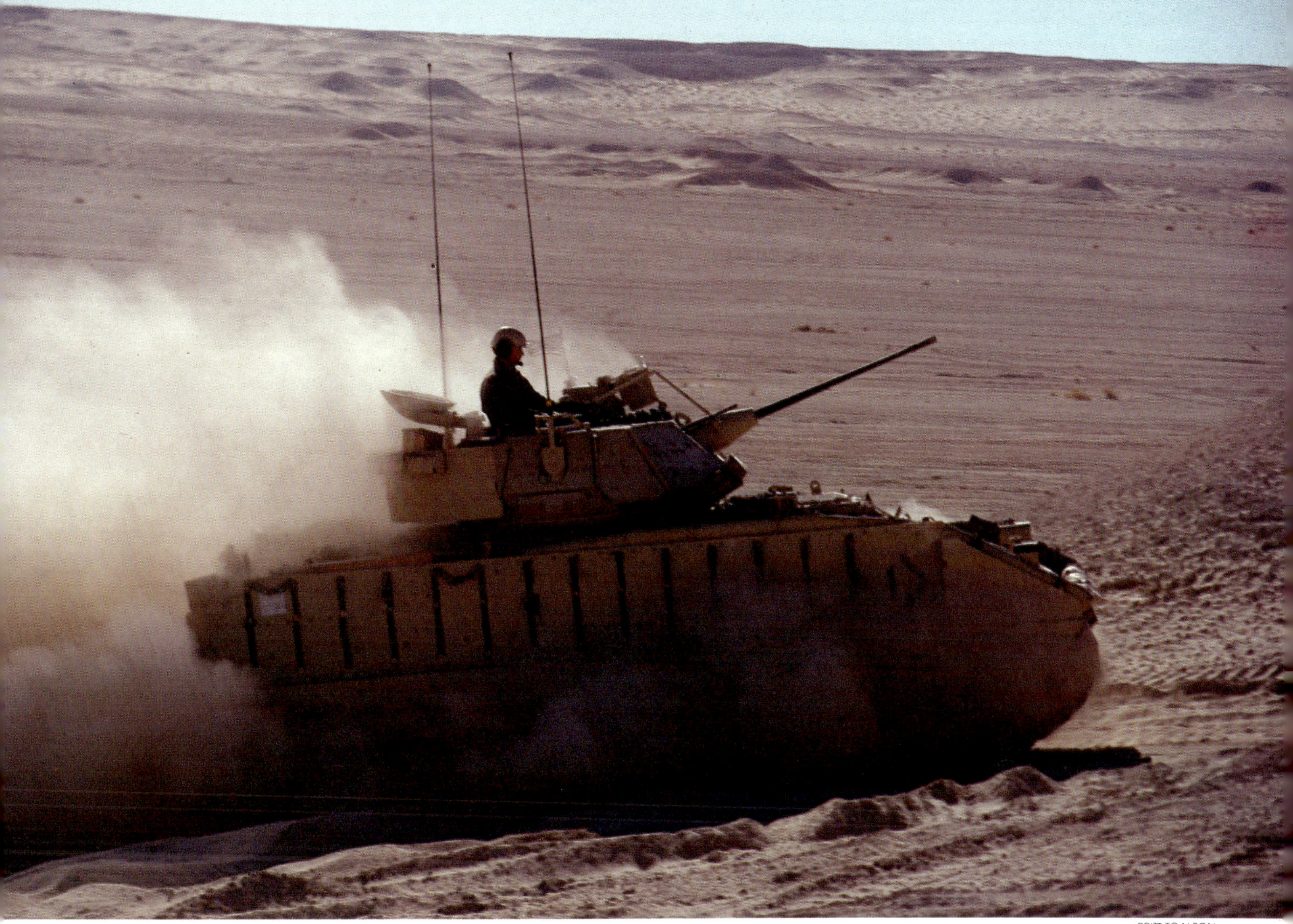

BRITT TOALSON

BRITT TOALSON

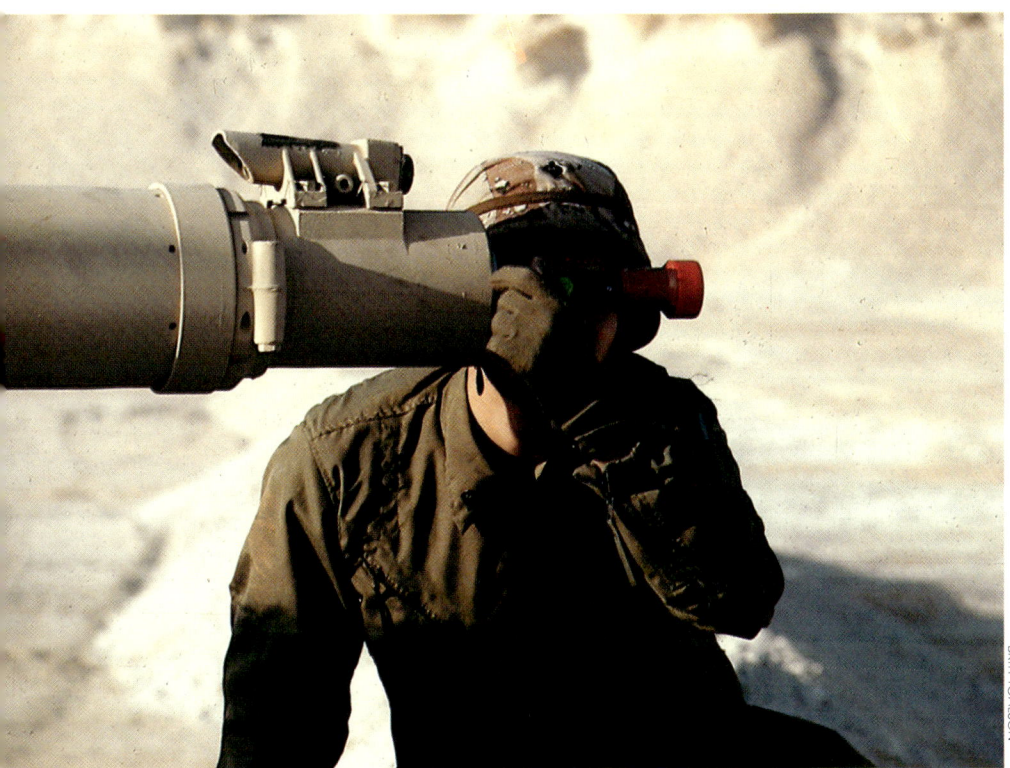

(Above) A Bradley Fighting Vehicle roars into firing position at Pegasus Range.

(Left) To bring the tank's adjustable sights into line with the cannon, the crew boresighted the system regularly. A tank commander places the crosshairs of a boresight device onto a target. The device shows exactly where the gun is aimed. With the gun's "lay" known, the gunner inside adjusts his optics to coincide, bringing both gun and sights into alignment.

after three months of dreaming about a simple french fry — it was almost too much. There was even cold Sharp's near-beer; good enough to drink!

Not satisfied with mere function, unit cooks, honestly overjoyed with the opportunity to stay up 24 to 36 hours to prepare their soldiers' gut-shot tastebuds something real, pulled out the stops ornamenting their mess tents. From the States had come banners and balloons. The Army had provided Thanksgiving menu programs. Each mess tent featured some sort of centerpiece table with a cornucopia overflowing with nuts, fruit, and candy. The NBC "Today Show" filmed 13th Signal Battalion's all-night preparation of the meal. Days before, ABC's "Good Morning America" had gone live from 1-7 Cav. In an interview with host Charlie Gibson, a cavalryman solemnly remarked that he thanked those back home who supported the soldiers, and those who he'd heard were protesting — well, he was in the desert defending their right to do so…

Thanksgiving fell squarely during the uproar over restrictions on religious practices and the freedom of chaplains. In the desert, the only real restriction was that the corps' chaplains had been told not to wear their cross emblems. A feisty bunch, many ignored even that rule. Religious freedom and practice were

If an army travels on its stomach, the First Team went far on Thanksgiving Day. Treating soldiers to a meal fit for their grandmother's, cooks across the division dished up turkey and ham, stuffing and potatoes with gravy, pies and cold "near-beer." Here, 2nd Brigade soldiers dig in.

CURTIS HOCOM

With desert-roughened hands, a soldier in TF 1-32 Armor serves the traditional Thanksgiving dessert. The division went through over 7,000 lbs of turkey, 4,400 lbs of canned ham, and 5,300 lbs of roast beef in a meal few would forget.

alive and well. At one unit on Thanksgiving, a visiting TV news crew seemed intent on exposing trouble by showing soldiers prevented from openly saying grace. The commander adroitly ended the matter by assembling his battery and before going into dinner, asking a well versed NCO to lead them in prayer — videocameras running.

Masked by the flurry of activity as the division celebrated the holidays and drew new vehicles, an exclusive cell of division planners quietly went to work on top secret plans which bore no resemblance to those they had crafted for the defense of Saudi Arabia. With VII Corps streaming in from Europe, the coalition dared to consider attack. The game, it appeared, had turned.

The success of Thanksgiving hinted at the magic that Christmas would work. The mail center in the soldier's mall was hit first. Unit trucks left its squat tents piled with parcels. The town of Tinley Park, Illinois, which had adopted the division, sent hundreds of Frisbees, hats, and "Any Soldier" cards. Their generosity wasn't unique. Public support from home found its greatest expression in the letters, cards, and parcels that were eagerly opened in the desert.

Christmas trees sprouted everywhere, as did sightings of Santa Claus. The trees, made from plywood sheets painted green, or camouflage nets draped over wooden frames, were festooned with decorations made of every imaginable bauble, from Christmas cards to dog tags. Young soldiers who had done little more than cruise the local mall the

THE SAUDI SANTA

The following is Capt. Dave Lemelin's account of a midnight visit from Saint Nicholas. Lemelin was commander of Headquarters Company, 1st Bn, 32d Armored Regiment throughout the campaign.

Santa visits TF 1-32 Armor.

On Christmas Eve, we dressed 1st Lt. Tom Deren up as Santa Claus. His crazy sister, a nun, had sent him the whole outfit. At midnight, the First Sergeant and I put Santa in my Humvee sleigh and drove off to all our farflung positions. The moon was brilliant and reflected off the sand like new fallen snow. At the first guard post, Santa answered the sentry's challenge with "Ho, Ho, Ho" and a flurry of candy, rather than the countersign. The startled guard let us by, probably figuring that use of deadly force was inappropriate against Santa.

Tom was a particularly ribald Santa and got a lot of laughs from the troops as we visited tents and command posts. Our final stop was at the battalion command group's sleep tents, where Santa nearly became a casualty. He startled the executive officer, big Maj. J.D. Thurman, who thought it was a terrorist assassination attempt and reached frantically for his pistol. We elves quickly calmed him down and no shots were fired.

We finished our Noel drinking non-alcoholic beer with Maj. Thurman and the rest of the command group, discussing the chances of us doing this same thing in the same place next Christmas...

Behold, a light shines in the darkness.

previous Christmas, carefully hung each decoration on their homemade tree, which radiated back the warmth of cherished memories, and guarded hopes.

Christmas dinner rivaled Thanksgiving. In the early afternoon as it ended, the wind rose and the sky grayed in the biggest sandstorm yet. It blew nearly all day, howling and flapping the canvas tent walls. It was a day to stay indoors, to enjoy friends and the booty brought by the mailman; cookies, Game-Boys, all manner of munchies, new cassettes, chips and salsa for the die-hard Tex-Mex crowd, books, and candy by the pound.

A week later, New Year's celebrations dotted the black desert, welcoming 1991. In the division rear area, on a bluff overlooking a New Year's Eve party, a huge "1991" in colored lights blinked on at midnight. Soon, the division would move north to Tactical Assembly Area Wendy, and a place called the Wadi al Batin, close to the enemy, a jumping off point for attack. Things had changed from the "speedbump" days of October. The coalition swelled with VII Corps armor, but Saddam had pumped up his forces, too: over 530,000 troops, 4,000 tanks, and 3,000 artillery pieces. They'd come far, but how much farther they'd go in this brand new 1991 no one knew.

CAV COUNTRY
FIRST TEAM

Vol. 2, No. 3   1st Cavalry Division   January 12, 199

THE DEADLY MORTAR

A 1-32 Armor mortarman prepares a mortar round as his platoon readies for a live-fire on Pegasus Range.
Curtis Hocom
Britt Toalson

By Robyn Gregory
1st Cav Div Public Affairs

"Hey, AT&T doesn't have anything on us, we can really reach out and touch someone," said Master Sgt. Dennis Minter as he watched his mortar platoon from the 1st Battalion, 32nd Armor Regiment live-fire at Pegasus Range.

Their touch with 4.2-inch mortars is meant to land destruction on an enemy in support of 1-32's maneuver elements.

"I'm aiming at a fly," said an enthusiastic Sgt. Daniel Scott, a mortarman, whose squad was next in setting up an aiming circle. Section sergeants set up these aiming circles to double-check each other's accuracy.

"The section sergeant lays in the direction of fire using a compass to exact mils," Minter explained. Normally, in hipfire or traveling we wouldn't do it.

"The guns could fire without the fire direction center and get an emergency round off within a minute."

Accuracy with the mortars requires good coordination, the platoon sergeant added.

"It's a team effort. The forward observers are the eyes, the FDC is the brain, and the crews are the muscles that put it down range. It takes all three working together," Minter said.

After receiving a call for fire from the FDC, Pfc. Jamison Foy begins cutting "cheese charges" that ignite the powder bags. Mathematics determine these missions will call for .25 charges.

The mortars begin hanging rounds and though the crews will never see them hit,
See Mortars, page 4

1-7 Cav updates technology, retains tradition

Mission remains same, newer methods used

By Daniel Maloney
4th Public Affairs Detachment

The mission of the cavalry scout has remained the same for over a hundred years: the "eyes and ears" of the command by providing reconnaissance and security.

What has changed is the way scouts of today conduct that mission and where it is conducted.

Unlike the scouts of the past whose missions took them across America's frontiers, the scouts of the 1st Troop, 7th Cavalry, are conducting their mission in the desert of Saudi Arabia as part of Operation Desert Shield. The mounts, too, have evolved to M2 Bradley Fighting Vehicles, OH-58 Observation Helicopters, and AH-1 Cobra Attack Helicopters.

Additionally, they receive support from attached elements such as 6th Combat Aviation Brigade, Fort Hood (air traffic control), 13th Signal Battalion and an Air Force Liason team that provides weather information and coordinates air support.

Although the technology has increased to a level old scouts would find incomprehensible, it is the tradition of the 7th Cav that instills the motivation necessary complete the mission.

The past is also heard in the language used by 1-7 Ca soldiers. The ground scouts speak of "mounting" an "dismounting" the Bradley, calling to mind the scout past mode of transport, the horse.

But among the three ground cavalry troops (two from the 2nd Armored Division's 2-1 Cav) and the two a cavalry troops, ties to the past are only part of the 7t Cav tradition.

Whether it's wreaking havoc as the Opposing Forc
See Cavalry, page

PRINTED BY TIHAMA - DAMMAM, TEL. 8420434

FIRST TEAM / CAV COUNTRY

Commander's Corner

Last Saturday, I observed a brigade conduct a battalion breach of a complex obstacle. The obstacle was a combination of mines, wire, a berm and finally a fire trench overwatched by an OPFOR. This mission once again highlights the meaning of the team and the requirement for teamwork. It required a fine-tuned racehorse to breach and break through this sophisticated defense. Detailed planning and aggressive execution by each soldier is what made the mission successful.

The obstacle resembled what we may encounter. The performance by the breaching battalion proves that training and working as a team makes the difference.

Friendly reconnaissance located the obstacle, immediately putting into action the battalion's breaching force. Combined arms units went into overwatch, calling in artillery fire, keeping our engineers free to move forward to the breach site.

Probing the belts of mines and cutting through rolls of concertina, the engineers opened lanes, a combat engineer vehicle following to proof the breach and plow over the berm. Only the fire trench remained.

Covered by tanks and infantry, armored vehicle launched bridges spanned the trench. Within seconds, the first Bradleys and Abrams poured through the gaps and the OPFOR's front line.

To successsfully overcome the obstacle, the individual parts of the battalion worked as a single force, as a solid team. Each element supported the others, each depended on the others. Success was never in doubt.

Nothing can stand in our way when we move as a team. Our collective strength as a team is far greater than our strength as many individuals.

It's no coincidence we're called the First Team! It's as a team that we'll continue to overcome the obstacles and succeed. It's as a team that we'll continue to earn our name. It's as a team that we stand ready to accomplish any mission.

First Team!

Brig. Gen. John H. Tilelli Jr.
Commanding General

Cavalry, from page 1

uring field exercises at Fort Hood, roviding accurate and timely recon nd security in the real-world mission f Operation Desert Shield, the tradi- on of hard, realistic training has lways made the difference.

When it comes to firsthand nowledge of enemy operations, the round scouts and the air cav scouts ain to keep their skills honed in the audi desert.

According to Hanson, the training is one in a cycle. While one troop is onducting maintenance another will e practicing reaction force skills and maneuver exercises.

In addition to keeping skills at an optimum high, the training keeps morale high, Hanson said. "Our training program keeps everybody busy and is a key to keeping morale up."

The training is also conducted with an eye on every possible contingency.

"We are on an operational mission now. Although we continue to train while we're here, the threat is real-world and tends to give everyone a sense of urgency." He added, "We're training on the war-fighting skills necessary to win."

The Oasis

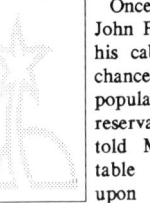

By Chaplain Dennis Camps
1st Cav Division Chaplain

Once early in his presidency John F. Kennedy and one of his cabinet members took a chance on getting a table in a popular restaurant without a reservation. The head waiter told Mr. Kennedy that no table was available. Where upon the cabinet member, sensing that the waiter did not recognize to whom he was speaking, told Mr. Kennedy, "Why don't you tell him that you're his president?" Mr. Kennedy replied, "If I have to tell him I'm his president, I'm not."

Mr. Kennedy rightly recognized that "president" is more than a title. It signifies a relationship. In much the same way, to be a chaplain means to be in a certain kind of relationship to a unit's soldiers and family members.

I believe that as a chaplain works, trains and shares the hardships and other common experiences with a unit, the relationship of chaplain is developed.

I am glad to have the title of "1st Cavalry Division Chaplain." I look forward to making the title a living relationship as we share the challenges and opportunities that lie before us.

First Team!

SAND HILTON

This Army-funded newspaper is an authorized publication for the soldiers of the 1st Cavalry Division supporting Operation Desert Shield in Saudi Arabia. Contents of Cav Country are not necessarily the official views of the U.S. Government, Department of Defense or the 1st Cavalry Division. Cav Country is a weekly publication of the 1st Cavalry Division Public Affairs Office and Tihama Advertising, Public Relations and Resarch, P.O. Box 2666, Dammam, 31461, Saudi Arabia, Tel: 842-0434.

1st Cavalry Division Commanding General..........Brig. Gen. John H. Tilelli Jr.
Public Affairs Officer .... Capt. Jeffrey E. Phillips
Public Affairs NCOIC .... Master Sgt. Thomas W. Fuller
Media Relations Officer ....Capt. Reginald Smith
Editor .... Pfc. Jose M. Zuniga
Assignments Editor...Spec. Robyn M. Gregory
Staff Writer.. Spec. Dean Welch
Photographers ....Sgt. Britt Toalson and Spec. Curtis Hocom

FIRST TEAM

CAV COUNTRY

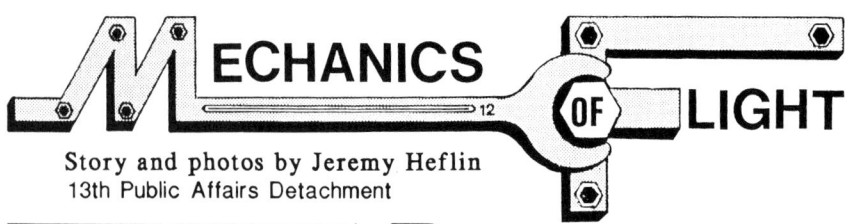

MECHANICS OF FLIGHT

Story and photos by Jeremy Heflin
13th Public Affairs Detachment

Maintaining the 1st Cavalry Division's fleet of helicopters is almost a 24-hour, seven-day-a-week job for Co. F, 227th Aviation Brigade's mechanics. (From left to right, clockwise) Private First Class Christopher Andrews removes the hot end off a UH-1 Huey turbine; Sgt. Jeff Barlow cleans a UH-1 rear tail rotor during a pre-flight inspection; maintenance personnel remove an OH-58D's engine to conduct a hot end inspection; and Spec. "Ziggy" Zeidner lubricates the main rotor assembly of a UH-1 turbine.

One of the most important parts of any unit's mission is maintenance, and in some cases the lack of it can be deadly. When a vehicle fails, it simply rolls to the side of the road and comes to a halt. If a helicopter fails, there is a drop of a few dozen to a thousand feet to correct the situation before an abrupt stop.

With that in mind, the soldiers of Company F, 227th Aviation Brigade hold the pilots' and passengers' lives in their hands as the main aviation maintenance unit for the 1st Cavalry Division. The Aviation Intermediate Maintenance (AVIM) company supports two attack aviation battalions, and all other 1st Cav aviation assets with parts and services including maintenance on the Army's most technical and sophisticated weapon, the AH-64 Apache helicopter.

Each portion of any helicopter needing repair has a platoon in the company specifically geared to take care of the problem. These platoons include: shops, avionics, forward support, production control, armaments, and supply and service as well as unit self support sections, the motorpool and a personnel administrative center.

"There's a lot of friendly rivalry between the aircraft crews," said Staff Sgt. Kirk Duggan, squad leader of UH-1 Forward Support. "We kid each other with friendly cutdowns between the different aircraft mechanics."

All kidding aside, the teams take their jobs seriously and consider themselves a tight group.

Captain Tammy Chamberlain, forward support platoon leader, explained that keeping all the helicopters up is something the mechanics feel balances with the protection provided by the equipment they maintain.

"They're the ones protecting us out here, so we are going to do whatever it takes to keep that force in place," Chamberlain said.

"That's how I feel about it, their lives and ours are on the line."

1-32 Armor cooks trade utensils for weapons

By Robyn Gregory
1st Cav Div Public Affairs

Fingers wrapped around M2 machine gun trigers, 1-32 Armor cooks practice the basics during a live-fire.
Curtis Hocom

You won't find these cooks frying eggs today — their fingers are wrapped around the triggers of M2 machine guns on Pegasus range.

The training for the 1st Battalion, 32nd Armor Regiment cooks and other headquarters soldiers ensures they could hold their own in their five-ton trucks.

"I'm a little nervous," said Sgt. Willie Macklin, a 1-32 Armor food specialist, while cleaning his .50 cal. "I'm kind of glad to go through this today. Being a cook, you don't get a chance for much training."

While fellow mortarmen lead concurrent training on weapon maintenance, one could not resist punning.

"Hey, could you pass the cooking oil?"

Humor prevailed and the cooks and mechanics didn't even seem to mind using their day off to fire.

"Training is more important than a day off," insisted Macklin. "If something should happen, I'll be ready now."

Pulling their trucks to the firing line, Macklin and the others put bullets tenaciously on target as easily as flipping an over easy egg.

Mortars, from page 1

somewhere the rounds are decimating a 50-meter zone, before untouched by civilization.

"In Vietnam, mortars were basically fired from firebases," explained the platoon sergeant. "This place is mechanized 100 percent."

The mortar platoon usually provides a wide variety of support for elements of 1-32 Armor ranging from making the enemy button up, to illumination, and also augments screening missions.

According to Minter, a delayed fuse causes more extensive damage on bunkers and dug in forces.

"If we had 300 rounds, we'd be making music!" Minter exclaimed.

"We'd get 10 rounds downrange and then we'd really bring hell on the target."

And that hell was apparent as 1-32's mortarmen witnessed their target's destruction downrange.

Testing
Staff Sergeant Richard Pugh, 3-82 FA, field tests a Bradley converted into a fire support vehicle.

4

"I've got indications there may be a pre-G Day attack coming down. First Cav, you're the only guy here. Go up there and link up with the 101st..."

— Lt. Gen. Frederick Franks
VII Corps Commander

TOW launchers in firing position, M3A2 Cavalry fighting vehicle crews of 1st Squadron, 7th Cavalry Regiment watch for the enemy from the division's forward screen line during the defense of the Wadi al Batin early in the air campaign. By late January, the division's front line had crept north, with 1-7 Cav mere kilometers from the border. J.E. PHILLIPS

RACE TO THE DEFENSE

Barely a week old, the new year brought crisis. Allied intelligence analysts revealed Iraqi units assembling north of the border near the Wadi al Batin, the area's natural north-south approach and that used historically by invading armies. The 10 kilometer-wide Wadi al Batin, a shallow valley, was the approach that Hussein suspected would bear the main Coalition attack.

Enemy units, missile launchers among them, were moving ominously toward the area. Unmistakably this was an army poised for a pre-emptive attack down the Wadi to destroy the logistic bases clustered around King Khalid Military City (KKMC) and the main supply route (MSR) running alongside the Trans-Arabian Pipeline, the "Tapline," which ended in outlets on the Mediterranean coast. These were the great logistic bases that would fuel Gen. Schwarzkopf's "Hail Mary" attack. If Hussein destroyed or even disrupted them, he could derail the Allied plan, and win crucial political and psychological prestige.

Although the coalition had nothing in position to stop an attack, in the process of moving 550 kilometers from AA Horse into Tactical Assembly Area Wendy, adjacent to KKMC, the 1st Cav was within reach of the area. Some units, 1st Brigade among them, had already arrived. At 9:00 a.m., Jan. 9, VII Corps Commander, Lt. Gen. Frederick Franks ordered the division, now under his control, to prepare to defend the Tapline Road. He attached the 2nd Brigade, 101st Airborne Division (Air Assault) to the division for the defense, boosting the 1st Cav's strength. Immediately, the "Screaming Eagles" began deploying from their assembly area near An Nairiyah. They would give the division an unusual mix of heavy and light forces.

The defenders arrived to find plate-flat desert, strewn with gravel and broken

CURTIS HOCOM

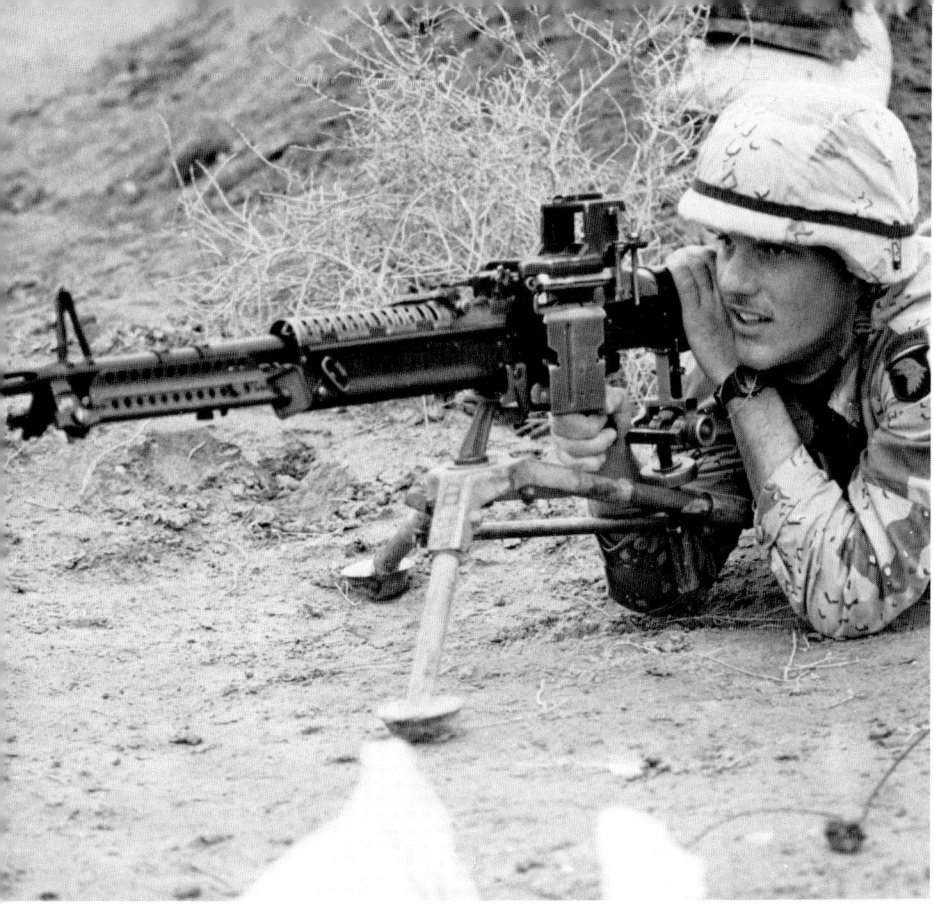

(Left) Defending the airfield, an M60 machine gunner of 2nd Brigade, 101st Airborne Division (Air Assault) checks his field of fire. Each defender had a specific zone to cover, zones interlocked to form deadly carpets of firepower all around El Qaysumah.

(Below) The Associated Press Radio reports on the aerial pounding of Iraqi units across the border in late January capture the attention of tankers in Delta Company, TF 3-32 Armor.

J.E. PHILLIPS

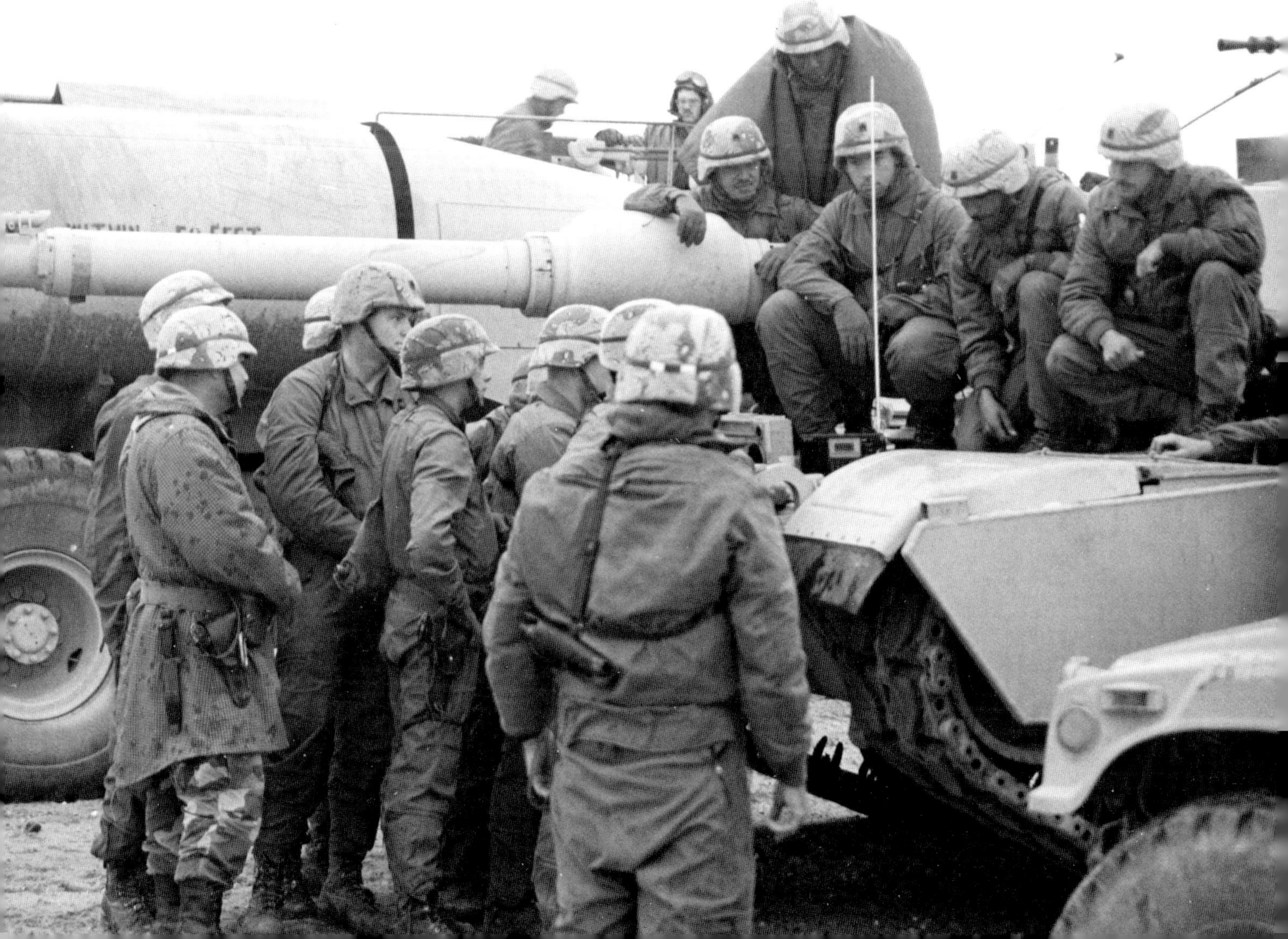

only by the sprawl of the town of Hafar al Batin and the Airfield at El Qaysumah, 13 kilometers to the east. The Tapline road, named main supply route (MSR) Dodge, connected the airfield and Hafar al Batin. Intersecting MSR Dodge at Hafar al Batin, MSR Sultan, also a two lane road, led south 60 kilometers to KKMC. Both roads were worn and pitted from the pounding traffic of an army preparing for battle.

Unusually heavy winter rain had flooded the Wadi al Batin. Its shallow trench was a mire, passage across much of its length impossible. Even the sure-footed Humvees bogged helplessly.

Intelligence indicated the Iraqis would attack with three mechanized or armored divisions. If they were successful, more would follow to exploit the penetration. Allied air attacks would destroy a substantial portion of the enemy — estimates ran to 80 percent — but enough would survive the aerial scourge, and within hours, Iraqi armor would be on the defenders.

The division's mission was to prevent the enemy from penetrating past MSR Dodge, protect El Qaysumah Airfield, the crossroads at Hafar al Batin, and the routes to KKMC. On its left was the French 6th Light Armored Division; to its right the 3rd Egyptian Division; to the northwest, Syrian forces.

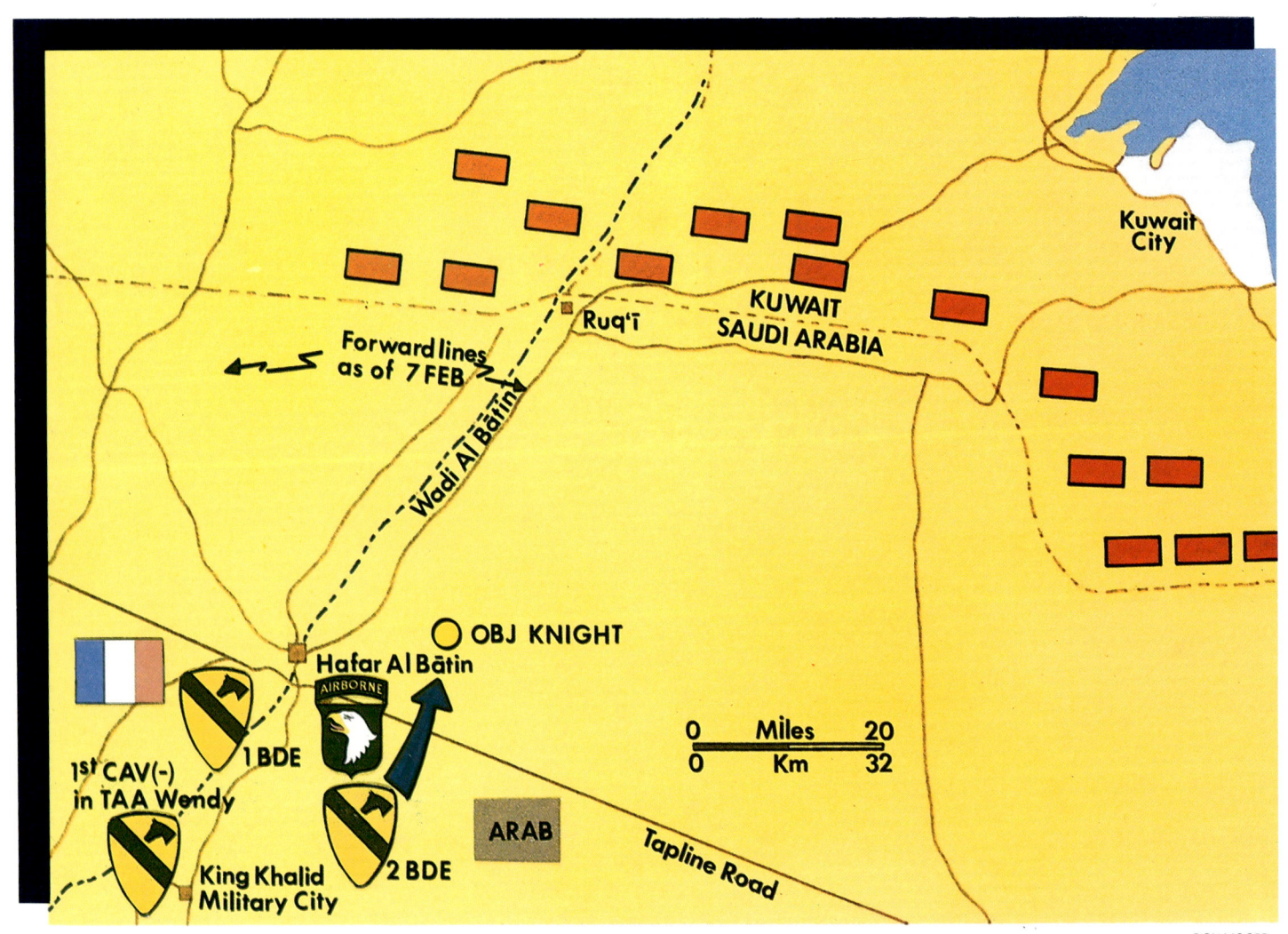

DEFENSE IN THE WADI

Situation on January 14, as defensive preparations along the Tapline road are complete. First Brigade has tied in with the 6th (French) Light Division on the left, 2nd Brigade, 101st Airborne Division (Air Assault) holds El Qaysumah Airfield and the Tapline to the 1st Brigade's right, 2nd "Blackjack" Brigade is prepared to counterattack into Objective Knight, destroying the enemy.

Soldiers from various nations inevitably compared equipment. American GI's weary of Meatballs in Spiced Sauce or Chicken a la King were only too happy to trade off their MREs for something more exotic. Liaison officers from the 6th (French) Light Armored Division enjoy the favorite pastime, comparing weapons with their counterparts at the 1st Cavalry Division main command post in January.

Liaison between divisions was critical. Promptly, liaison teams of sergeants and officers loaded up Humvees and slid off into the desert, heading for the command posts of allied headquarters, French, Egyptian, and Syrian among them. As they left, teams from adjacent units arrived.

After weeks of planning for their own attack, the division staff now reversed course and launched into planning a defense. The plan called for tight coordination: the enemy, prodded along by French and U.S. air and artillery strikes, would slide east along the Tapline road, a wall barbed with tanks and Bradleys from 1st Brigade. He would then reel into a kill zone surrounded on three sides by 1st Brigade,

Desert fog, a "Shamal," a particularly vicious sandstorm, hits the division's rear CP, coating bunkers and driving grit in a tempest packing enough wallop to collapse sandbagged tents.

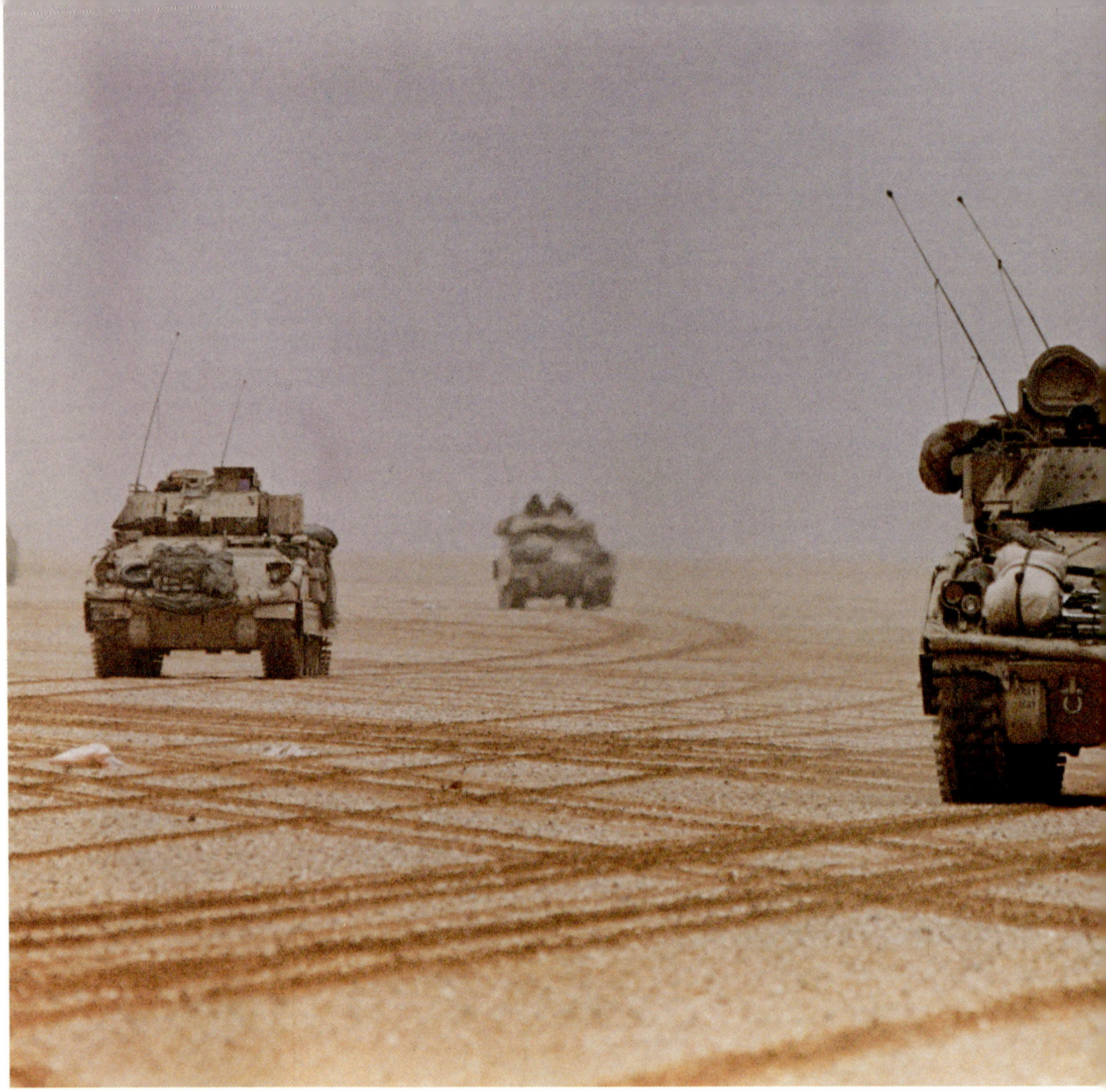

J.E. PHILLIPS

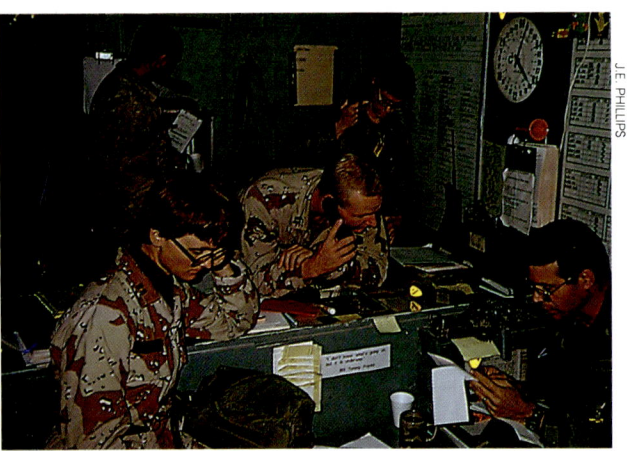

As war dawns on the morning of Jan. 17, Major Gary Moore and operations officers in the division's main CP monitor activities in the tense hours following the opening of hostilities. Soldiers had prepared for combat since August, but its final onset left some in disbelief, many wondering what would happen next.

1ST CAV PAO

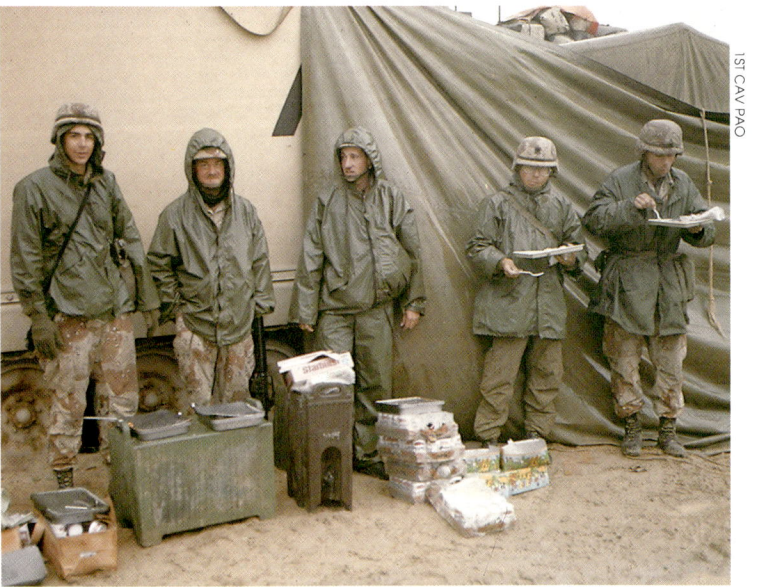

(Right) Cold chow and rain — all too familiar sights in the Wadi — greet TF 1-32 Armor Commanding Officer Lt. Col. James Methered (fourth from left) and members of his command post taking a break for supper "al fresco."

STEVE ELFERS

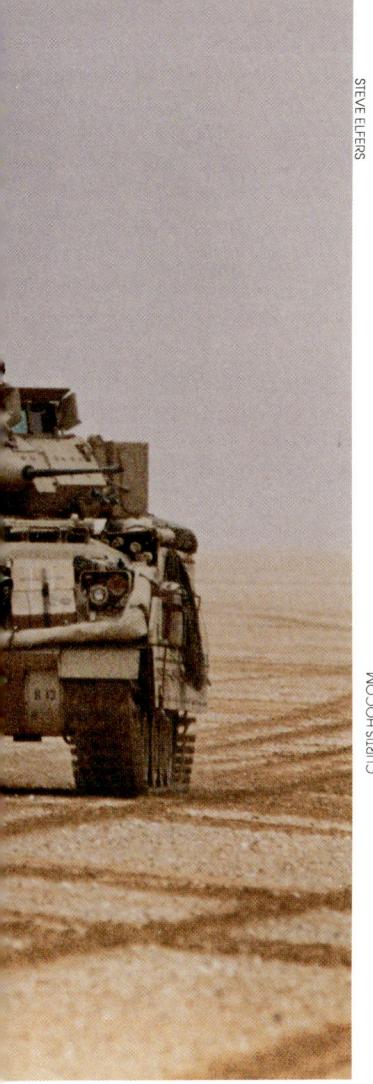

Business end of the combat wedge, Bravo Company, 2-5 Cav practices the attack formation used throughout the division. Placing tanks and Bradleys on a wedge-shaped front, nine kilometers wide, the wedge enabled the brigade battle task force to move swiftly and react instantly to contact. Artillery and engineer units were centered and logistic elements trailed. Well drilled artillery batteries fired from the march, halting only briefly.

CURTIS HOCOM

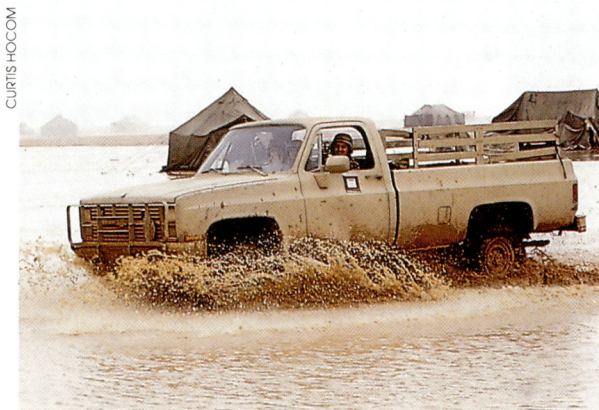

Far cry from October's heat, the ceaseless rains of January and February saturated the desert, bringing up patches of green. Troops destined to fight on the ground were anxious over the impact of rain and clouds on the success of Air Force bombing.

(Below) In a war of watching and waiting, those who could see in the night had the upper hand. A mortar crew has installed an infrared sight on their .50-caliber machine gun.

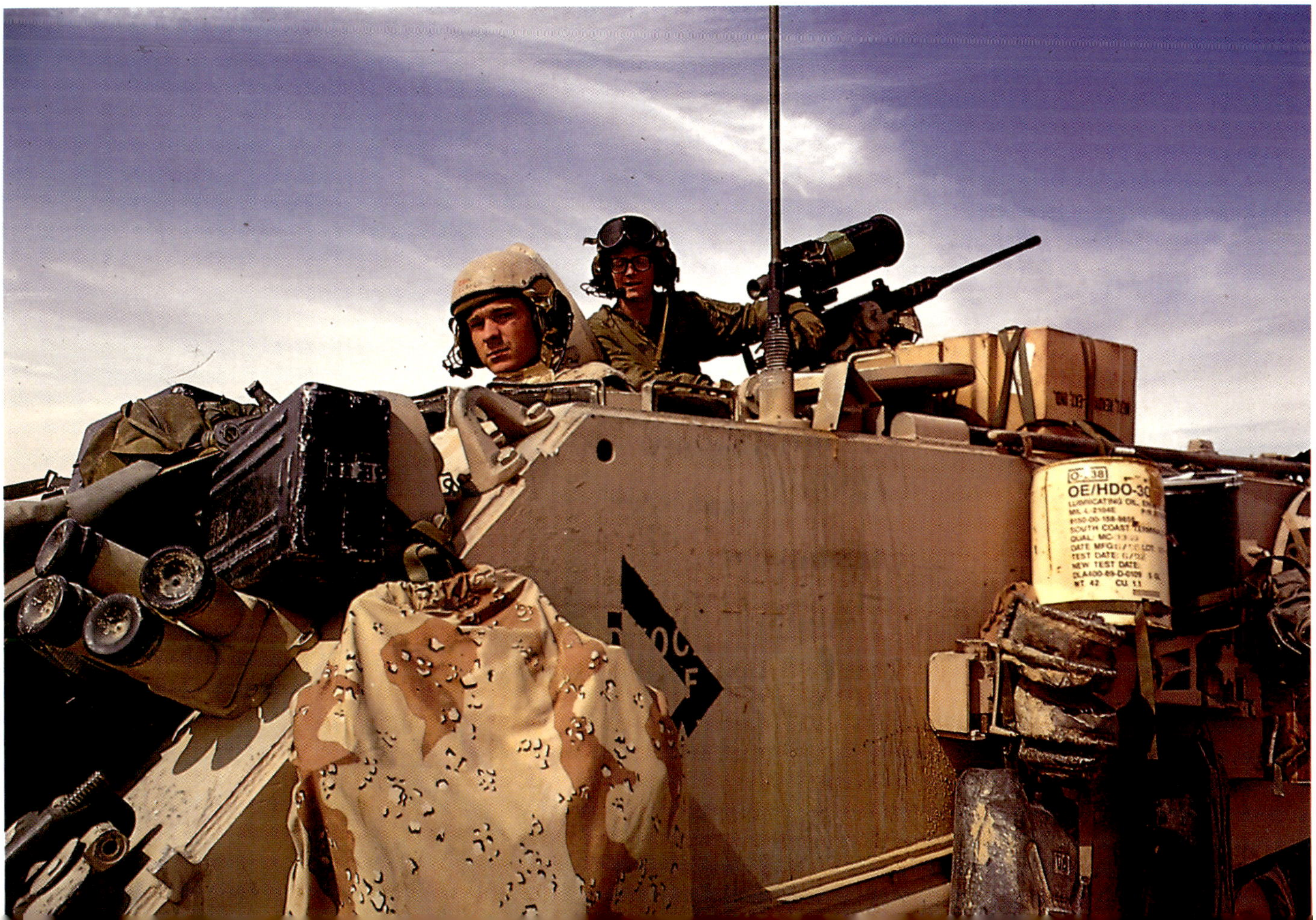

BRITT TOALSON

Their headrests specially upholstered by their crew chief, Chief Warrant Officer Mike Butler (L), pilot, and Capt. Mike Klingele, copilot and commander of Charlie Company, 1-227 Aviation, prepare to take up their Apache.

the 2nd Brigade, 101st Airborne, and the Blackjack Brigade counterattacking from south of the Tapline, to the east of the airfield, and into Objective Knight on the enemy's left flank.

Rain pelted the desert as 101st Airborne troopers arrived at El Qaysumah Airport. In a battle against time and weather, they dug in. Combat engineers, operating their own equipment as well as abandoned civilian dozers and backhoes, dug alongside the infantry. In 48 hours, an anti-tank ditch ringed the defenders for 13 kilometers. Bright yellow Caterpillar tractors on the battlefield were a jarring sight, but no one complained.

Moving to the critical place, Brig. Gen. Tilelli directed preparations from his tactical command post on the Tapline. On the 13th, in a night move through blinding rain, armor from the 1st Brigade and what had arrived of the 2nd was flung north into the line. The brigades had less than 12 hours to dash from partially established positions in TAA Wendy and secure battle positions along the Tapline. Entire units pulled out in the gathering dusk and downpour, leaving behind tents and shelters, field showers and latrines, cots and Christmas packages. They marched through the southern reaches of the Wadi, working through the quagmire in the impenetrable blackness, making it through sheer tenacity.

Lt. Col. Murray Williams, a U.S. liaison officer

An artilleryman adjusts his M9 aiming circle as his crew practices occupying a firing position from the march.

The Avenger, based on the HMMWV, could fire eight Stingers from the turret before reloading, or its crew could dismount and fire from the shoulder, away from the vehicle. For self-defense, it mounted a .50-caliber machine gun. Stinger anti-aircraft missiles ready, a 4-5 ADA Avenger keeps watch near the division main CP.

Fuel HEMTTs, laden with 2,500 precious gallons, cross the Wadi headed for an evening rendezvous with TF 1-8 Cav's thirsty tanks and Bradleys. The relatively new HEMTT proved durable and capable, a welcome sight to armor crewmen in a division consuming some 300,000 gallons of fuel daily.

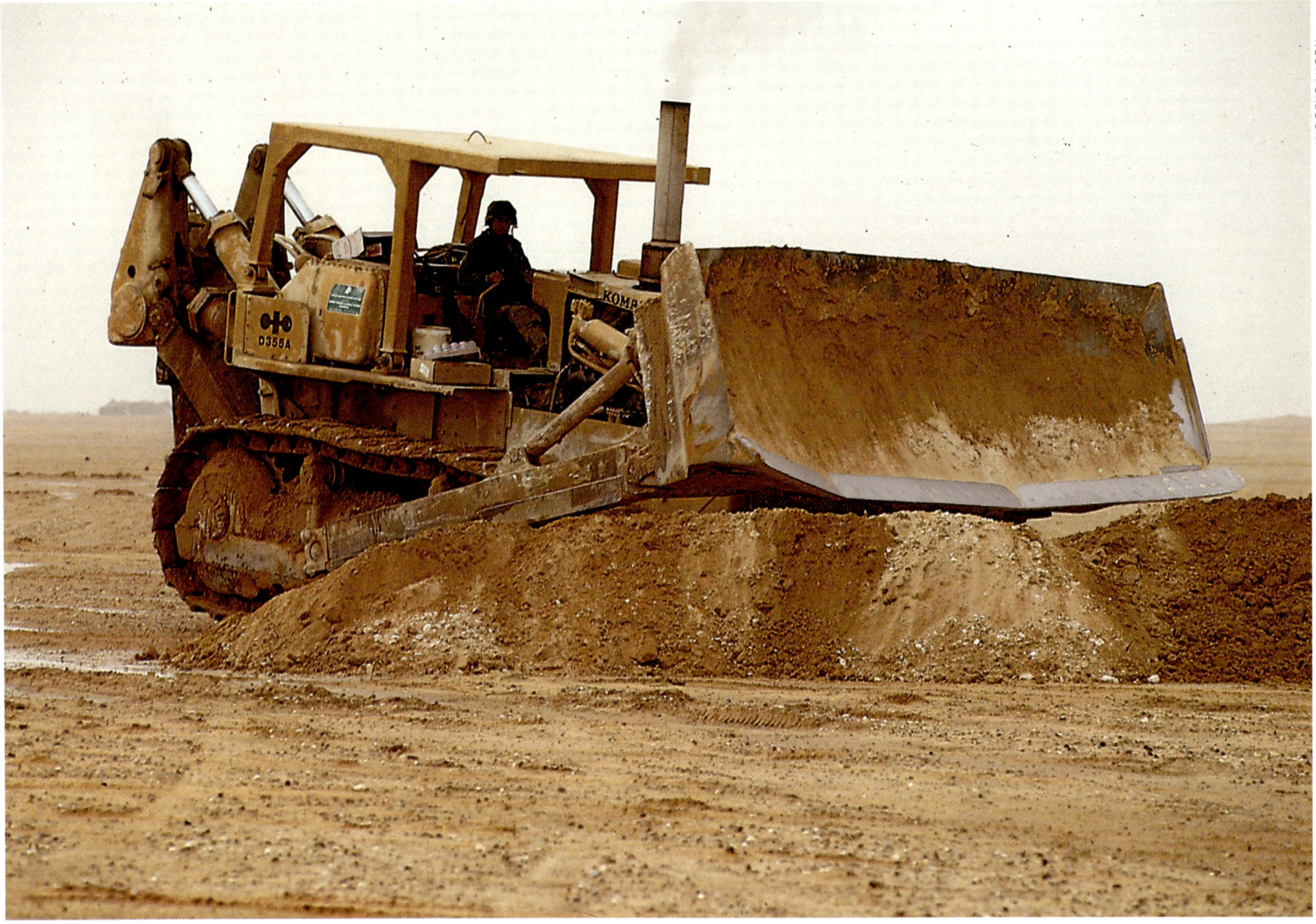

ROBYN GREGORY

Eighth Engineer D7 bulldozers dig in the defenders at El Qaysumah Airfield.

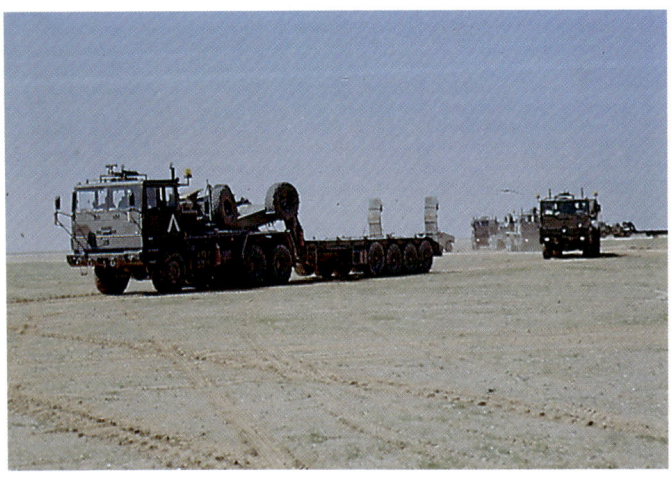

Heavy equipment transports of 43d Corps Support Group return to AA Horse to load tanks destined for fighting positions along the Tapline Road. In the early days of the defense, the 43d CSG was the 1st Cav's "Red Ball Express," recalling the all-out transport effort of Gen. George S. Patton Jr.'s Third Army in WWII.

(Right) Military traffic headed for VII Corps units deploying from Europe travels on the Tapline Road.

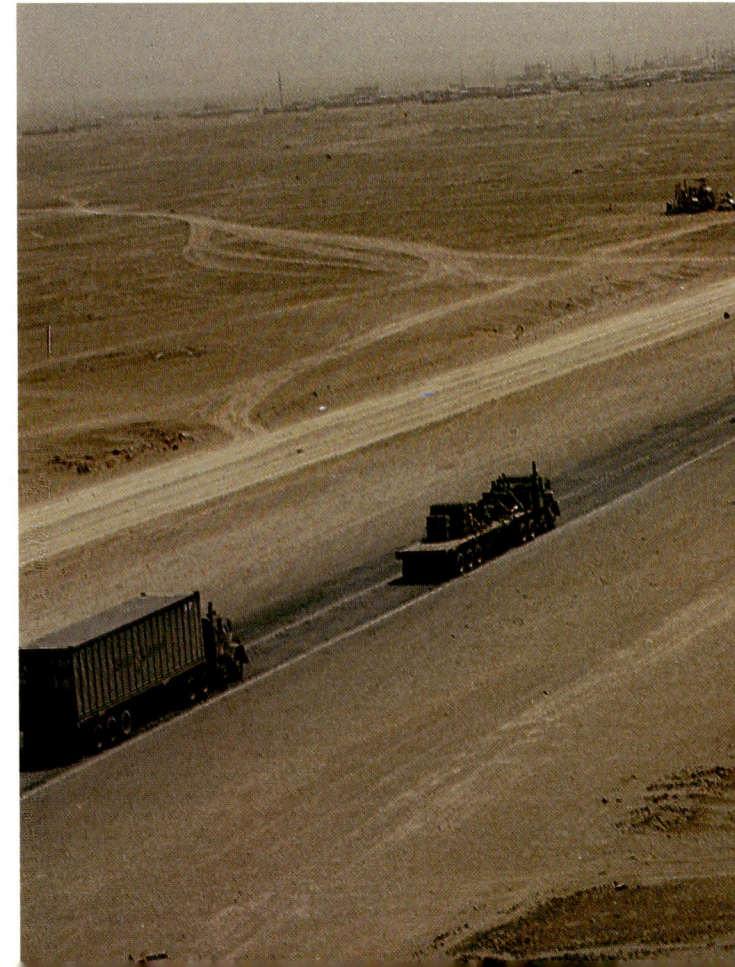

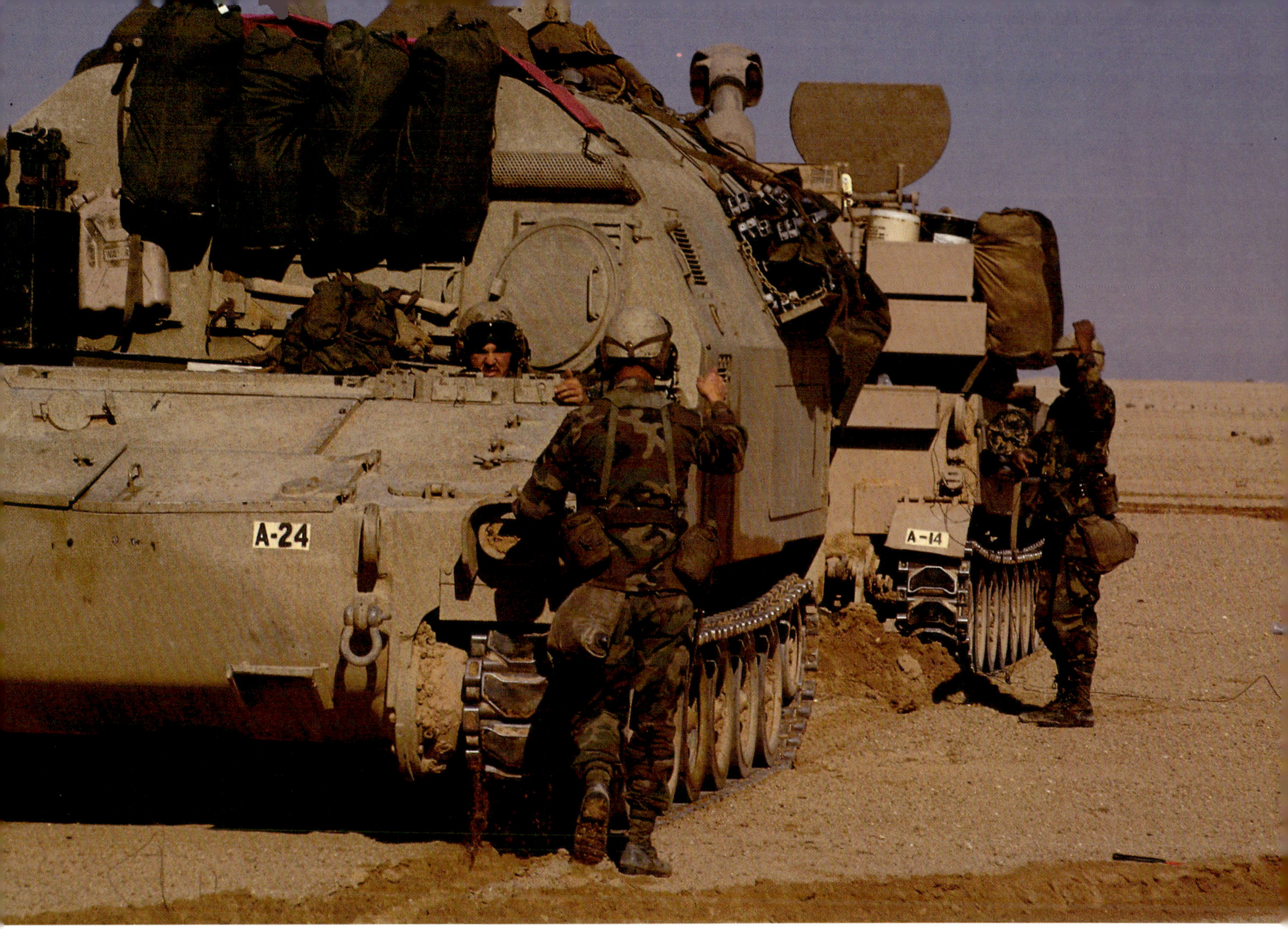

ROBYN GREGORY

(Above) The crews of a 3-82 FA howitzer and ammunition-laden Field Artillery Support Vehicle (FASV) drill in the Wadi. Only 3-82 FA had the fast, new FASV; other artillery units in the division were still equipped with the slower M548 ammunition carrier.

CURTIS HOCOM

J.E. PHILLIPS

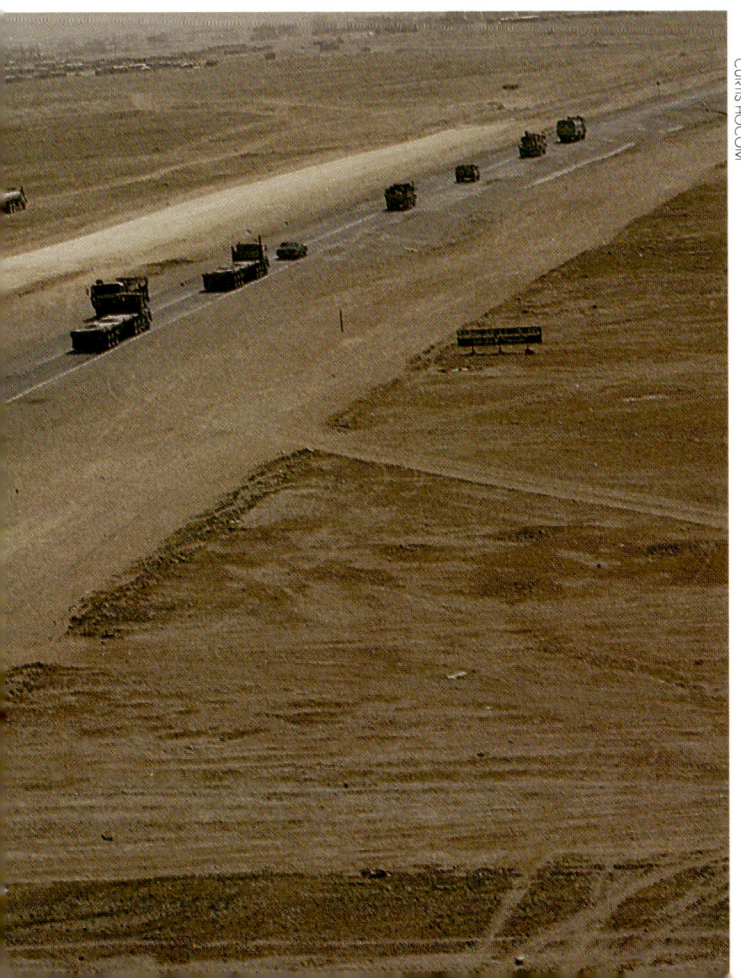

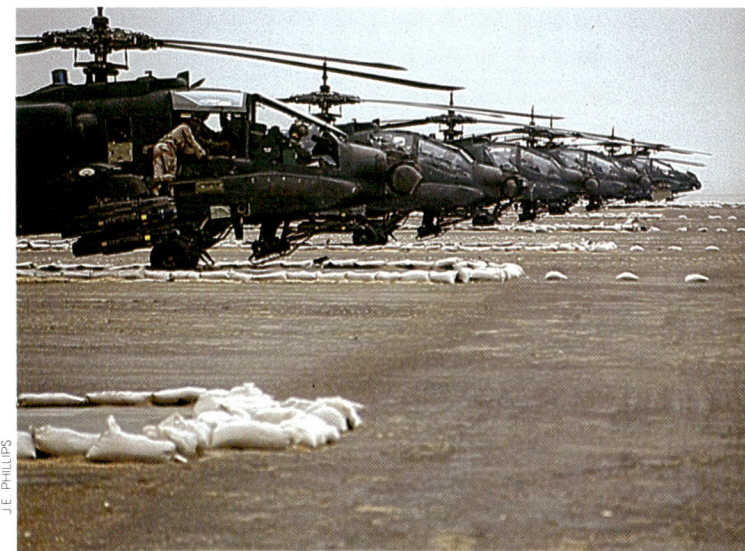

In late January, an AH-64 Apache crewchief prepares the cockpit of his silent warrior as 1-227 Aviation awaits the alert.

Fuel, lifeblood of armored operations, came to 1-7 Cav once daily. Seeking to conceal their positions, crews fell back several kilometers to meet the tanker, brought in by the troop's first sergeant.

with the Egyptians on the right flank recalled, "I knew units were moving that night, but the next morning I was amazed to find a whole brigade had dug in during the night." Lt. Gen. Franks told Brig. Gen. Tilelli, "Your division sure does move quickly."

While the division threw up its wall in the sand, much of its combat vehicles and support equipment sat useless aboard flatbed trucks and in convoys, crawling north along a crowded supply route. The division's support command, bearing its logistic support, was still in AA Horse. Should the enemy attack, it would not arrive in time to support combat. At best, Tilelli's defenders would have six hours' warning of an attack. With laden C-130s landing at their backs, Screaming Eagle troopers gouged out fighting positions at the airport. Their division had held the enemy in a desperate defense in the Ardennes 46 years before, and now, for all its contrasts, this scene recalled Bastogne.

Without its support command, the division would not last long. The 43rd Corps Support Group (CSG), itself at KKMC, stepped into the gap. Establishing fuel points along the supply route from AA Horse to TAA Wendy, it kept the convoys rolling north. The 43rd CSG simultaneously helped the departing Tiger Brigade as it moved east to join the Marines and assumed the role of a forward support command. Day and night, its heavy transport trucks hauled fuel and ammunition, food and water — whatever cargo had to move. Drawing heavily on the very stocks

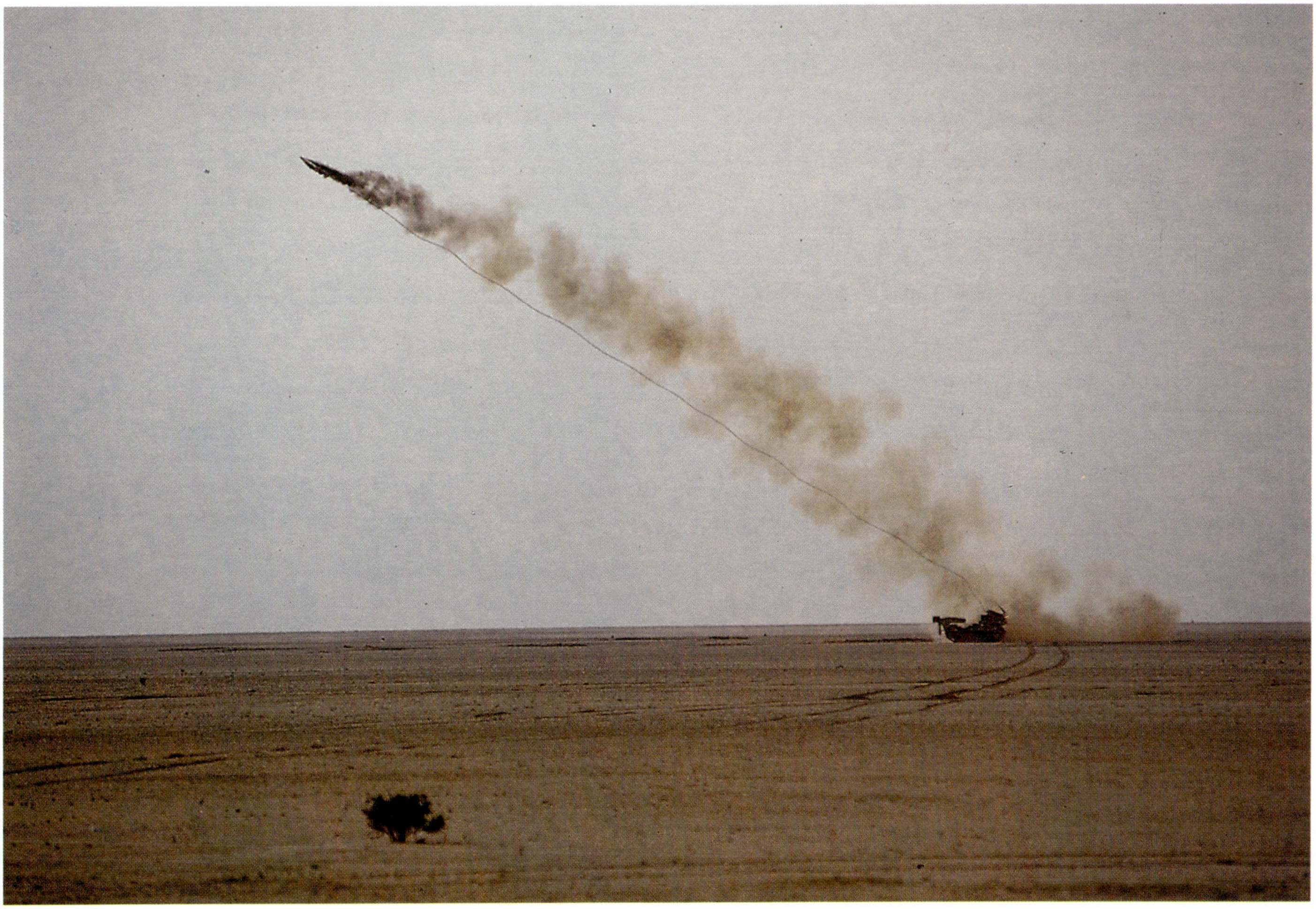

BRITT TOALSON

BRITT TOALSON

BRITT TOALSON

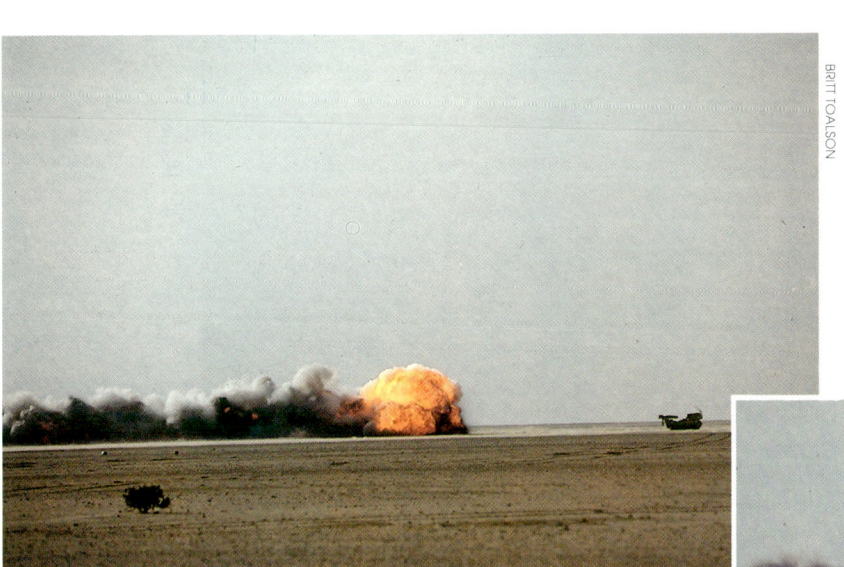

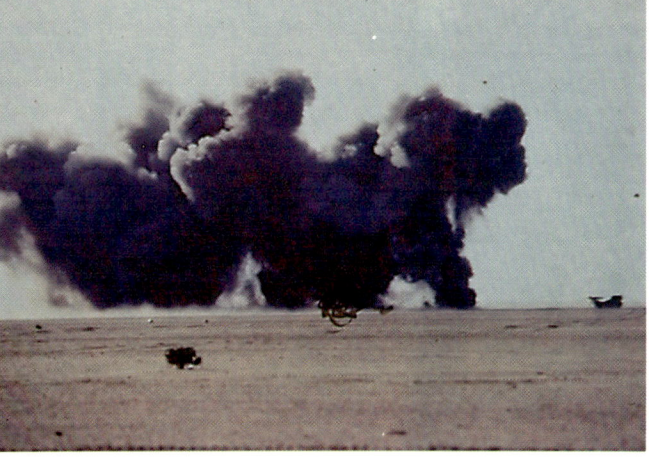

Ripping open a dummy "enemy" minefield, a rocket-launched mine clearing line charge (MICLIC) arcs overhead and explodes as it settles. The overpressure of the explosive opens a lane wide enough for a tank. The Tiger Brigade's crossing was aided by MICLICs. The 1st Cav did not need any as it crossed into Iraq through breaches cleared by the 1st Infantry Division.

threatened by the attack, the 43rd CSG kept the defenders supplied.

As liaison officer for 2nd Bde, 101st Airborne, Capt. Steve Olsen had called the 1st Cav's tactical command post (CP) home since January 9. An experienced paratrooper, he spoke with authority, helping the 1st Cav's staff fit his light brigade into the structure of an armored division. Olsen told the staff that there would be resistance if it directed the airborne brigade's attack helicopter battalion to operate separately, as part of the division's aviation brigade: in the 101st, brigades retained close control on their helicopters. The plan was changed accordingly…

As paratroopers and engineers finished preparing the strongpoint at El Qaysumah, the remainder of the division's armor slid into fighting positions along MSR Dodge. By the 14th the defense was prepared. From then until the opening of the air campaign, three days later, the division's front line crept north, adding a cushion of time and terrain. Tensions and readiness rose on the 15th, as President Bush's deadline for Iraqi withdrawal from Kuwait came and quietly passed.

The night of January 16 fell without distinction. Cold and clear, it soon clouded over. At about 2:00 a.m., soldiers in TAA Wendy awoke to the "whoosh" of rockets. One recalled that emerging from his snug sleeping bag he looked towards the southwest, from where the sound of rockets had roused him. Another "whoosh," this time directly overhead, but he could see nothing. He figured it was merely Arab Cobra pilots firing night gunnery at KKMC and retired again. When he awoke again at 6:00 a.m., it was to the voice of Peter Jennings reporting pre-dawn strikes on key Iraqi targets by U.S. cruise missiles fired off the Saudi east coast, missiles that would fly a path taking them over a slumbering TAA Wendy.

To soldiers and commanders expecting the worst from an enemy still respected, January 17 began an ordeal where every unidentified vehicle was enemy, every loud noise was incoming artillery, every night held at least a few nightmarish hours in a gas mask and chemical suit, as a chemical alarm accidentally went off somewhere. Maj. Phil Savoire, deputy staff judge advocate, was leading a convoy north from AA Horse when word of war reached him. Within moments, convoys headed south appeared, their drivers all wearing gas masks. Savoire, fear welling up, was on the verge of ordering his group into their masks when some civilian trucks passed by, their drivers blissfully clear of masks — or ill effects.

The horror of chemical war, never fully experienced during the war, brushed against many soldiers that first week. Falling asleep dreading the electronic beep of the chemical alarm, soldiers knew it was a good bet they'd be jolted awake within hours by the cry "Gas, Gas, Gas!" Flying into their mask and thick charcoal lined suits, rubber gloves and boots, they would lie in their cots waiting for word. In a tent or turret filled with buddies, the near total sensory deprivation of the chemical mask and suit in the pitch black brought on an unnerving sense of isolation and vulnerability. For endless hours — or minutes — the sound most audible inside the rubber and glass wall of the mask was one's own precious breath, a reminder of the fragility of life.

In late January, as the air campaign mounted, the threat of enemy attack faded. Growing numbers of Iraqi soldiers, pounded from the air, took the lonely, dangerous walk south into the division's lines to surrender and escape Hussein's "Mother of All Battles." The defense mission ended. On the 25th, the Screaming Eagles left, and in the Wadi al Batin, the First Team neared combat.

As the January moon rises over the Wadi, an artilleryman calls it a night.

J.E. PHILLIPS

5

"The Security Council...noting that, despite all efforts by the United Nations, Iraq refuses to comply with its obligation to implement resolution 660...in flagrant contempt of the Security Council,...authorizes member states cooperating with the Government of Kuwait, unless Iraq on or before 15 January 1991 fully implements the foregoing resolutions, to use all necessary means to uphold and implement resolution 660 and all subsequent relevant resolutions and to restore international peace and security in the area."

— United Nations Resolution 678

The multiple launch rocket systems and howitzers of DIVARTY would account for most enemy destruction, pumping 1096 rockets and 4960 shells into Iraqi positions from the war's first artillery strikes in early February through the close of the ground campaign. A 1-82 FA howitzer hits the enemy on Feb. 16, as Operation Red Storm rages. BRITT TOALSON

DECEPTION IN THE WADI

In 205 B.C., Han Xin wanted to attack Wei Wangbao across the Yellow River. Han's intention was to attack Wei from the rear at Anyi from faraway Xiayang. But he created a diversion by collecting materials for crossing the Yellow River at a nearby place called Linjing, as if he planned to cross the river there. Wei Wangbao was fooled and deployed his main force along Linjing, and left Anyi unguarded. Consequently, Han Xin's troops crossed the river at Xiayang without resistance. This was one of the main campaigns between the Chu and Han states.

— General Tao Hanzhang,
Sun Tzu's Art of War

Just before 5:00 p.m. on February 5th, enemy gunfire arced out from near a solitary border observation tower, missing a 1-7 Cav AH-1 Cobra flying reconnaissance. The pilot sent five 2.75" rockets into the area, scoring two direct hits. Two days later, another pilot watched as soldiers entered the tower; he instantly radioed his discovery. Thirteen minutes later, a "Copperhead" laser guided round from a 1-82 Field Artillery 155mm howitzer slammed into the tower. Several enemy soldiers bolted from it. They got as far as a nearby truck before disappearing in the explosion of a TOW missile streaking in from one of the Cobras. The unlucky sentinels were victims of the first use of Copperhead in combat. They were also among the first to feel the presence of Gen. Schwarzkopf's deception plan.

With the air campaign in its third week, Allied intelligence still indicated the presence of over 40 divisions in the Kuwait Theater of Operations. Like Han Xin, Schwarzkopf decided to improve his odds by fooling his enemy. The 1st Cav, still guarding the assembling VII Corps to the south, was ordered to begin a deception in the Wadi al Batin. As 2nd Brigade Commander Col. Randy House described it, the division would pull a "head fake," drawing Hussein to focus his forces on the Wadi while the main attack gathered in the West.

The scheme played on Hussein's own belief that Hafar al Batin and the Wadi would be the avenue of the Coalition's main effort, the site of his "Mother of All Battles." As Brig. Gen. Tilelli told his commanders, "It's always easier to deceive an enemy into buying something they already believe is going to happen."

The division had by now crept north from the Tapline Road, well forward of any other U.S. division. Mere kilometers separated 1-7 Cav's screenline from the border. To their front, at the border itself, isolated outposts from the division's Long Range Surveillance Detachment watched for the enemy from sunken, invisible bunkers.

Strung out on a line 70 kilometers long, 1-7 Cav's Bradleys hunkered in fighting positions over a kilometer apart in the flat, featureless desert. Stretched to its limit, the squadron could not afford to offer its crews relief from the solitary vigil. It seemed like the top of the world — or the end of it. Only the disembodied voices of buddies and commanders on the radio, the low howl of a Bradley engine, the conversation of the crew, or the wind interrupted the quiet. Each day, the first sergeants arrived at the fighting positions with fuel trucks, chow, and mail.

Squadron Executive Officer Maj. Mike Masterson was getting concerned about the continual operation of the squadron's Bradleys without maintenance. At least his Cobra gunships, flying the screenline, but landing to the squadron's rear, were examined by mechanics on a regular basis. He wasn't sure how long the Bradleys — or the troopers — would be able to keep up. Masterson and squadron commander Lt. Col. Walter "Skip" Sharp took to flying along the screenline in a scout helicopter "just to show them we were there and cared," Masterson recalls. "As we passed over each Bradley, the crew would wave like crazy. Their morale was incredible."

A healthy dose of stoic good humor helped. "My

Pfc. Brian Hartner, 1-7 Cav, makes cocoa.

Until 1-7 Cav's forward screen line was reinforced by elements of 1st Brigade in late January, troopers of "Garryowen" (the 7th Cavalry Regiment's nickname) barely left lonely outposts within sight of the border. Here, crews briefly pulled back get some hot chow (note Saudi snacks and drinks), fuel, and mail, and hear the latest rumors.

Days after the start of the air campaign, Iraqi soldiers began surrendering. They walked south into 1-7 Cav's screenline, waving surrender leaflets, white sheets, even fragments of white signal flare parachutes. Taken to an interrogation site in 1-7 Cav's rear, they volunteered valuable intelligence. Eventually, the division collected almost 1,800 enemy prisoners of war (EPW). The Tiger Brigade, in more densely populated Kuwait, took over 4,000.

mother wrote me a letter," Pfc. Brian Hartner told a journalist visiting his Bradley. "She said that my cousin is over here and I ought to look him up; that it'd be real nice. He's on the U.S.S. Missouri. It's no sweat; I'll just go over and look him up."

As tough as it was for the unrelieved soldiers on the Saudi frontier, it was proving tougher on the Iraqis facing them. The war overhead was flattening them. "It's quiet, except at night. Then the A-10s and the bombers take care of that," one soldier said. At night the airstrikes lit eerie domes of brilliant light on the northern horizon. A rapid series of subsequent blasts indicated something had been hit and was exploding, eliciting both winces and cheers from watching cavalrymen. The concussions followed, sweeping across miles of desert to buffet soldiers watching awestruck from the screenline. The quiet ended simultaneously with the thump of distant explosions. That anyone could survive what came to be called "the Northern Lights" was beyond understanding.

Within days of the air campaign's opening, enemy deserters appeared on the empty horizon, walking south, some holding scraps of white cloth. None knew what lay before them; many expressed surprise at finding Americans. One said his commander had told them he would turn his back if any of his unit wished to leave. Others risked a bullet or retribution on their family as they threaded their way through their own obstacle systems to get away. By early February, deserters straggled in almost daily, arriving singly and in small groups — happy just to be alive. They were among the lucky few. In days, the 1st Cav would add its fire to the maelstrom consuming the enemy in the Wadi.

As the time for combat drew near, Division Artillery Commander Col. James M. Gass had gathered his soldiers in Alpha Battery, 21st FA, his battery of Multiple Launched Rocket Systems (MLRS), to talk to them about war. Gass, a combat veteran, had brought these soldiers to the desert and trained them, in the process earning their complete trust. Now he offered them his counsel and insight.

"Now, if you'll let me pretend that I'm the coach and you're the team, and we're getting ready to play the Super Bowl — I'm talking about mental readiness — You have to prosecute violently, with great vigor and force to break the will of the enemy,"

On February 13, against enemy artillery positions, the soldiers experienced their baptism by fire. The Iraqis possessed a huge reservoir of artillery, boasting field pieces capable of ranges far greater than U.S. howitzers could manage. Virtually all could deliver chemical rounds. This made the destruction of Hussein's artillery a high priority, while reinforcing the deception.

Capt. Hampton Hite waited for the go-ahead in his battery command post, wondering if this was going to be "it." Hite, commander of Alpha Btry, 21st FA, had led his team through several false starts in the days following the division's creep north into the Wadi. To Hite, however, this time looked real.

He was right. Just before dusk, he moved out in his Humvee, his ten tracked launchers in tow. Traveling approximately 20 kilometers, they arrived at the

Colleagues under the uniform, Doctor (Lt. Col.) Cecil White (R), 413th Civil Affairs Company, and an unusual Iraqi prisoner, a Baghdad physician, compare notes enroute to an evacuation hospital, where the Iraqi proved helpful.

After months of preparation, combat neared. DIVARTY soldiers listen to their commander, Col. James Gass, talk about war.

(Below) Sgt. Stewart Royals (foreground) and Sgt. Michael Bey, Alpha Battery, 21st FA, prepare their launcher for an afternoon raid.

Before firing, MLRS crews checked the on-board navigation system, identifying the precise pre-designated firing point. Here, self-propelled loader launchers (SPLLs) move past guides to the checkpoint enroute to their firing position.

(Right) Reviewing a plan for history, the first MLRS strike of the war, Capt. Hampton Hite (R), Alpha Battery, 21st FA commander, briefs his officers before they head north to firing positions on Feb. 13.

(Left) In an ageless ritual, every crew named their launcher. Sgt. John Cox waits aboard "General Lee," flying the appropriate standard. JEREMY HEFLIN

final global positioning system initialization point, a gently sloping stretch of desert on the left shoulder of the Wadi. A deepening rose sky greeted each launcher as it pulled up to a fire direction sergeant to confirm its location and check its on-board positioning system. The dry air was electric — this mission had already gone farther than any of the previous attempts.

The word was "go." Hite moved out in the gathering dark to the firing position, a wide flat area from which he could watch each launcher move into its pre-selected position and pivot left to face the last glow in the west. On ten launchers, ten box-like rocket pods, each containing 12 rockets tilted up and slowly swivelled right in unison, until all aimed north.

The night sky burned blue as each launcher disgorged fire and steel. Rockets exploded from the pods in a thunderous "whoosh," tracing a laser path skyward every three seconds. The battery emptied its pods in under a minute. Each rocket carried 644 bomblets, each capable of peppering 100 square

An MLRS raid from the enemy's vantage point. A T-55 tank struck by the bomblets called "steel rain" by MLRS crews. Soviet-built tanks like the T-55 showed an unpleasant tendency to shed their turrets when hit.

(Right) A battery of 10 firing Multiple Launch Rocket Systems (the division had an extra MLRS) turned the night sky a deep blue, as their rockets roared away in seconds. Alpha Battery, 21st FA, launches Operation Red Storm.

"WE WERE THOSE LIGHTS..."

Lt. Col. Michael Starry, DIVARTY executive officer, recalls the war of "Steel Rain," Alpha Battery, 21st Field Artillery.

"Nobody had ever aggressively approached the berm. We figured we'd punch them in the eye and see what they'd do.

"We'd send cannon batteries up during the day and bring MLRS up at night. The cannons would move back and prepare for the next day while the rockets throttled them by night.

"It was thrilling to take the fight to the enemy, to be the first. No one had really locked horns with this guy, yet. We stood back and threw rocks at him. We did it with a grin on our face. it was the maneuver guys who had to go up there and look him in the eye.

"Our soldiers were all rock hard, never even blinked. There was no guilt. It was automatic from the first raid to the last. After every mission, the Alpha Battery, 21st FA guys would stow the rockets and slap an ace of spades they'd ordered from a playing card company on the ground. Then they were off.

"We built our confidence in the Wadi, we put on our game face during the deception. That's where we steeled ourselves for the upcoming battle. It was calming to finally fight after all those months.

"We whipped them day after day and what worried us is we're thinking, 'What the hell is this guy up to? Why isn't he fighting back?'"

"You see, Saddam was leading from his bunker and getting reports in from the field. So he looks up on the board and sees all these lights blinking and they're blinking in the Wadi. We were those lights."

(Above) Enveloped in the blast of their own launch, the SPLL crew operated from a tightly shuttered cab. Shown here, an MLRS strike from Battery Commander Capt. Hampton Hite's perspective.

(Right) An MLRS fires while a Howitzer awaits the word.

meters. Seconds later, they exploded over eight Iraqi artillery units and an infantry company just settling into their evening routine.

Instantly, Hite ordered the battery out, a precaution against counterbattery fire. Engines screaming, the launchers pulled out of position, pods barely stowed. In single file, the battery sped to a rally point several kilometers back, and out of immediate danger. A supporting rocket battery from VII Corps was ready to attack any enemy artillery which might fire back, using target locations supplied by Alpha Battery, 333rd FA, with DIVARTY's target acquisition radar. But this time there was no return fire. As Hite's battery passed by, the supporting rockets loosed a volley on additional targets, providing his crews the spectacular view they had missed from within their shuttered cabs.

Evidence of Hite's success, secondary explosions erupted in the target area long into the night. The war's first MLRS raid was history.

Now the missions came in quick succession. Intelligence indicated that Hussein had begun to focus on the Wadi. The deception went into full swing. The 8th Engineers went forward to blow holes in the border berm, making it look like the site of an attack. Their first mission, Berm Buster I, took place on the 14th. Covered by 1-7 Cav, the engineers moved up to the berm, blowing three lanes open with cratering charges and the 165mm cannon of their tank-like combat engineer vehicle. Later, the same weapon destroyed three border observation towers near the berm.

(Right) Clambering to the crest of the berm, 8th Engineer "sappers" rig explosives during Operation Berm Buster II to blow open a lane and convince defending Iraqis of an imminent attack. Behind the man to the right, a TF 1-32 Armor Bradley overwatches, its dismounts covering from perches on the berm. (inset) Friendly artillery airbursts over enemy positions suppress the defenders while the engineers work.

Bonne Starry

Donn,

Mike hasn't seen this book yet so write something in it — However, do look on pages 61 — picture of Mike & pages 106 — all his quotes — Hope you enjoy the book

Love, Bonne

Berm Buster II followed the next day. Just after 3:00 p.m. on the 15th, 3-82 FA pounded the area across the berm, destroying at least one observation post. Then TF 1-32 Armor moved up to secure the breach area, Abrams tanks from Alpha Company and Bradleys from Charlie Company. Even the battalion's riflemen took up positions on the crest. Now the combat engineers dashed forward to the berm in their personnel carriers, dismounting to scramble up the 15-foot slope and place their charges. Thirty-five minutes later the explosions blew open nine lanes. The ruse was enhanced by the placement of dummy tanks and a loudly played recording of vehicle noises. By 6:00 p.m., the mission was complete and the breach force gone. A

Many prisoners related the terror of a rocket raid. One said that the first — and last — clue was the "pop" of sub-munitions overhead. Horrified at seeing the vehicles beside them blow up without warning, many Iraqis simply gave up. Here, what is left of an Iraqi headquarters in the Wadi after a raid.

Wreathed in smoke, a 1-82 FA howitzer sends the deception's message from the Wadi al Batin into Iraqi positions in mid-February.

Using "red bag," a potent propellant charge used so infrequently its trajectory had to be confirmed by 1-82 FA, the division's artillery pounded enemy targets day and night. DIVARTY used range-extending rocket assisted projectiles to strike targets up to 23.5 kilometers away. Here a crew prepares red bag-propelled smoke rounds used to mark targets or obscure enemy observation of friendly movement.

surveillance team remained to watch for enemy reaction, but reported nothing.

That night, the division's artillery, accompanied by the 42nd FA Bde, attached from VII Corps, moved again into firing positions. In a massive raid called "Red Storm," howitzers and rockets pounded 28 targets — enemy maneuver forces, artillery, and anti-aircraft sites. As Red Storm lifted, Apache attack helicopters from the 11th Aviation Brigade went in to finish the destruction. They passed low over Hite's returning rocket launchers, ghostly shadows against the starry night.

Over the next few days, the division continued its uproar in the Wadi, developing the deception and inflicting significant enemy losses. Until the 16th, the division had suffered no combat losses, but at 10:30 a.m. that day, an M1A1 of TF 2-8 Cav struck a mine at the berm while the battalion was moving up. No one was injured. The tank was quickly recovered and repaired.

Occupying their new positions, 1st Brigade's tank crews were forced to scrape three to four feet of sand from the berm's crest to gain a clear view of the desert beyond. Wasting no time, the engineers blew three lanes into the berm and by the 18th, the Brigade had sent several mounted and dismounted recons into enemy territory. That afternoon, enemy artillery hit a TF 2-8 Cav foray. They withdrew through the lanes without loss. In moments, USAF A-10 airstrikes silenced the artillery.

The engineer CEVs did more than blow up dirt berms. One levelled an Iraqi border check point suspected of controlling sporadic artillery strikes in the 1st Brigade area. From near the CEV, 2nd Lt. Kenneth Cary, an Abrams platoon leader in Alpha Company, TF 2-8 Cav, watched as the first 165mm round struck the building harmlessly. "It was a dud. And then this black cat came tearing out. The next round blew down the entire wall."

Early on the 19th, TF 2-8 Cav moved out on a recon, returning after destroying an enemy ammo cache. That evening, 2nd Lt. Rick Davis, leading a platoon of TF 2-8 Cav M1A1s, reported enemy vehicles and soldiers moving to his front. 1-82 FA pumped illumination rounds over the area. After waiting nearly an hour for confirmation that they were hostile, Davis was ordered to engage. His tanks opened fire, hitting one vehicle. TF 2-5 Cav's Bradleys joined in, hitting an Iraqi MTLB ammunition carrier with a TOW missile as TF 2-8 Cav mortar fire pelted the dismounts. The next morning, infantry swept the area, capturing several enemy survivors.

The torrent of alerts had slackened since January.

Council of war, on the eve of the ground offensive, Chief of Staff Col. Leon Laporte (speaking at front) briefs Brig. Gen. Tilelli, his commanders and staff. From left, Lt. Col. Van Winkle, Lt. Col. Feuge (standing), Col. Harmeyer, Lt. Col. Steele (partially hidden), Lt. Col. Bishop (standing), Lt. Col Armstrong, Lt. Col. Gunlicks (standing), Col. House, Lt. Col. Sharp (in flight suit), Lt. Col. Harris, Col. Cadorette (foreground), Col. Gass, Maj. Townsend (standing), Col. McGill, Col. Fousek, Brig. Gen. Franks, Lt. Col. Schneider (standing), Brig. Gen. Robles, and Brig. Gen. Tilelli. Note the Saudi Pepsis, lower right.

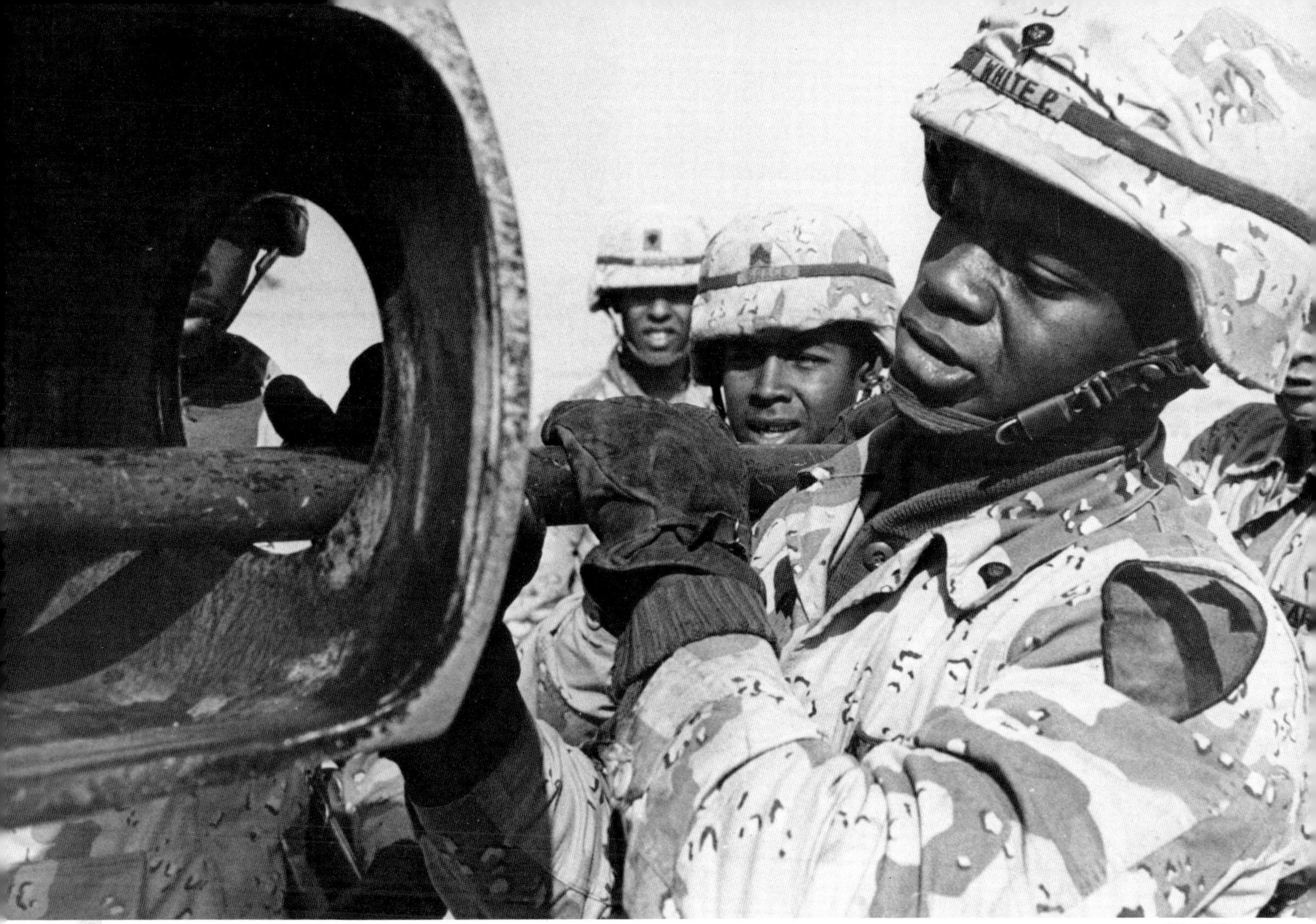

JEREMY HEFLIN

"Punching the tube," a howitzer crew cleans carbon from their howitzer's cannon after firing into enemy positions from the Wadi.

CURTIS HOCOM

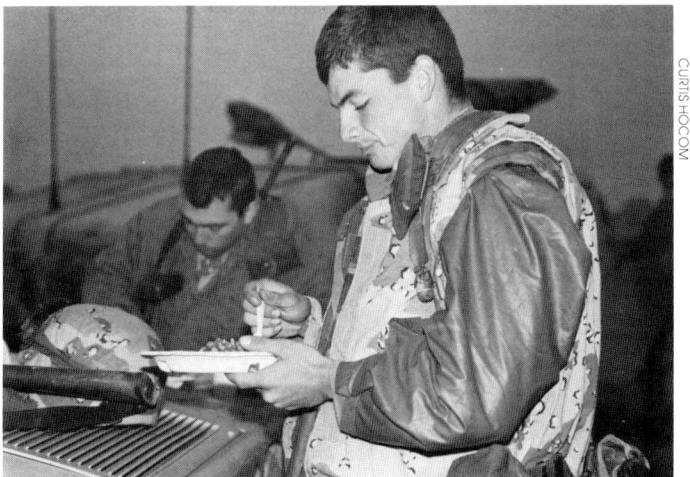

With winter's rain and plunging temperatures, the value of hot food rose. The sacred duty of company first sergeants, the chow run (made once or twice daily, situation permitting) brought in rations, mail, and spare parts. It was a long day's high point. Here, a TF 3-32 Armor scout downs his chili-mac.

CURTIS HOCOM

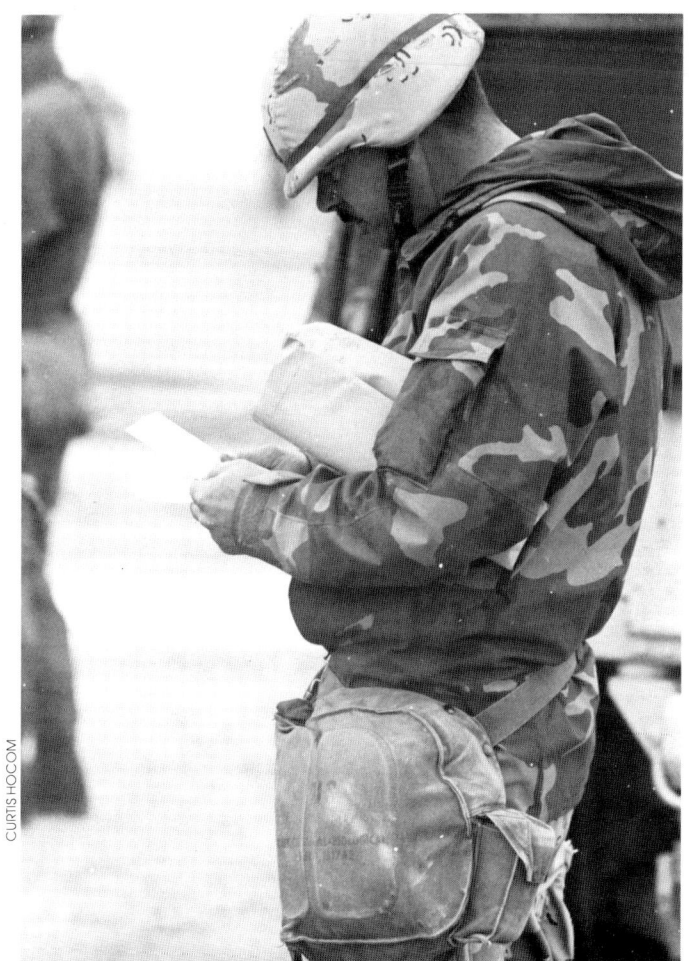

(Right) Putting the war on hold, a soldier pauses to read news from home.

MEDICS

The following is Spec. Jose Zuniga's account of TF 2-8 Cav's medics in action.

"'Let's go, let's go,' growled Command Sgt. Maj. Marvin Loris as he approached us around midnight. 'We've got a mission.'

"We were to support a recon into Iraq, retrieving the injured or dead. I drove our personnel carrier. As we inched along the berm, my commander reminded me that one jolt on the gears could send us over a mine.

"The lead tanks rolled across the berm. Artillery lit the sky. We medics knew we'd be busy, but the mission ended without friendly casualties. The task force did take several prisoners and we treated them.

"The Iraqis were so glad to see us. They were starving and it was raining. They were cut off from their lines. A lieutenant tearfully told us in English how grateful he was that he didn't have to be in the rain anymore. We brought them to the battalion aid station, worried about having the enemy in vehicles with us. They were so tired and miserable, however, the last thing on their minds was escape.

"One Iraqi had been shot, but most of them had trench foot and other problems from exposure. Their socks stuck to their rotted feet and we had to peel them off. I don't know how they managed to walk.

"We completed treatment and sent them to the prison camp, wondering about their fates. Anyway, our mission was over."

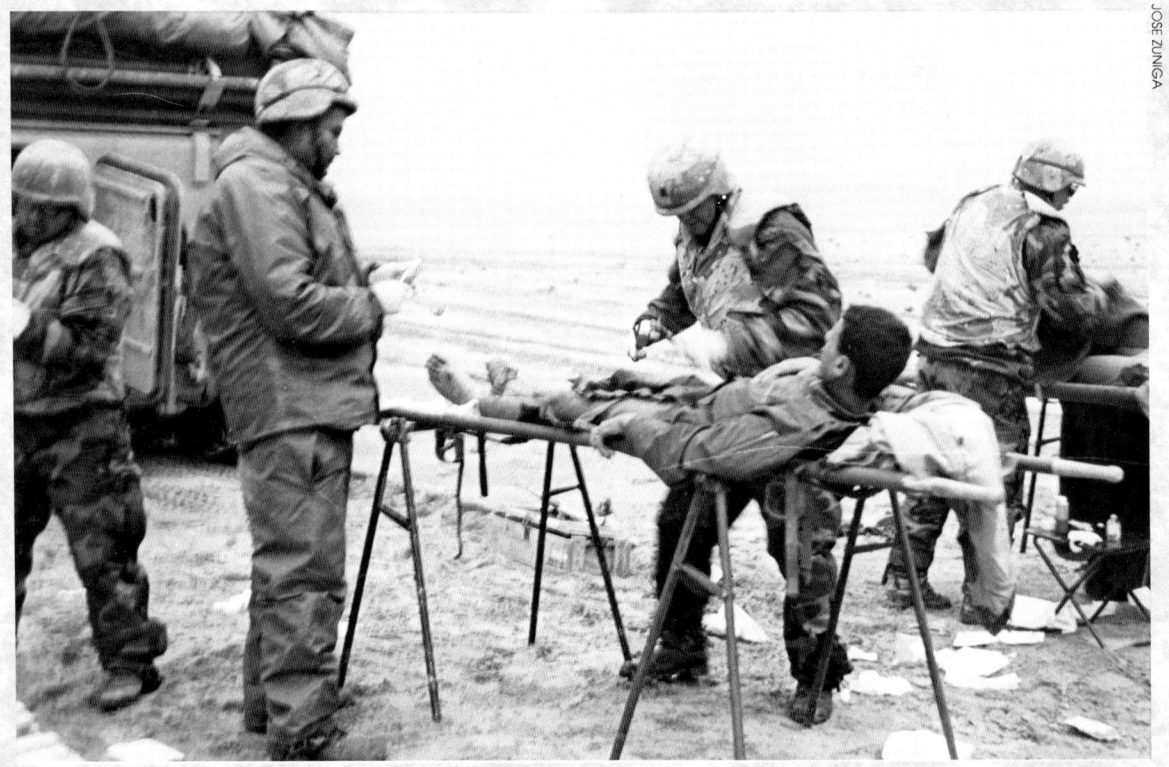

Exemplar of Hippocrates' Oath, a 1st Brigade medic, hands flying, patches up a prisoner wounded in a border action. Medics made no distinction between friend and foe.

While the reports of Scuds hitting Dhahran, Riyadh, and Tel Aviv caused concern, those were distant places. As long as Hussein was flinging only high explosives and not chemicals, the admittedly tragic hits on cities had little effect on life on the frontier. That changed on Valentine's Day. While soldiers of TF 1-32 Armor were at the division's shower point in Hafar al Batin, luxuriating in the first shower many had taken in weeks, a Scud slammed into an auto parts store across the street, one of two fired into the area. The explosion tore the building apart and sent soldiers flying for cover. But the siren call of running water proved irresistible, and the grimy soldiers soon resumed their hard-won showers.

Over the next few days, DIVARTY continued to hit high payoff targets — maneuver units, artillery, anti-aircraft, and command posts — with shells and rockets. Watching the almost nightly displays of pyrotechnics was the evening's entertainment among units in the Wadi area.

At the main command post, soldiers gathered on the perimeter berm, applauding the strikes as though they were watching their favorite ball team putting the visitors away. Essentially, they were.

CURTIS HOCOM

Valentine's Day gift to Hafar al Batin, the wreckage of a Scud hit symbolized Hussein's cynical, pointless campaign against the cities. More disruptive to 2nd Brigade soldiers yards away at a shower point was the (momentary) interruption in a long-awaited scrub.

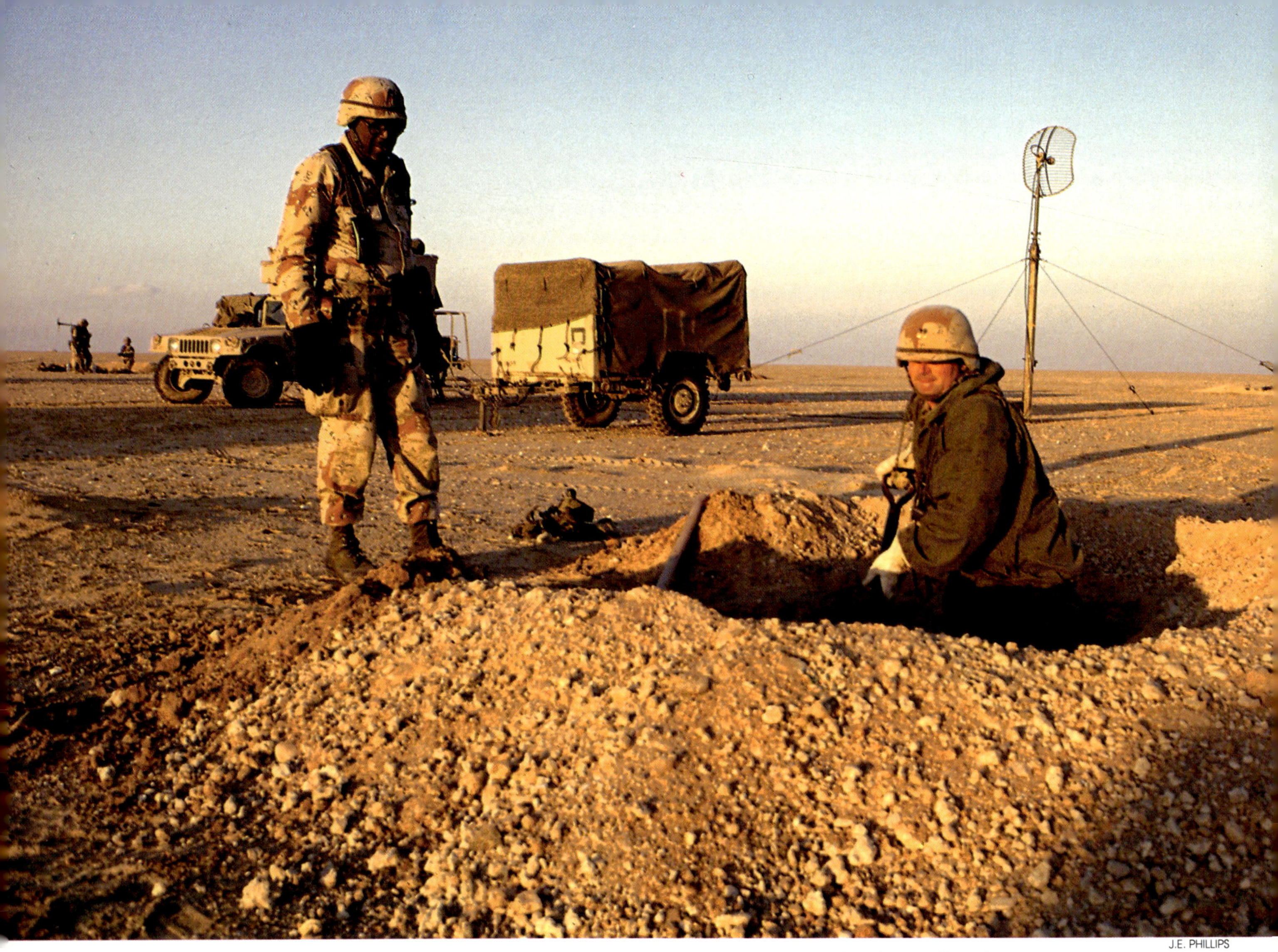

J.E. PHILLIPS

With constant Scud launches and ranged by powerful enemy artillery, soldiers dug bunkers without complaint. Here, in early February, members of DIVARTY's signal site dig in moments after erecting their antenna. A passage from the 13th Signal Bn. combat log shows the close proximity of signal soldiers to the fight, "(Node center) R51 reporting approximately 24 EPW are at their doorstep wanting to surrender."

CURTIS HOCOM

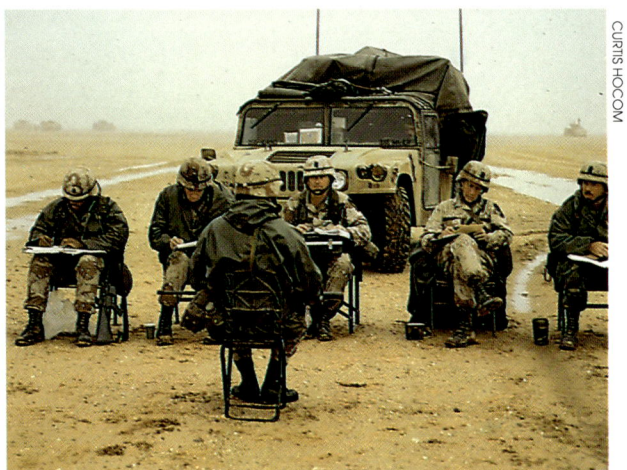

Facing a fearful sight, a soldier in TF 3-32 Armor undergoes an oral examination given by the battalion's first sergeants to determine his readiness for promotion.

(Right) Bradleys line up for fuel in the Wadi. Next stop: the chow line.

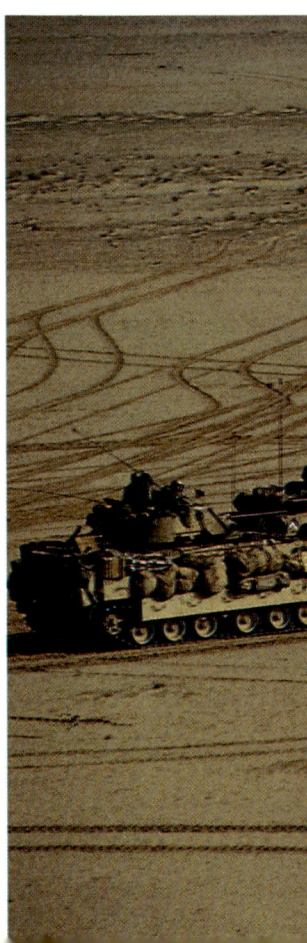

(Left) Late Christmas stocking stuffers, new AT-4 anti-tank missiles are inspected by 2nd Brigade infantry preparing for the drive into Iraq. The AT-4 was an improvement over the LAW, with greater range and penetration.

A 1st Brigade tank crew catches chow on the fly during maneuver drills to the west of the Wadi al Batin in February.

(Left) Training to the final hour, infantry fire light anti-tank weapons at an improvised range in the Wadi. Most hoped they'd never have to use the short range LAW against anything more lethal than a wooden target.

Immediately following Operation Red Storm, the volume of enemy radio transmissions spiked, an indication to intelligence officers that the raid had a significant impact. Only later would they discover that February's strikes decimated three enemy divisions and supporting forces. A 312th Military Intelligence Bn. specialist listens in.

On the 15th, Iraq's Revolutionary Council tried to slow the Allied pace. Baghdad offered to pull out of Kuwait after a cessation of all operations against Iraq. President Bush called it a "cruel hoax." Lt. Gen. Franks, commanding VII Corps, to which the 1st Cav was still attached, ordered all operations to continue. His corps was now nearly in position to the west of Hafar al Batin.

Prisoners continued to dribble into the division's lines, primarily 1-7 Cav's positions. They were questioned initially by a team located with the squadron. Willing to talk, they provided invaluable intelligence, confirming that Hussein was thickening his forces in the Wadi. At least four divisions faced the 1st Cav, all smarting from the strikes hurled out since early February.

The Iraqis had bitten; it was time to set the hook. On the 19th, Col. Randy House was ordered to conduct a reconnaissance in force across the border the next day to "determine enemy location, composition, strength, and intent." Stealth wasn't a priority; House was instructed to elicit an enemy response, but not to get mired in decisive combat. As darkness fell on the 19th, a company of TF 1-5 Cav reconned the crossing sites on the berm and probed three kilometers beyond. It returned, having found nothing. At noon the next day, Knight Strike I, named for the 1-5 Cav "Black Knights," kicked off.

TF 1-5 Cav moved north in a diamond, the Scout Platoon's cavalry fighting vehicles on point, followed closely by Alpha Company's Bradleys, leading and centered, Bravo Company's tanks on the left, Delta Company's on the right, and Charlie Company's Bradleys trailing. Tucked into the formation were the task force's two platoons of 8th Engineers and its Vulcans and Stinger teams from 4th Battalion, 5th Air Defense Artillery. The brigade's field artillery remained at the berm, where it would fire 536 rounds in support of Blackjack.

BLACK KNIGHTS STRIKE

The following is from a statement made by Staff Sgt. Christopher Cichon, an Alpha Company, TF 1-5 Cav Bradley commander, after the Feb. 20 Knight Strike I attack.

"I was neck-high out of the hatch scanning for a new target, when the noise and pressure wave from the executive officer's vehicle (Bradley A-51) getting hit caused me to look back. I saw smoke and flame coming off his turret and burning pieces going everywhere. The C.O. called... saying, `My Black 5 element is hit.'

"I figured we had to do something quick, and guided the driver alongside A-51 with intentions to evacuate the casualties. I counted heads and came up short the gunner. I found out from the scouts that the gunner on A-51 was dead. A glance confirmed that...

"I was working on Sgt. Thompson when I saw an orange blast and billowing cloud of smoke surround my own vehicle. I watched everyone hitting the ground and covering the wounded with their own bodies. That's what Pfc. Cooper was doing because his helmet was blown off. He was about 10 feet from the explosion and I recognized his bright red hair. He was across the man he was trying to give aid to at the time.

"Pfc. Cooper stood up halfway, looked at me, and then...fell over.

"I was shocked and angry. I thought to myself, we've gotta' get out of here or we're all dead meat. Sgt. Jones loaded up the casualties, then I checked the area for anyone else.

"Despite the fact we were all under some intense fire, no one was just laying on the ground, cowering.... I am extremely proud of my soldiers. They handled the wounded properly and remained calm. These men...all kept with the highest of military standards despite imminent danger..."

Staff Sgt. Cichon received the Silver Star for his valor, as did Sgt. Ronnie Williams, Cpl. Calvin Clark, Pfc. Daniel Sheets, and Pfc. Ardon Cooper (posthumously).

Two other soldiers fell during the battle: Sgt. Jimmy Haws, Charlie Battery, 4-5 ADA, killed when his Vulcan was struck, and Sgt. Ronald Randazzo, Alpha Company, TF 1-5 Cav. Nine soldiers were wounded in the action.

Eleven Bronze Star Medals with V-device for valor were awarded to other Black Knight soldiers who assisted in the evacuation of casualties under fire.

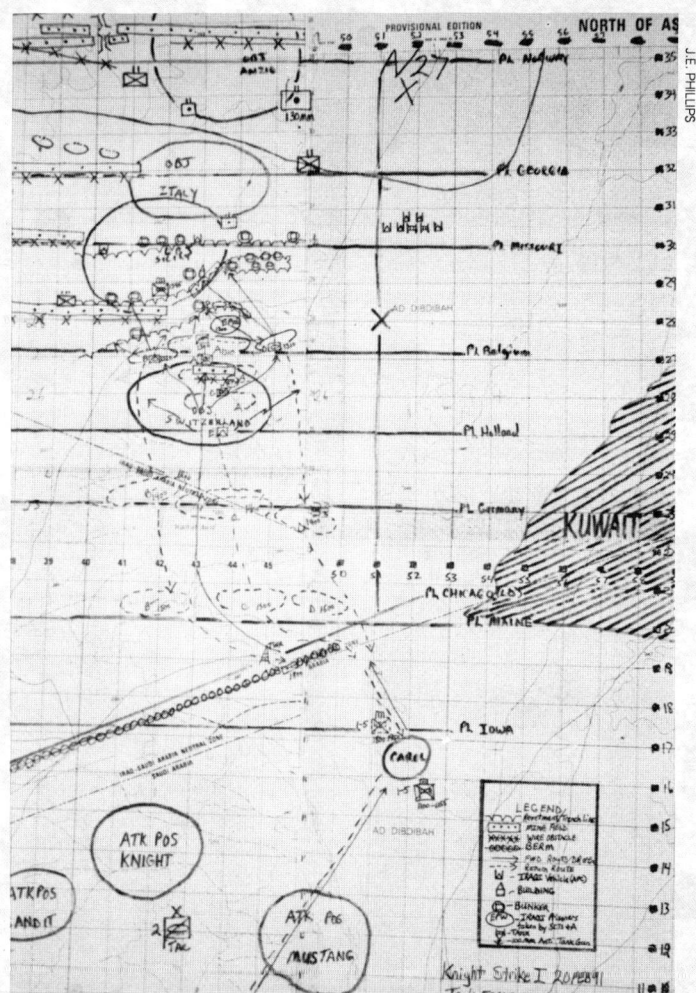

Portrait of an attack, a battle map of Lt. Col. Michael Parker's shows graphics marking TF 1-5 Cav's Knight Strike I fight in the Wadi on Feb. 20. Centered above Objective Switzerland, at Phase Line Belgium, is Alpha Company. Directly above it and the enemy prisoner of war symbol, the deadly anti-tank gun.

Silhouetted against smoke from the burning fire trenches, a TF 1-5 Cav Bradley moves cautiously forward under fire during Operation Quick Strike, its TOW missile launcher up and ready.

The Iraqis prepared elaborate obstacles, alternating belts of mines, trenches, berms, and barbed wire. Here, an infantry trench, abandoned in the bombardment of the Wadi al Batin. To its front are belts of wire and mines, to its rear, shell holes.

Second Brigade struck north in Operation Quick Strike to cement the deception and probe for soft spots in the Wadi defenses that the division could exploit. Instead, the brigade ran into a spirited defense and the towering inferno of fire trenches, some lit by its own tracers. Here, Abrams tanks of TF 1-32 Armor move north on the attack's second day.

House accompanied the task force in his command vehicle.

Task Force 1-5 Cav moved on. About 10 kilometers past the berm, Alpha Company made contact. The Bradleys instantly laid a base of fire while the tank companies raced up. The task force struck savagely, destroying an enemy battalion in minutes. USAF A-10s swept away over 100 Iraqi artillery pieces entrenched and invisible from the ground. The task force started taking in prisoners.

Then Knight Strike turned ugly. The rounds struck while the Scouts and Alpha Company were collecting prisoners. Suddenly artillery was falling on the engineers and Alpha Company was taking direct fire. "All of a sudden, I'm about a thousand meters back… observing with my binoculars from my command track… and the Vulcan that's behind me takes a hit. And I can hear, and then I can see, rounds going through my antennas," House recalled. In quick succession, enemy direct fire hit two Alpha Company Bradleys. "I was neck-high out of the hatch [of my Bradley] scanning for a new target when the noise and pressure wave from the X.O.'s vehicle [the Bradley of the Alpha company executive officer, 1LT Christopher Robinson] getting hit caused me to look back to my left rear. I saw smoke and flame coming off his turret and burning pieces going everywhere," wrote Staff. Sgt. Christopher Cichon after the battle. Moments after seeing Robinson's Bradley struck, Cichon, dismounted, watched his own take a hit.

The Scouts took fire, too. House watched the Scout platoon leader in action. "I could see his track getting the s— shot out of it and he was talking like he was at the beach. He says, 'Taking fire, returning same.'" TF 1-5 Cav's tanks quickly regained firepower superiority while Charlie Company moved up to help with the prisoners. Shortly before 2:00 p.m., an artillery smoke screen covered the task force's

Much of Hussein's armor was unprepared for artillery and air strikes, as this T-55 and MTLB offer mute testimony.

As 2nd Brigade struck north on Operation Quick Strike, it ran up against fire trenches — walls of flame and oily smoke. Here, their burnt-out remains belie the hellish specter they presented Americans and Iraqis alike. With their staggered arrangement, attackers threading between trenches would be trapped in a kill sack.

withdrawal, ordered by Brig. Gen. Tilelli. That night, and for the next four days ending in the start of the ground offensive, heavy air strikes pounded the Wadi.

On the 24th, hours after Gen. Schwarzkopf launched his "Hail Mary" attack, House was ordered back up the Wadi. The Allied offensive was meeting with unanticipated success; the enemy defense was fast disintegrating and Schwarzkopf needed the enemy forces in the Wadi held down.

Blackjack moved out at approximately 5:00 p.m. House was to move north in a limited attack to fix the enemy's focus on the Wadi. He also was to feel for soft spots through which the division could charge due north, thus avoiding the longer route taken by VII Corps. The division was now Theater reserve, subject to be recalled if needed. Consequently, House was directed to be careful and preserve his forces.

Night fell as rain and sand whipped the advancing armor of the brigade's desert wedge. House recalled running into enemy defenses soon after nightfall. Calling on A-10s and artillery, adjusted by the division's OH-58D laser designator-equipped helicopters, Blackjack fought to the enemy's fire trenches. The oil-filled slits, hundreds of meters long, blocked progress up the Wadi. Emplaced in two staggered ranks so that they overlapped, the only way through burning trenches was around the edges, and into prepared enemy kill sacks. Lit as Blackjack approached, they burned convulsively in the wind. Clouds of acrid oil smoke

Spec. Keith Owsley, a scout in TF 3-32 Armor, takes a break from atop his HMMWV, watching the battalion's tanks maneuver over the tabletop desert west of the Wadi.

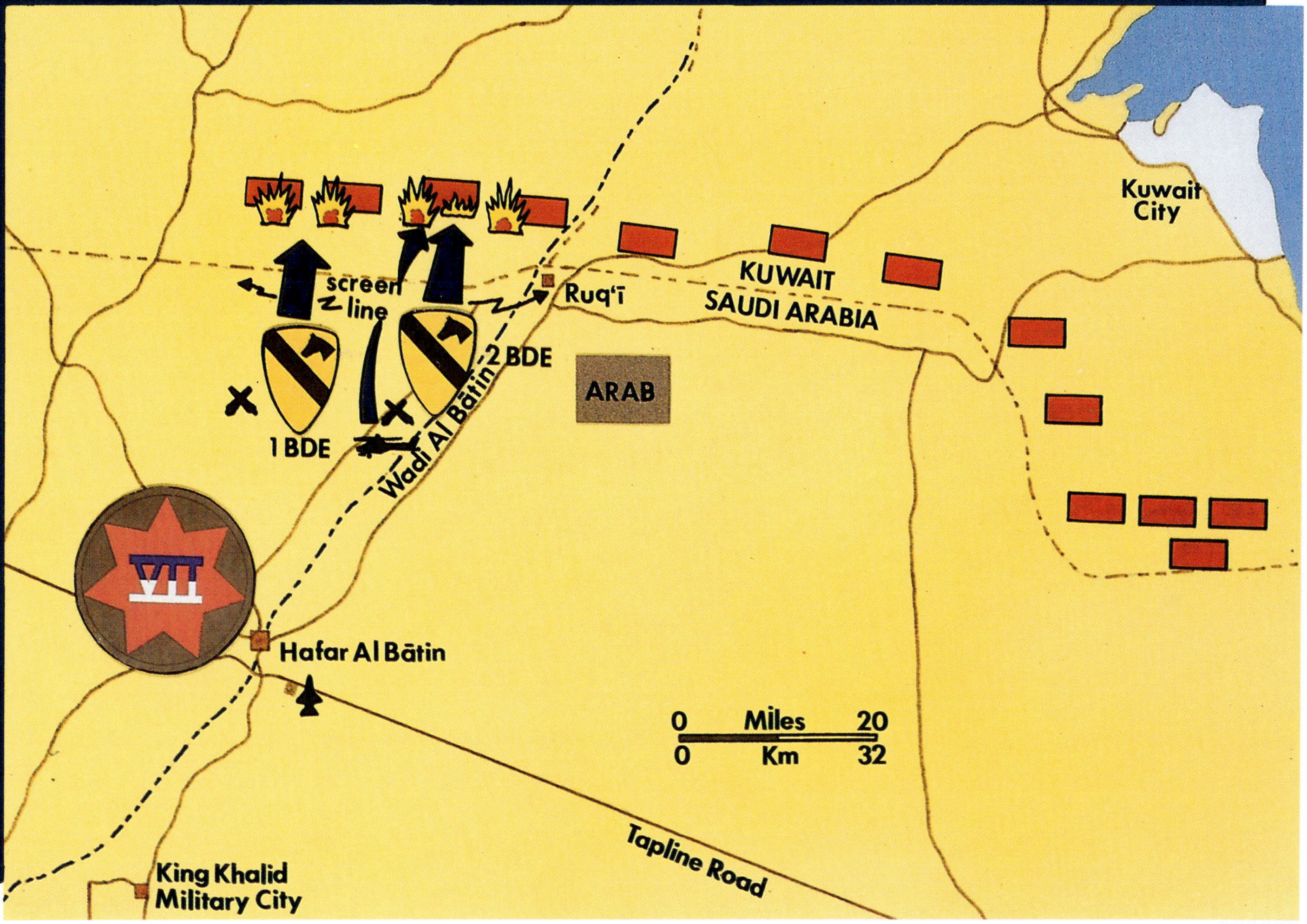

DON MOORE

DECEPTION

Situation during period 7-25 February. The 1st Cav's lines have crept north since the defense, are now just below the border. Both 1st and 2nd Brigade task forces and supporting artillery conduct reconnaissance, artillery raids, and "Berm Buster" obstacle reduction missions. On Feb. 20, 2nd Brigade conducts Knight Strike I, 10 kilometers into Iraq. In Quick Strike, on Feb. 24-25, with Aviation Brigade support, 2nd Brigade penetrates to enemy fortifications, fire trenches.

ROBYN GREGORY

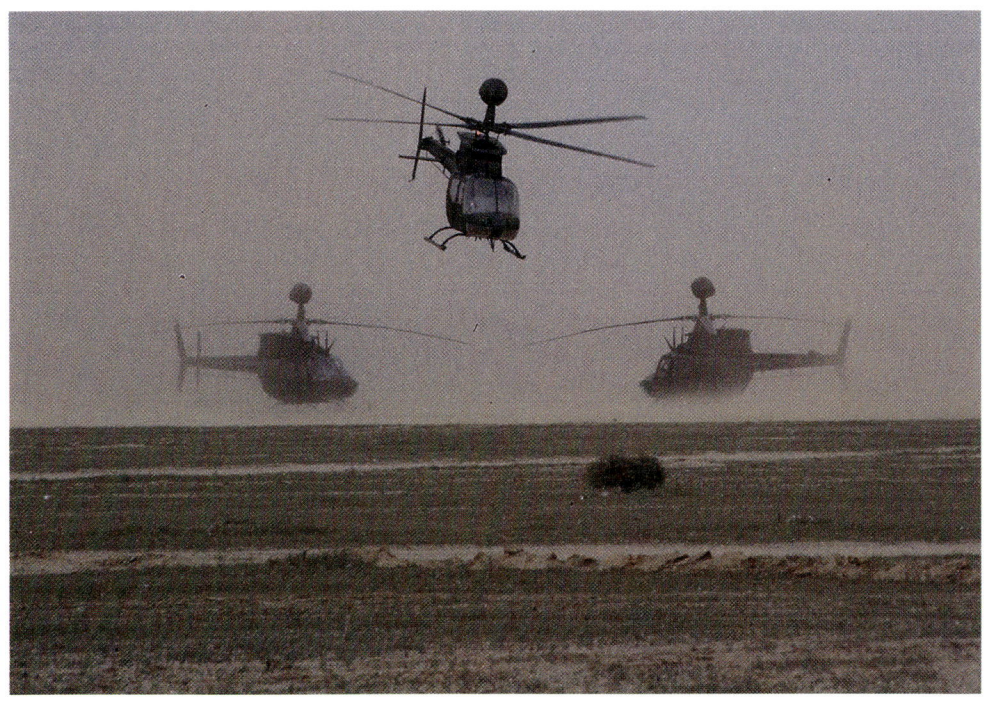

Capable of hovering hidden, with only their bulbous mast sight exposed, OH-58D helicopters of D Company, 227th Aviation spotted distant targets and "painted" them with a laser code. "Reading" the code, a Copperhead round or Hellfire missile would zero in.

FIRST ATTACK

Playing in the last act of the deception, Aviation Brigade Apaches delivered dozens of Hellfires into the bunkers along 2nd Brigade's attack route. Here, an AH-64 departs, fully loaded.

The 1st Battalion, 227th Aviation pilots were as ready as they could be. The word came on Feb. 24. "My mind worked overtime drafting guidance and instructions to give to my staff that night," recalled Maj. Marline Johnson, operations officer. "I gave them a hasty warning order and told them to load Hellfire-heavy."

With that guidance, crewchiefs went to work by flashlight on the birds that would fly into killing range of the 27th and 28th Infantry Divisions.

The phone rang — mission postponed until 3:00 a.m. It would be postponed two more times that night. The pilots anxiously hovered around their tents, writing a last letter, a few scribbling out a will. The unit mailbox filled.

With the final change, fear stabbed the crews: the mission would occur in the morning without cover of darkness, without air support.

The battalion launched into the damp, cold dawn. Worried crewchiefs watched their aircraft shrink to spots in the grey sky.

Passing across the berm and over the 2nd Brigade, pilots could make out tankers below waving and cheering the "tank killers" on. Moments later, eight Iraqis held up tattered white flags. Bravo Company's "Grim Reaper" scouts landed their OH-58's to watch them until Blackjack could collect them.

As Bravo Company moved forward a kilometer, Chief Warrant Officer Mark Mullen locked onto an enemy tank and fired a Hellfire, exploding it. To his right, Charlie Company's "Vampires" crept forward as enemy mortars exploded near him. Anti-aircraft fire joined in.

"At first they couldn't see us. They were standing outside of their bunkers until the first Hellfire hit. Then they started shooting just about everything at us," said pilot Chief Warrant Officer Brian Amos.

Meanwhile, the battalion was hitting the enemy hard, destroying tanks, trucks, mortar and artillery pieces, fuel tankers, and soldiers.

As the fire escalated, the dreaded radio call froze everyone for an instant,

Iraqi fire downed the AH-64 piloted by Capt. Mike Klingele and Chief Warrant Officer Mike Butler during "Quick Strike" on Feb. 25. The two flew out under enemy fire, clipped onto a rescuing Apache. Here Butler, bloodied in the crash, shows off the lifesaving sling every 1-227 Aviation Apache crewman wore.

"We're hit, we're hit, we're going down!" It was Charlie Company Commander Capt. Mike Klingele.

"I saw the ground rolling and pulled pitch," recalled Chief Warrant Officer Mike Butler, pilot. "It was a hell of an explosion and we were thrown violently. The canopy exploded and the flying glass cut us up. My first thought was, I'm alive."

Their wingmen, 1st Lt. Robert Johnston and Chief Warrant Officer Ed Sanderlin, saw the crash and suppressed the enemy, already beginning to move toward the wreck. While his company continued suppressing, Johnston flew forward, fearing the worst. Then, in the shattered cockpit, he saw movement.

Butler and Klingele pulled themselves out and scrambled through enemy fire to Johnston's Apache, hooking onto the wing using the sling with which the battalion had practiced. Johnston took off, the two hanging onto the wing. Butler transferred to the battalion's UH-60. Klingele hopped onto an OH-58 scout and re-entered the fight.

Later, Butler planted his feet firmly on the ground and a huge kiss on the faces of his rescuers. "Getting shot at was the easy part. Getting pulled out was the hard part. In 20 years of flying, I've never seen such professionalism as in this company at this time," he said.

For their heroism, Johnston and Sanderlin were each awarded the Distinguished Flying Cross.

The battalion regrouped and made two more runs against the Iraqis before their relief by 1-3 Aviation's Apaches. The tally for the day: 31 bunkers, one tank, three howitzers, five trucks, a radar site, and two grateful survivors.

"Our firepower overwhelmed them," recalled Chief Warrant Officer Brian Amos of the luckless enemy chalked onto his Apache fuselage. From 7,700 meters, Amos' Hellfire missiles destroyed five bunkers, two 120mm heavy mortars, a T-55 tank, a fuel tanker, and an unknown number of enemy troops.

Artilleryman take the edge off a chilly dawn.

and flying sand reduced visibility to the front of one's tank. The brigade came on and as they did, the enemy fought back. "All night long, moving firing… getting through minefields, marking those minefields, getting those units through, and right before light the next morning… the Apaches came in," recalled House. The Apaches struck at bunkers and enemy in and amongst the fire trenches and on the flanks of the brigade. Now House attacked straight at the fire trenches, pulsing strips of towering flame and smoke vivid against the grey dawn before him. Artillery pounded the defenders; Copperhead rounds destroyed four tanks and a ZSU 23-4 anti-aircraft gun. Apaches came in low, forming in battle lines, engaging with 30mm cannon and Hellfire missiles. One took a hit from an anti-tank gun and went down, its crew whisked out under fire, clinging to a rescuing Apache's wings.

The enemy stiffened, refusing to yield. House

With the deception underway, details of the impending attack came under close scrutiny. Standing on a map in the sand, Brig. Gen. Tilelli (pointing) and his commanders review plans for the ground campaign's breach crossing during a "sandtable exercise" Feb. 9. Over 6,000 vehicles would cross, potentially facing both conventional and chemical attack.

knew he could pierce the trenches, but there was no soft spot; it would take time and losses to open a route for the division. At about noon on the 25th, Tilelli ordered the brigade back. The main attack in the west was going better than expected; the Iraqis had been diverted with results beyond all expectations. The deception had destroyed elements of the Iraqi 12th Armored Division, 25th, 27th, 28th, 31st and 47th Infantry Divisions, and a corps artillery group. The enemy had focused on the Wadi, weakening his flanks, and missing entirely the movement of VII Corps. There no longer was any need to slug it out in the Wadi al Batin.

In the rain, Blackjack returned to Saudi Arabia, refueled and prepared with the rest of the 1st Cav to launch into the final assault.

(Left) Communications in the desert varied from difficult to what should have been impossible. In the deception, radio and mobile subscriber equipment coverage was stretched over an area 70 kilometers wide and 80 deep. By Feb. 27, depth went to nearly 300 kilometers. Here, a signal "node" at DIVARTY headquarters.

(Below) Taking his ritual dousing, a newly promoted artillery sergeant knocks out a few push-ups while comrades wet him down. In the uncertainty and danger of combat, traditions forged links to a more familiar, secure world.

6

"SECRET
SCHWARZKOPF SENDS
SUBJ, ATTACK
1. (S) SEND IN THE 1ST TEAM.
2. (S) DESTROY THE REPUBLICAN GUARD.
3. (S) WE'RE GOING HOME."

— Official Order

Exiting the refuel on the move (ROM), 2nd Brigade Bradleys prepare to press north to the breach. The turret of the Bradley in the foreground is blackened from machinegun and cannon fire. Sand bags supplement the armor in front of the driver. On the laden vehicle's side, a crewman has slung a case of MREs. J.E. PHILLIPS

TO THE EUPHRATES

As Col. Randy House's Blackjack Brigade withdrew from the burning Wadi, Division Chief of Staff Col. Leon LaPorte was airborne, skimming east over the rain-beaten, tawny sand toward the division's eastern flank and the 3rd Egyptian Division command post.

Late on the 23rd, the division had left the control of VII Corps to be the Army reserve. In the early hours of the 24th, Schwarzkopf attacked. Two corps of armor flew through the berms and poorly defended obstacles and began to roll up the enemy's flank. Caught totally by surprise, focused on the Wadi, the Iraqi defense disintegrated, accelerating the Allied timetable.

And now House had returned from his Rubicon. Tilelli knew the division could still be ordered up the Wadi, attacking directly north, or — he could be sent west to reinforce VII Corps. Reading his boss, LaPorte sent a liaison team from his Operations and Plans staff to the Egyptians. Their job was to arrange the division's passage north. Their HMMWV had been gone just 30 minutes when Army headquarters alerted the Cav to join VII Corps in its attack on the Republican Guard. Unable to reach the team he had dispatched, LaPorte tore off in his ancient "Huey," catching them as they were entering the Egyptian CP.

Returning to the division's main CP in the cramped, vibrating Huey, LaPorte briefed the confused team over the intercom. His words came in clipped bursts. The plan for an attack to the west with VII Corps was a "go." The 1st "Ironhorse" Brigade would launch toward the breach sites opened in the berm by the 1st Infantry Division. Already, Ironhorse had pulled off line and was assembling, while 2nd Brigade caught its breath, refueled, and re-armed. The division would initially keep its rear headquarters and base in Saudi Arabia; to move it now would disrupt support. It all seemed unreal; the berm that for so long had represented the frontier past which lurked a virile enemy, now lay broken and empty.

To Col. John Sylvester, whose Tiger Brigade was waiting to the east below the Kuwaiti border for the word to move, the early hours of the 24th were a time to reflect on what he sensed would be his brigade's moment in history. "There is one thing this brigade does well...and that is move very quickly. I don't think there is any unit faster. But right now I just want to get us rolling through the breach," "Tiger Six" told his staff.

The "Tiger Battle Team" as Sylvester called it, had joined the 2nd Marine Division as the 1st Cav rushed to the defense of the Wadi al Batin. With its Abrams, Bradleys, and self-propelled artillery, it was now poised to attack north in support of the lightly armored Marines.

At 5:30 a.m., the Marines breached the border berm and pushed forward, clearing six narrow lanes through a network of minefields and trenches. The word for which they waited reached the Tiger Brigade that afternoon and at 2:00 p.m. the command post moved through the 30-foot cut in the berm. Ninety minutes later, Task Force 3-41 Infantry crossed in column, buttoned up and wearing chemical suits. Mine plow-equipped tanks led, widening the lanes. Within fifteen minutes, TF 3-41 Infantry cleared the first of two minefields safely. The others began to move, TF 3-67 Armor on the left and TF 1-67 Armor on the right, to bring them out from the six lanes in a brigade wedge, with 1-3 Field Artillery trailing in the center. Seconds later, an Abrams in TF 3-67 Armor disappeared in smoke and sand as it struck a heavy mine. The explosion severed the left track, but left the crew unhurt. The crossing continued. The brigade moved on into the nightmar-

At 3:30 p.m., Feb. 24, the Tiger Brigade Battle Team rolls into Kuwait.

ish dreamscape of southern Kuwait. The debris of the air war littered the flat desert: spent bomb casings, unexploded rockets like quills in the sand, wrecked and blackened equipment. Once only distant flashes and rolling thunder, now the war enveloped the brigade. Choked with the pall of burning oil wells, at least four dozen surrounding them, the air was an eerie purple, as if viewed through dark sunglasses. Against it the sand almost glowed. It seemed like the fires of Hell were burning Kuwait away.

Three eternal hours after jumping off, the Tiger Brigade cleared the obstacle belts and continued north into the cauldron.

The brigade met little resistance; except for sporadic, ineffective artillery, it was all too easy. Where were the chemical mines, the fire trenches, the dug-in fanatics? At 7:30 p.m. a 502nd Military Police Company HMMWV struck a mine, killing the driver and wounding the gunner. Across the brigade, nerves that had slackened snapped taut again.

At 9:00 p.m. they halted for the night. Enemy artillery fired blindly, coming nowhere close. Other enemy soldiers had better aim: over 200 found the Tigers and surrendered.

At dawn, with the brigade awaiting orders to attack north, TF 3-41 Infantry hit a bunker complex spotted the night before. In an approach repeated over the next two days, tanks and Bradleys pounded the bunkers from up to 2,500 meters away, then sent in dismounted infantry. The defenders, totally dispirited, gave up readily. They quickly realized, as one said, "We have nothing that can touch you."

Just after 1:00 p.m., the battle team attacked with TF 3-41 Infantry on the right in the main effort, TF 3-67 Armor on the left in a supporting attack, and TF 1-67 Armor following as reserve. Abrams gunners, eyes glued to their thermal sights, immediately picked up "hot spots," the glowing silhouettes of enemy armor in the distance. From nearly two miles away they fired, torching T-55s and T-62s before the bewildered crews could even see their tormentors.

"The fighting was quick and violent," said TF 3-67 Armor Commander Lt. Col. Douglas Tystad. "We'd hit them at 3,000 meters. They'd send a round in the name of Saddam, and then they'd give up. When they see their T-55 and T-62 tanks blow up at a range of 3,000 meters and they know they only have a range of 1,200 meters, they don't fight long."

Within ninety minutes, the fight was over. For the second time since crossing his Rubicon, Sylvester accepted the surrender of a brigade commander and his entire unit (the first followed TF 3-41 Infantry's bunker fight). "They've got no fight left in them," Tiger Six declared. He'd soon discover that his assessment wasn't entirely correct.

The wind came up early on the 26th, and with it the sand. As the sand mixed with the rain that had resumed, visibility in the Wadi al Batin plummeted; but with Iraqi defenses collapsing everywhere, the Cav's soldiers were gripped only with thoughts of attack. Still the Army reserve, Tilelli asked to go straight north through the defenses, exploiting the enemy withdrawal that had begun even as House returned from the fire trenches. Permission was denied; at 10:00 a.m., the division was re-attached to VII Corps. Tilelli was directed to take the cavalry and charge west.

Though the storm kept Tilelli's and Franks' helicopters grounded, LaPorte had gotten airborne before it hit. Now, while 2nd Brigade assembled, he launched Col. George Harmeyer's 1st Brigade to refuel on the move (ROM) sites set up by DISCOM south of the breach crossings. Blocking Harmeyer from the ROM, and his gateway to Iraq, however, was a huge concentration of British armor in col-

Buttoned-up against artillery, the Bradley of Lt. Col. Walter Wojdakowski, commander of TF 3-41 Infantry, moves into Kuwait.

umns, itself waiting to move. LaPorte saw the potential for a multi-national traffic jam of breathtaking size. In minutes, he had coordinated passage with the British headquarters; the solution was simple, yet to the chief of staff watching from overhead, it made for a memorable sight.

"[The] 1st Brigade came on and the British vehicles turned ninety degrees to open passages through the columns. The 1st Brigade passed right through. The British soldiers were standing on their vehicles, waving and cheering. As far as you could see there were vehicles on the move."

At the ROM, Col. Richard Fousek's DISCOM

Col. John Sylvester, 1st "Tiger" Brigade Commander (R) and MG William Key, Commander, 2nd Marine Division. To their rear left, Lt. Col. Michael Johnson, Commander of TF 1-67 Armor.

As the Tiger Brigade moved into Kuwait, it moved into an apocalyptic world of hellfire with more than 500 oil wells set ablaze by the Iraqis before they capitulated. The smoke drifted north, darkening the sky over the 1st Cav near Basrah and the Euphrates River valley.

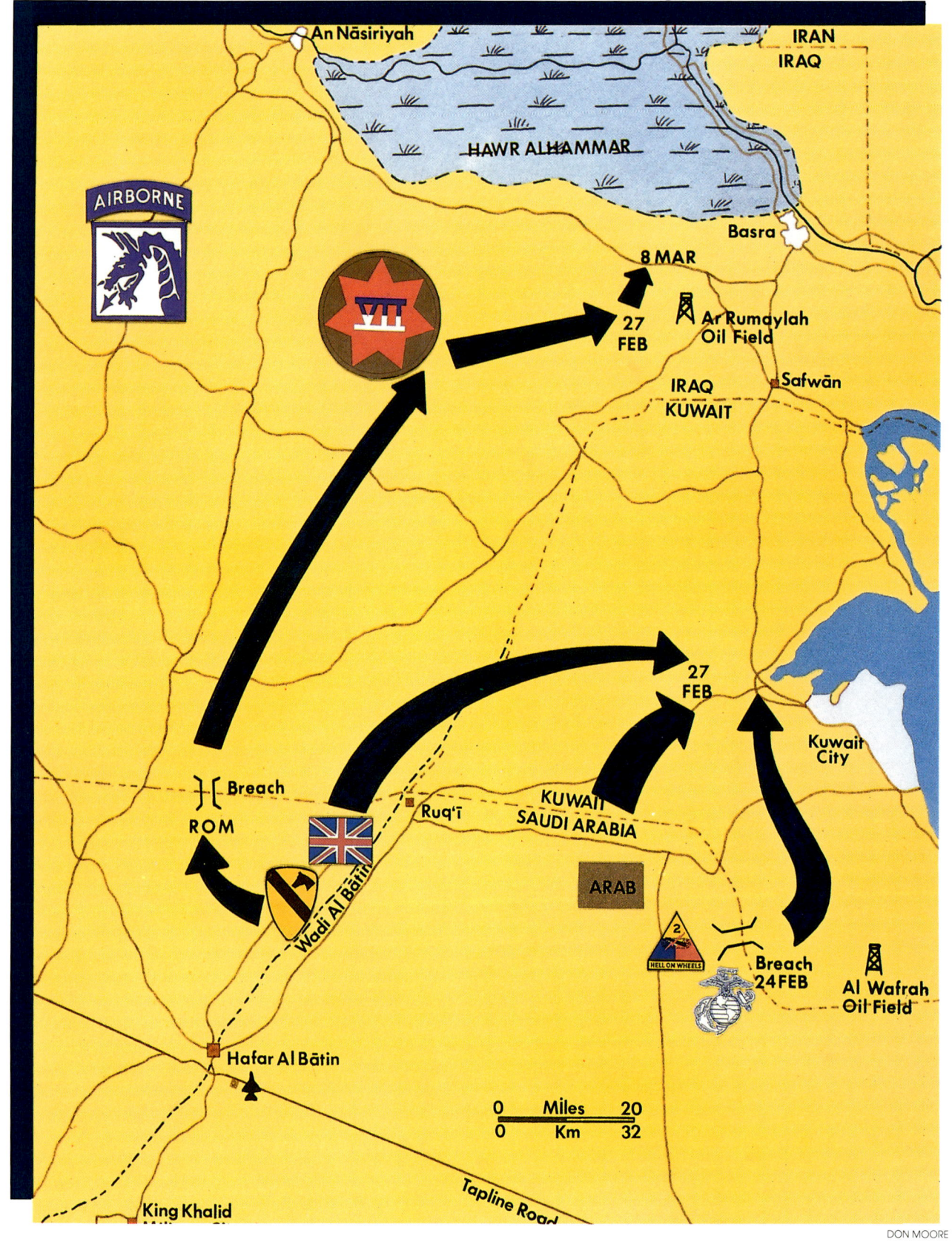

ATTACK

The "Tiger" Brigade attacks into Kuwait with 2nd MARDIV, Feb. 24. Continues north, meeting resistance in vicinity of Mutla Ridge, Feb. 26, defeating it and closing escape routes from Kuwait City. On Feb. 25, 1st Cav withdraws from Iraq, begins swing to the west at noon, Feb. 26, conducts refuel on the move, crossing 1st Infantry Division breach sites late Feb. 26. Halted at noon, Feb. 27, the 1st Cav has moved 300 kilometers in 24 hours. On March 8, 1st Brigade moves north, sealing Highway 8.

and elements of the 43rd Corps Support Group waited out the afternoon and the approach of the division. The ROM was designed to refuel moving formations without disrupting their momentum. At each of four sites, 24 parallel columns of vehicles pulled up, halting with each vehicle alongside a fuel point where a support soldier manhandled a hose. As each vehicle came to a stop, a crewman vaulted out, grabbing the proffered hose and jamming it into the filler neck. Tank and Bradley crewmen never touched ground. Engines stayed running; the whine of 1,500 horsepower Abrams turbines rising above the shouted exchanges of soldiers and the howl of the desert wind. An entire company refueled every 15 minutes. Then, with the refuelers cheering them on, the vehicles moved out and another column filed in.

The rest of the division, hot on 1st Brigade's trail, closed on the ROM sites as rain yielded to leaden skies. Endless lines of armor continued to file in; DISCOM continued to pump.

By the next evening, with the passage of the last elements of the division going north, the ROM had pumped 400,000 gallons of fuel into 6,100 vehicles headed for the breach, Iraq, and the Republican Guard.

In Sylvester's command post, the 26th began with a preparatory order from 2nd Marine Division; the Tigers were to attack north to Al Jahra on the western outskirts of Kuwait City, cutting off and destroying enemy forces trying to escape from the capital. Passing the order to their units, the brigade staff sat down to "war-game" their options. They settled on a plan placing TF 3-67 Armor on the left, attacking to seize Objective Colorado, and the Al Mutla police station. TF 1-67 Armor attacked on the right to seize Objective Kansas and secure the cloverleaf at Al-Jahra. The infantry followed, tasked to seize Objective Nebraska, the high ground northeast of the Ali Al Salem Airbase. The brigade's howitzers trailed.

To supply the 1,000 tons of fuel the division gulped daily, tankers were pooled, forming "Task Force Cofer," named for its commander, Lt. Col. Robert Cofer. TF Cofer pushed fuel forward to the brigades, reducing their transport burden. A similar group under Lt. Col. Joe Hart pushed ammunition. Following the ROM, TF Cofer sustained the division's operations in Iraq. 2nd Brigade vehicles at the ROM on Feb. 26, enroute to breach sites.

On the eve of the ground war ("G-Day"), Lt. Col. Thomas Suitt, commander of TF 2-5 Cav, briefs his company commanders.

Cavalry fighting vehicles of 2nd Armored Division's 2-1 Cav, attached to 1-7 Cav, screen the division's northern flank during the attack. The two troops — company-size units — of 2-1 Cav increased "Garryowen's" ability to screen and provide reconnaissance.

With the air campaign, vehicles display orange panel markers and inverted 'V's identifying them as Allied. Both are visible on these TF 1-32 Armor tanks, halted in Iraq, their crews in chemical suits. As standard operating procedure, the tanks carry three extra 120mm rounds in tubes on the turret. The box on the rear houses an auxiliary power unit, which would be gutted for storage if it broke.

Obstacle-level view of a mine plow. The rakes, set track-width apart, scooped up mines, sloughing them off to the sides. The chain-hung roller, called a "dog bone," detonated tilt rod mines designed to explode under the driver. The plows proved effective without seriously degrading the tank's performance.

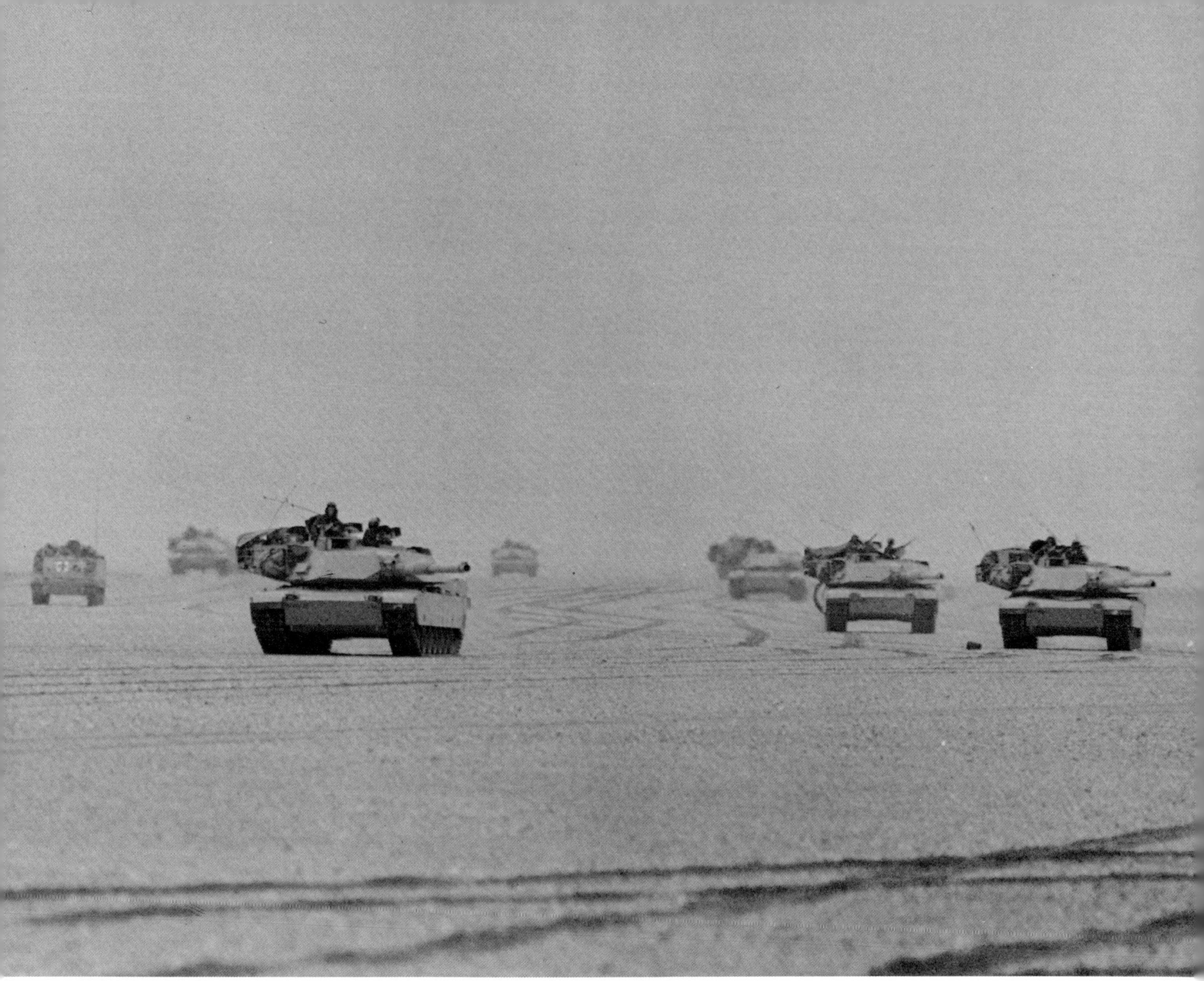

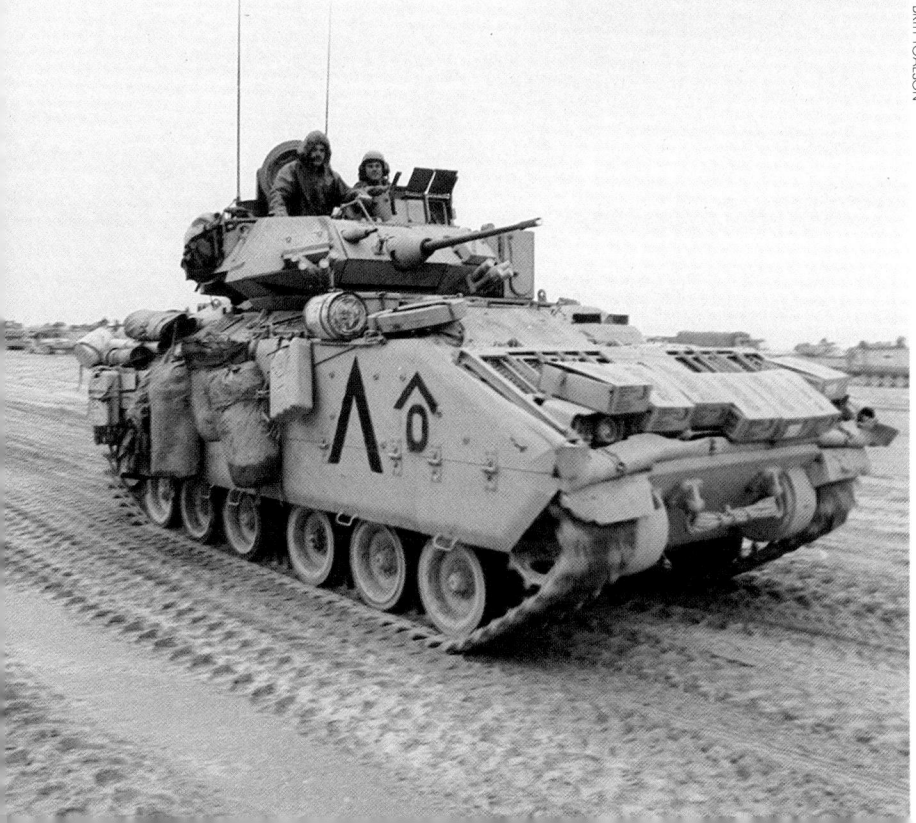

Task Force 3-32 Armor attacks in a battalion wedge.

BRIT TOALSON

(Left) What couldn't fit inside a Bradley, fit outside — or wasn't worth carrying. This cavalry fighting vehicle of TF 1-8 Cav's Scout Platoon carries MRE cases on the front, duffle bags on the side, and even an Iraqi gas can on the right rear side skirt.

At noon, the brigade attacked. Driving north at over 20 kilometers per hour, its crews fired into enemy positions observed during the night, eliminating any attempt at resistance. TF 1-67 Armor came on a bunker complex and dug-in tanks, oriented to the east. The enemy was destroyed with tank gun and TOW missile fire.

Pushing north, the Tigers approached the outskirts of Al-Jahra. And Iraqi resistance stiffened. Southwest of its objective, near Ali Al Salem Airfield, TF 3-67 Armor encountered an enemy strongpoint and what appeared to be a minefield. Tystad ordered one company to breach the minefield with its mine plows while two others provided covering fire. A fourth shot through the breach, securing the far side. As it crossed, enemy fire from the strongpoint opened up, but was silenced by the overwatching force. Within an hour of making contact, the brigade was moving north again, the enemy now quiet behind them.

Following TF 3-67 Armor, TF 3-41 Infantry assaulted its objective, mastering light resistance and securing Nebraska. TF 1-67 Armor raced on and seized key terrain controlling the cloverleaf. For TF 3-67 Armor, the battle continued. Moving in column

JOSEPH DECARO

Feb. 26 was a day of heavy fighting for the Tiger Brigade, as it attacked to secure the area of Al-Jahra and the highway cloverleaf critical to Iraqi units trying to escape from Kuwait City. Here, dismounted infantry of TF 3-67 Armor assault the Al Mutla police station, site of stiff room to room combat.

on the road toward Objective Colorado, its lead crews spotted enemy armor trying to escape north on the road later called "the highway of death." Losing not a moment, Tystad ordered the lead company to engage the Iraqis and block the route. Their opening volley left three enemy vehicles, two tanks and a howitzer, burning. The remaining crews surrendered.

Now came the infantry's moment. With tank and Bradley support, the task force's dismounts assaulted the police station as a 1-3 FA barrage lifted. Fighting room to room, they secured the building, killing or capturing 40 defenders outright. The next morning 52 more dead Iraqis were discovered.

It was during the fight that the brigade lost a second soldier. Sgt. First Class Harold Witzke III, traveling with the task force command post, was attempting to find a spot from which his CP could control the battle. As his vehicle stopped, automatic fire opened up. Witzke, trying to defend his soldiers, was mortally wounded.

With the end of resistance at the police station, the task force turned to the cloverleaf, meeting some residual resistance and crushing it.

The brigade spent the rest of that day and the following day consolidating positions and clearing the area of the enemy. Iraqis continued to surrender, their numbers in the hundreds, but it was the highway out of Al-Jahra that bore mute testimony to the Iraqis' defeat. For two kilometers, some 1,000 vehicles, civilian and military, lay in wreckage, most destroyed from the air while they were trying to escape.

As members of Sylvester's Tiger Battle Team looked out on the congestion of destroyed enemy along the highway of death in Kuwait, the First Team entered the breaches secured by the 1st Infantry Division. For most crews, it was dark as they slid up to the berm. There was no mistaking the lanes, however. Each route through bore an illuminated sign, positioned so that only traffic approaching from the south could see the light. Along the lanes, empty fuel drums marked the way. The enemy had fled from the area days before and was now in a rout, but for many, the breach symbolically opened the book of war (in fact, the enemy was folding so fast that a battle plan written by the division late on the 26th was obsolete by the next morning).

Emerging from the lanes, the division continued north through the night, making for Objective Lee, 90 kilometers away. Only through night vision devices and thermal sights could crews make out the formations in which they travelled. The expectation of contact, announced in a shower of tracers or a flash on the horizon, was overwhelming, yet none occurred.

Just after 4:00 a.m., the last unit arrived at Objective Lee. There they donned chemical suits and popped nerve agent pre-treatment pills. The little white pills would reduce — but not eliminate — the effects of poison gas; masks stayed close at hand.

Ninety minutes later, Tilelli ordered the division on to Objective Horse, 100 kilometers further into Iraq. From there it would head east in an attack on the Republican Guard's Medinah Division, a tank force equipped with the fabled Soviet T-72, Iraq's best armor.

As Saudi Arabia fell far behind, and with it the Mobile Subscriber Equipment "nodes," the tactical cellular phones in the commanders' HMMWVs failed. And then the division outdistanced radio communications with the main command post. Without missing a beat, the brigade commanders started talking directly to each other, relaying information and forming an electronic community in the black void that is the desert at night.

The division reached Objective Horse by 11:00 a.m. Two hours later, after a final review of battle plans, Tilelli started the attack. From its forward screen, 1-7 Cav slipped above 1st Brigade, securing the division's northern flank. The brigades spread into battle formation, 2nd Brigade in the south in its proven wedge, TF 1-5 Cav leading, TF 1-32 Armor and TF 1-8 Cav on its wings, 3-82 FA following. The 1st Brigade moved in a box led by TF 2-8 Cav and TF 3-32 Armor, with TF 2-5 Cav and 1-82 FA following.

On a sand sea, against the grey of a desert storm, the steel armada moved east. First Cavalry Division armor extended to the horizons, gliding noiselessly. Somewhere up ahead the enemy waited. Up ahead there was fighting. The 2nd Armored Cavalry Regiment had hit the Tawalkana Division with heavy enemy losses. Over the intercoms, rumors of a cease-fire swirled. The formations passed the first destroyed positions. A Bradley arrowed out to a collapsed bunker, returning with a huddle of dark figures on it carrying what looked like a white flag. The flying rain stung eyes aching with lack of sleep. How much longer before contact? The formation glided on.

The battle was not to be. Arriving on the heels of the 1st Armored Division, Tilelli ordered his units into hasty defensive positions. They had come 300 kilometers in 24 numbing hours. Tilelli had the order to prepare to continue the attack the next morning, this time against the Republican Guard Hammurabi Division, trying to escape to Basrah. At 11:58 p.m., VII Corps announced a possible cease-fire for 5:00 a.m. That soon changed to 8:00 a.m.

Two hours before the tentative cease-fire, 1st Armored Division kicked off the attack. Preceding it, in the cold hours before dawn, a massive artillery

J.E. PHILLIPS

"As far as you could see, there were vehicles on the move," said Division Chief of Staff Col. Leon Laporte of the 1st Brigade. Here, the "Ironhorse" Brigade on the move in Iraq.

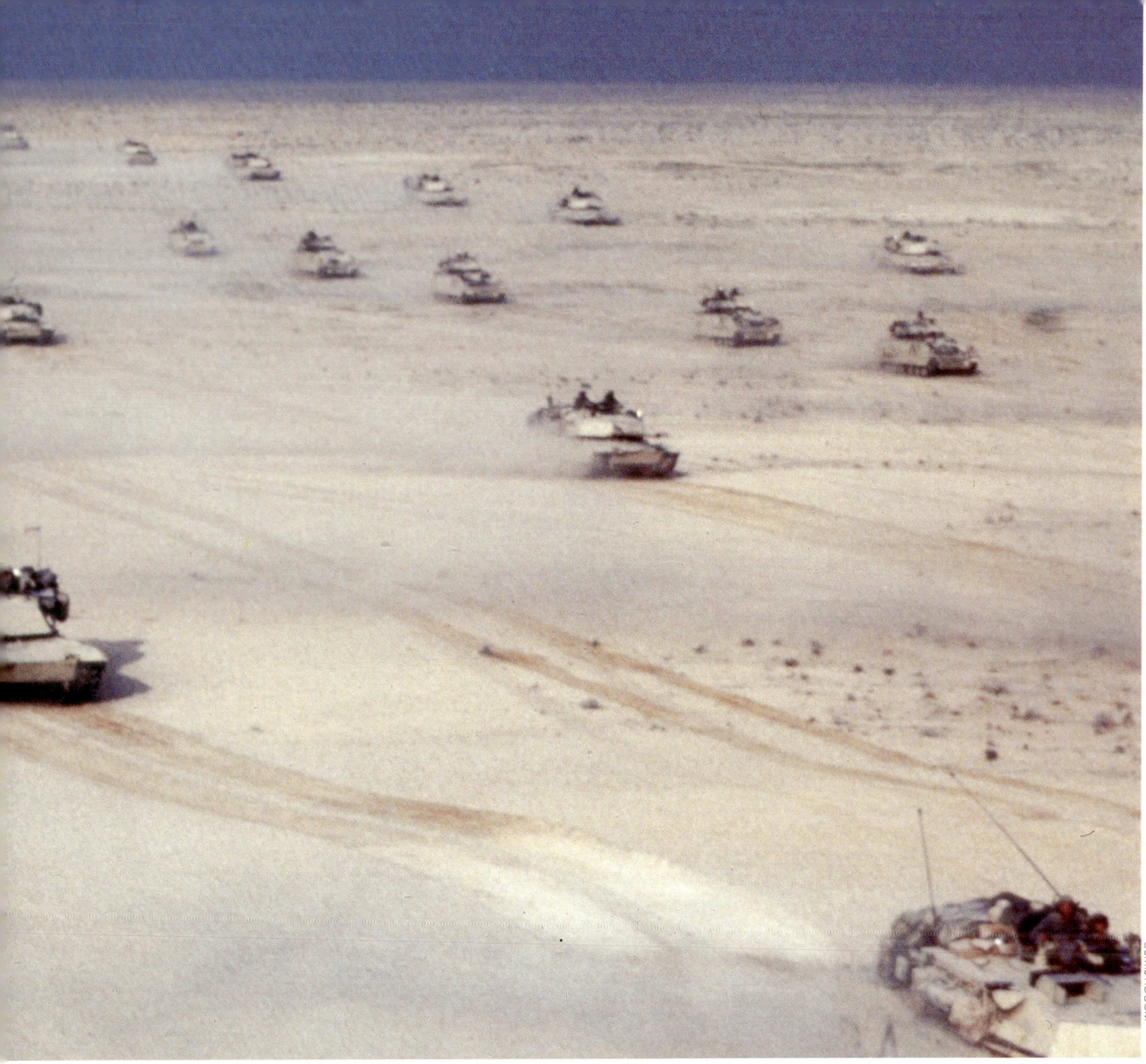

CURTIS HOCOM

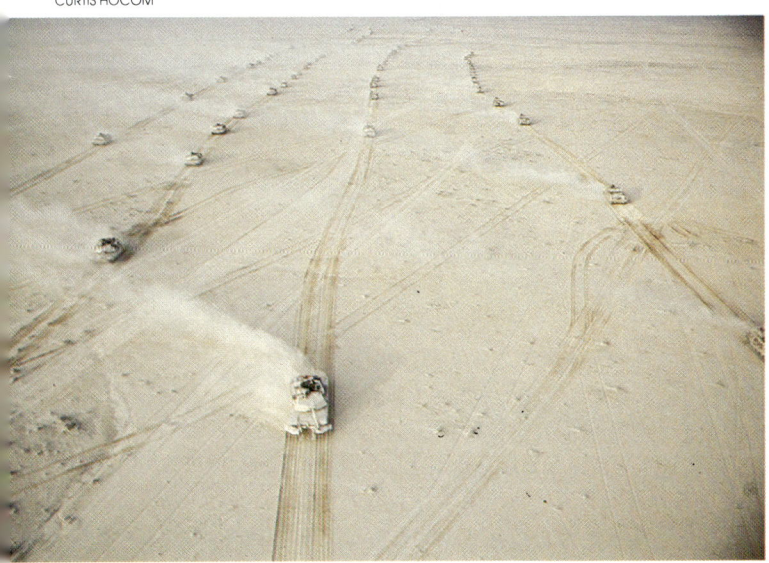

CURTIS HOCOM

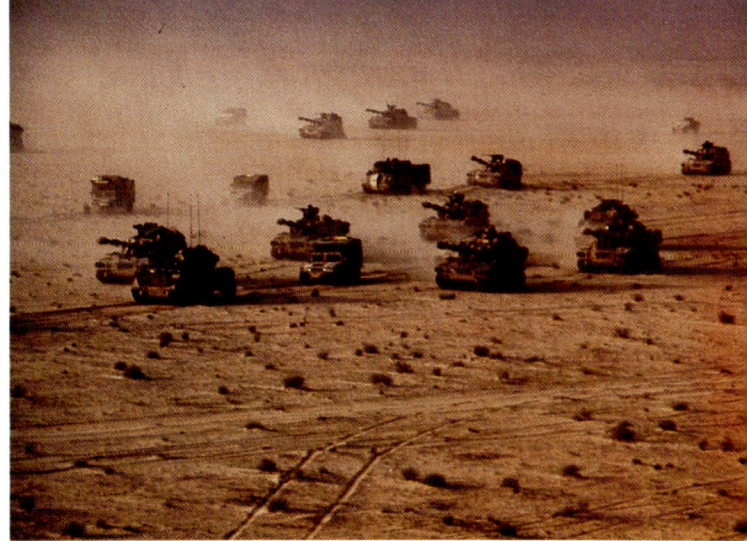

CURTIS HOCOM

preparation split the night. A cease-fire seemed remote. Soldiers half hoped for one, knowing they might have far to go; half hoped for battle, knowing how far they had come.

At 8:00 a.m., the cease-fire was ordered. The fighting officially stopped. But the dying continued. In the night the division had entered an area studded by unexploded munitions, remnants of countless artillery and air strikes. Within hours of the cease-fire, four soldiers were wounded by exploding bomblets. Two died. "The most dangerous time is after the cease-fire," said Lt. Col. Parker, commander of TF 1-5 Cav as he reflected on the losses, three of them his own soldiers who had made it through the battle in the Wadi and the marathon drive into Iraq.

As the cease-fire was issued, the mission of the 1st Cavalry Division shifted from destruction of the enemy to force preservation. It was an article of faith that deep in the Iraqi desert, word of peace had not reached every defender, nor was it implausible that some fanatics would fight on. Deliberately, units began clearing bunkers in their vicinity, unearthing stores of weapons, food, munitions, and more prisoners. The desert around the division looked like the impact zone of a world-class target range. Soldiers moving from one unit to another threaded their way between and around mines, bombs, bullets, rockets, and wreckage, walking in footprints or vehicle tracks. Stories of booby-trapped war trophies abounded, tempering the hunt for treasures like black Republican Guard berets or a secret-looking diary or map...

Then, with the cease-fire just hours old, explosions sent an old fear flooding back — had it all resumed? But the cease-fire held; the explosions came from the division's engineers blowing enemy

Intended as their route of escape, the highway leading from Kuwait City to Basrah came to symbolize the grisly rout of the Iraqi army, earning the nickname, "Highway of Death." As it secured the vicinity of Al-Jarah, on the capital's outskirts, the Tiger Brigade participated in the carnage, but the vast majority of damage came from air strikes.

141

equipment and stocks of munitions. A select few vehicles were preserved to make the long trip west to Fort Hood as museum pieces, relics from the "Mother of all Battles."

For several days after the cease-fire the Aviation Brigade flew over the destruction wrought by the deception raids, photographing the results. The sight was chilling, a carpet of devastation.

In the final mission of Desert Storm, 1st Brigade moved north to Highway 8, in the Euphrates River basin, assuming the 24th Infantry Division's positions astride the main supply route between Baghdad and its shattered army. The 24th Infantry Division, along with the rest of XVIII Airborne Corps, headed south and home.

And then it was the 1st Cav's turn. The 3rd Armored Division, from VII Corps, took over the 1st Brigade's sector and the division began moving south. On March 13, the Ironhorse Brigade crossed the border berm a last time, passing into Saudi Arabia and joining the assembled division on the plain of the Wadi al Batin. For the First Team, Operation Desert Storm was over.

A soldier uses his global positioning system (GPS) satellite assisted navigation aid to pinpoint the location of enemy dead for later burial.

(Left) American soldiers, suckers for kids and animals, found orphans to adopt, even in the depths of the desert and the well of destruction. Here, a trooper holds a puppy whose litter was discovered in an enemy ammunition dump and rescued moments before destruction.

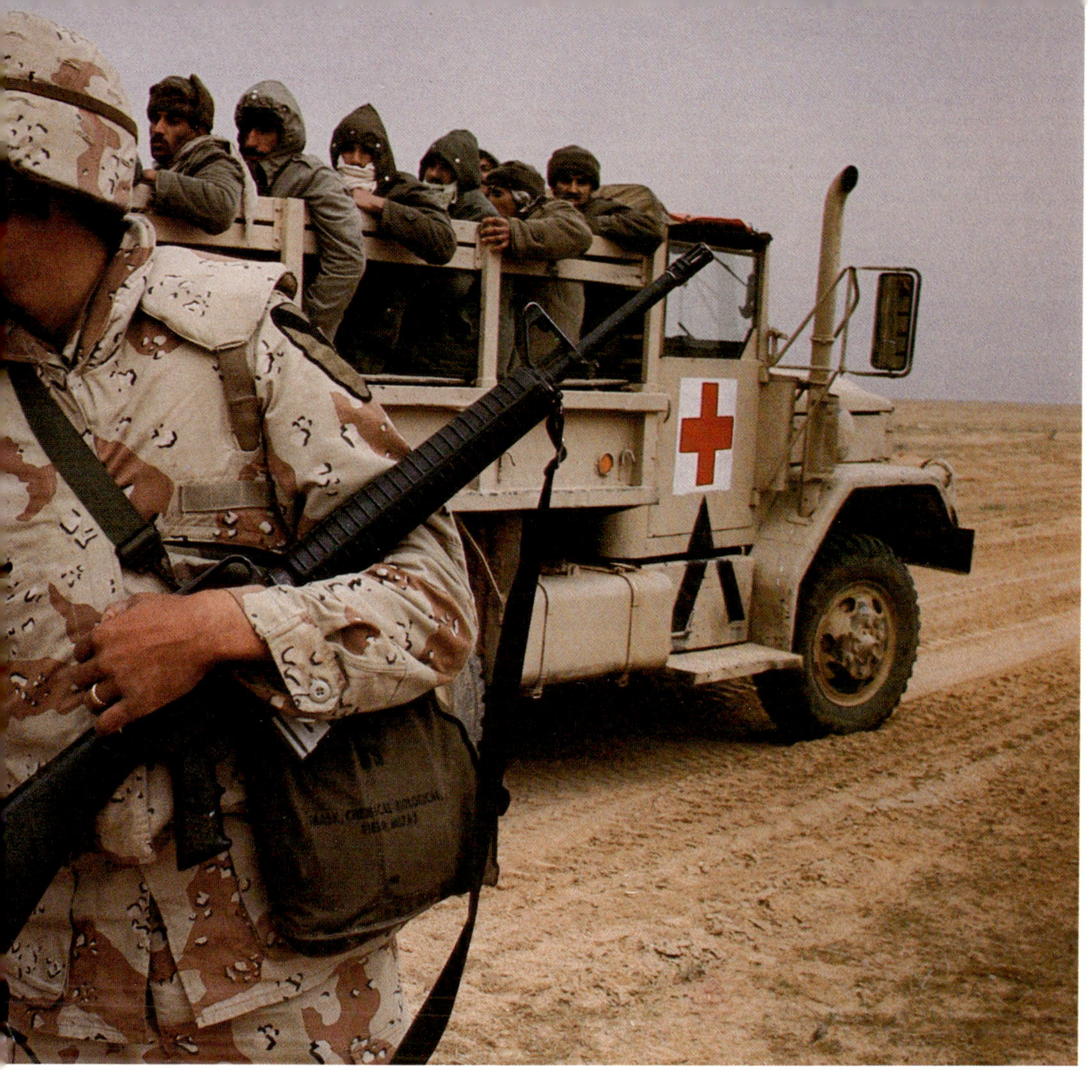

(Left) Finding adequate transport to move the large numbers of prisoners taken in the ground campaign proved a tough challenge. Spec. James Gamble and Spec. Steve Jones, TF 3-32 Armor, relax after loading Iraqis onto a truck.

STEVE ELFERS

Aftermath.

BRITT TOALSON

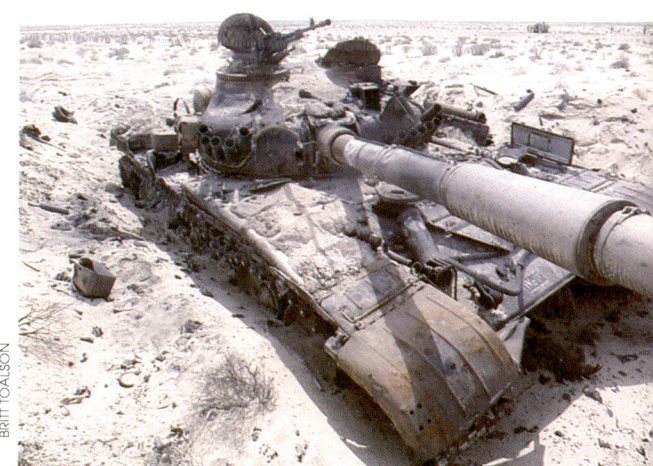

Shattered illusion, a Republican Guard T-72, pride of Hussein's armored corps and flagship of Soviet export weaponry, lies wrecked southwest of Basrah, victim of U.S. airstrikes. The T-72, which amassed a fearful reputation before the war, proved dramatically inferior to western armor. Many were killed by Abrams tank crews before their sights could even detect the Americans.

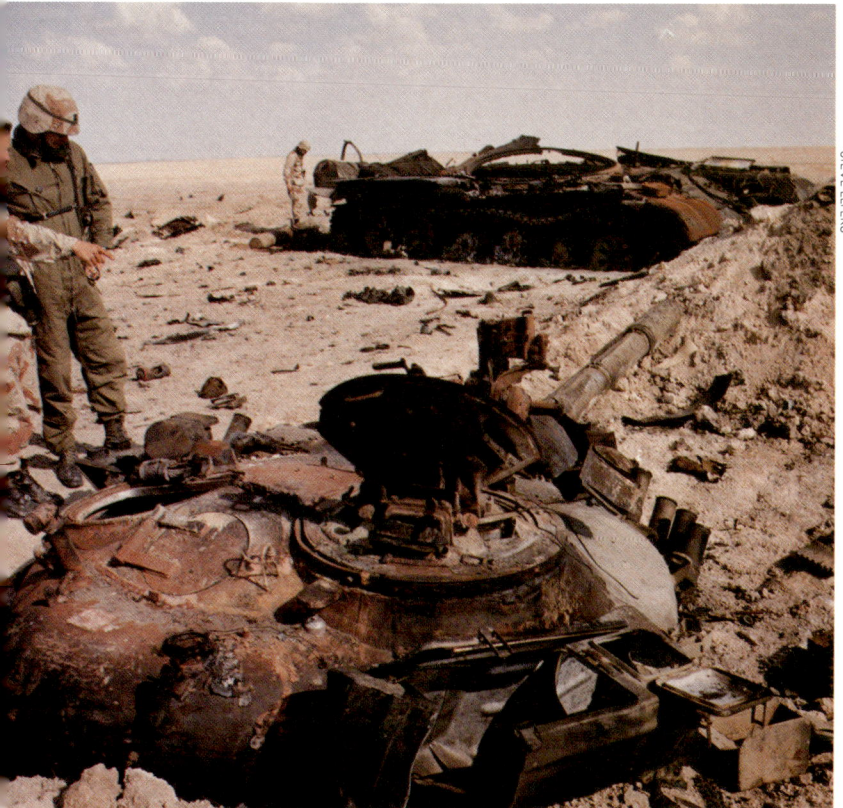

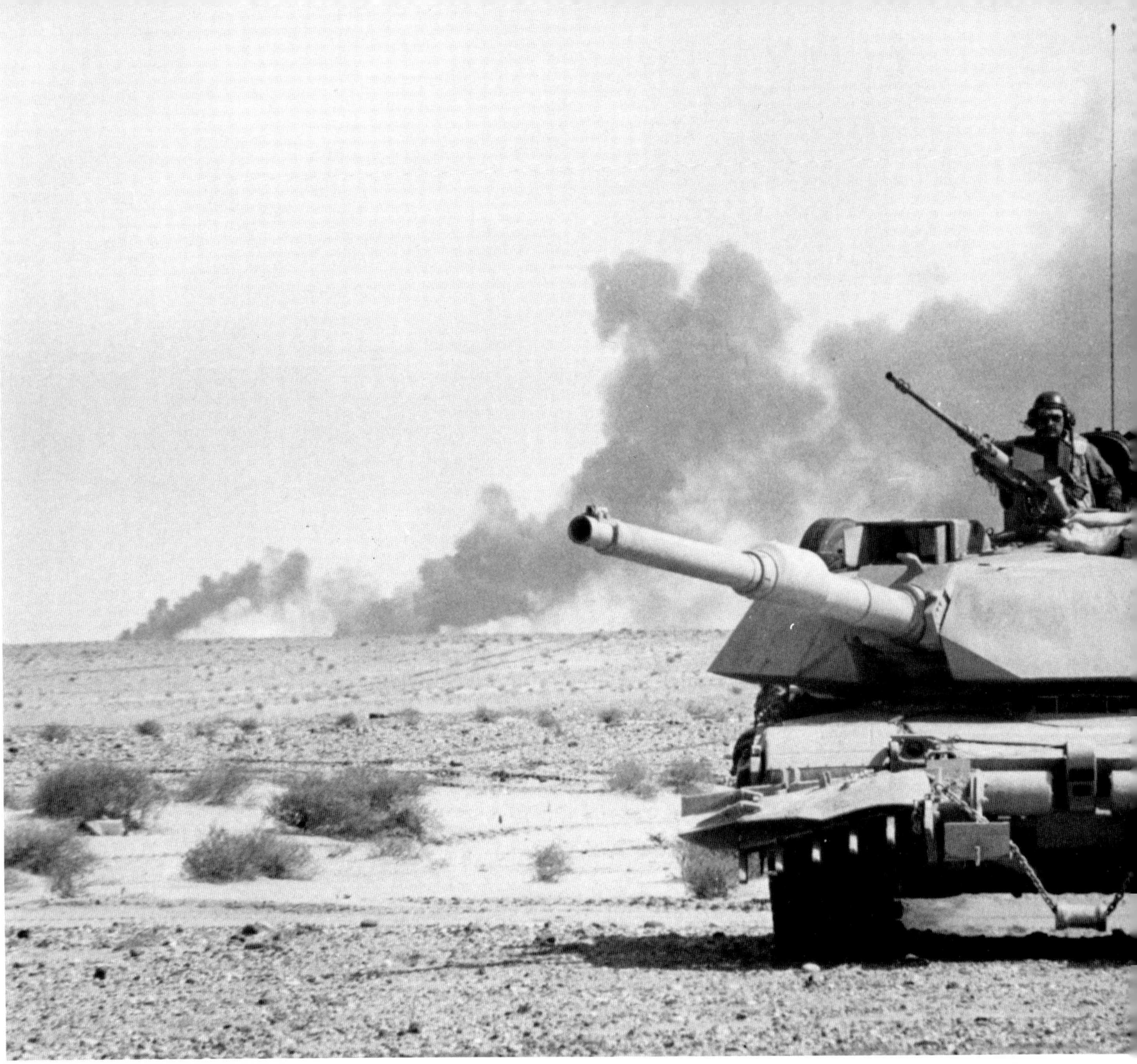

Alert for mines and defenders not yet ready to surrender, an Abrams crew moves past burning enemy equipment.

JEREMY HEFLIN

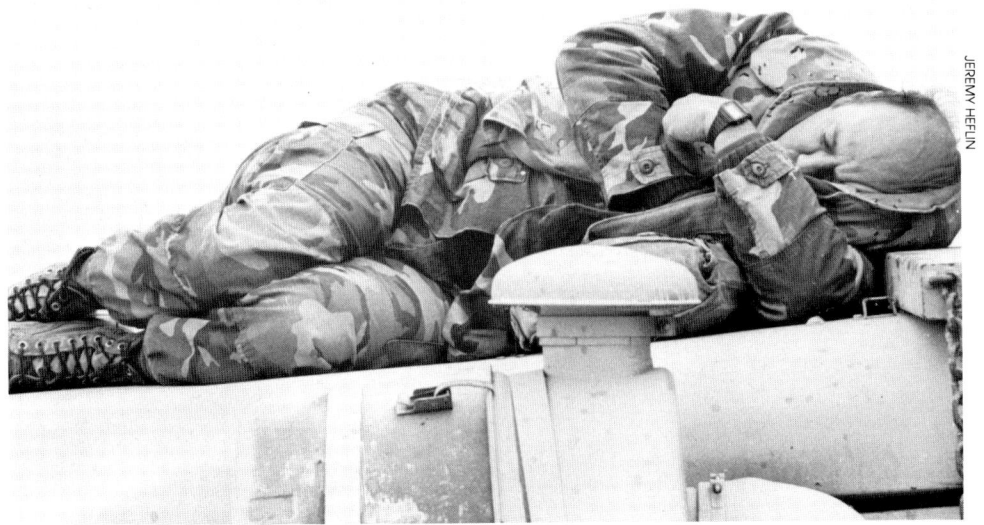

Exhaustion — February 27.

Following the cease-fire, the preservation of friendly forces was high priority; bunkers and positions located throughout the division's area had to be checked and cleared.

(Below) Checking his map before the next drive, 1st Lt. Court Horncastle, Scout Platoon Leader, TF 1-32 Armor, shows the fatigue of sleepless days and nonstop movement.

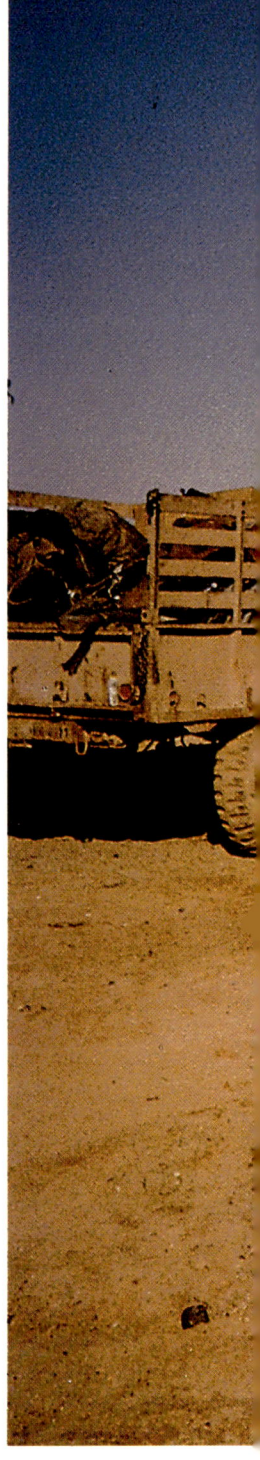

(Right) Celebrating ceasefire, 1-7 Cav troopers hoist their colors and cheer the possibility of getting back home.

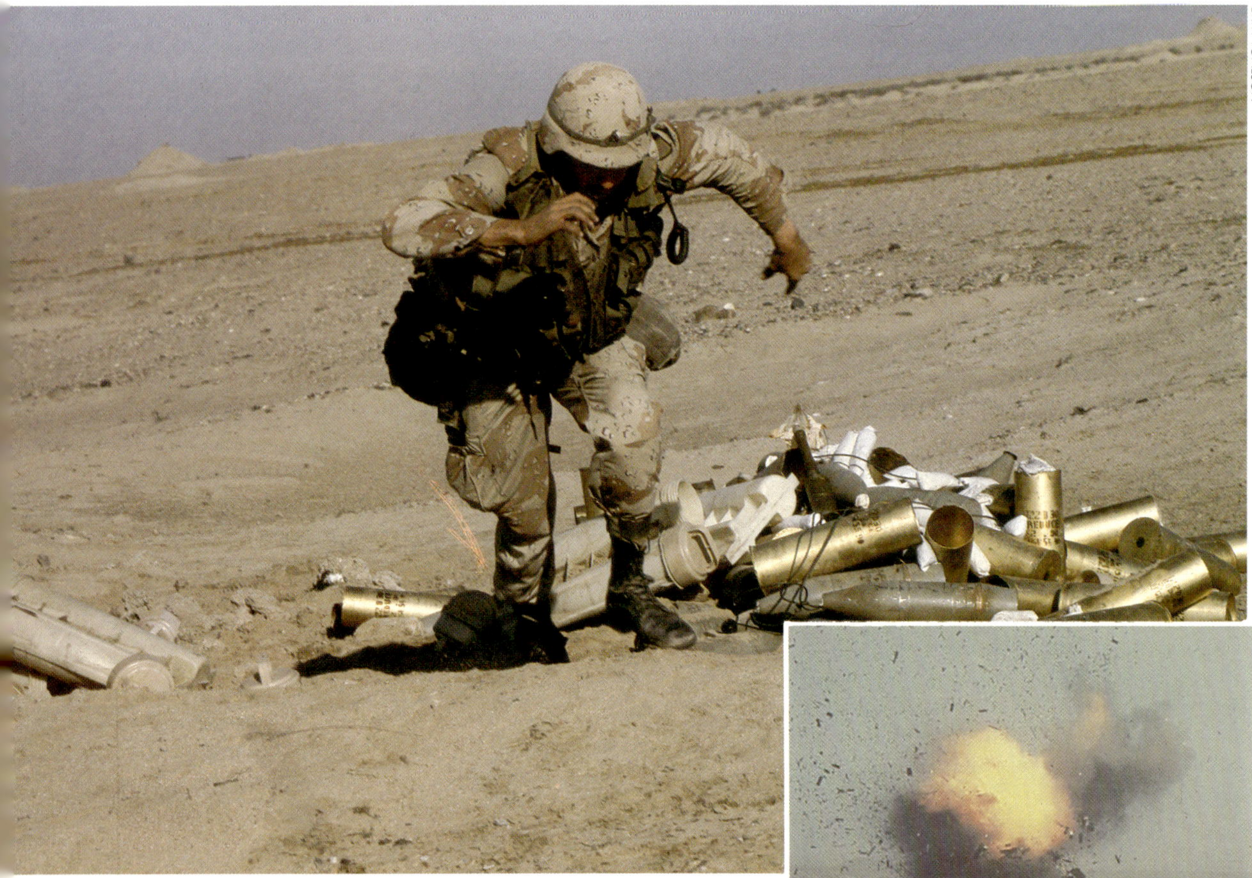

BRITT TOALSON

BRITT TOALSON

Enemy equipment, vehicles, and huge stores of munitions littered the desert in the wake of defeated and fleeing Iraqi forces. (Above) An infantryman bolts from a pile of munitions wired for demolition. (Inset) "Fire in the Hole!"

BRITT TOALSON

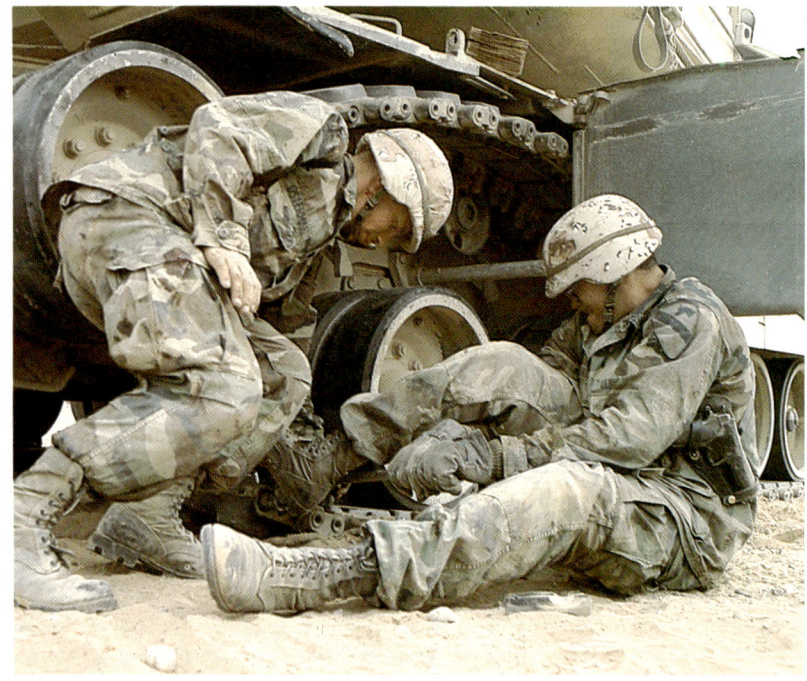

From noon on the 26th to noon on the 27th, the division travelled 300 kilometers. A tribute to the quality of equipment and maintenance, every tank and Bradley made it, even those repaired from mine damage just days before. Crews checked their equipment at every halt; no one wanted to be left behind.

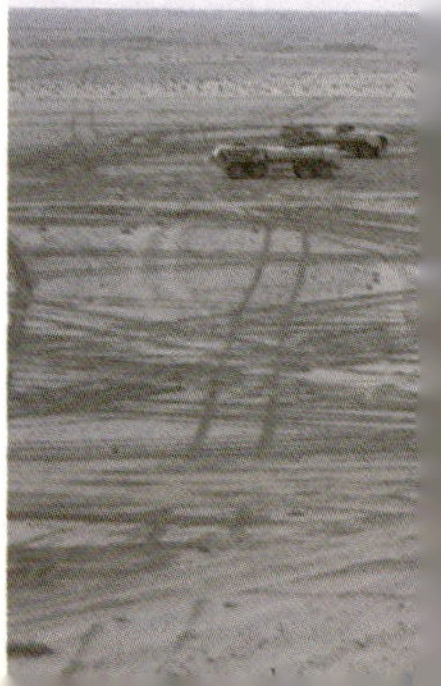

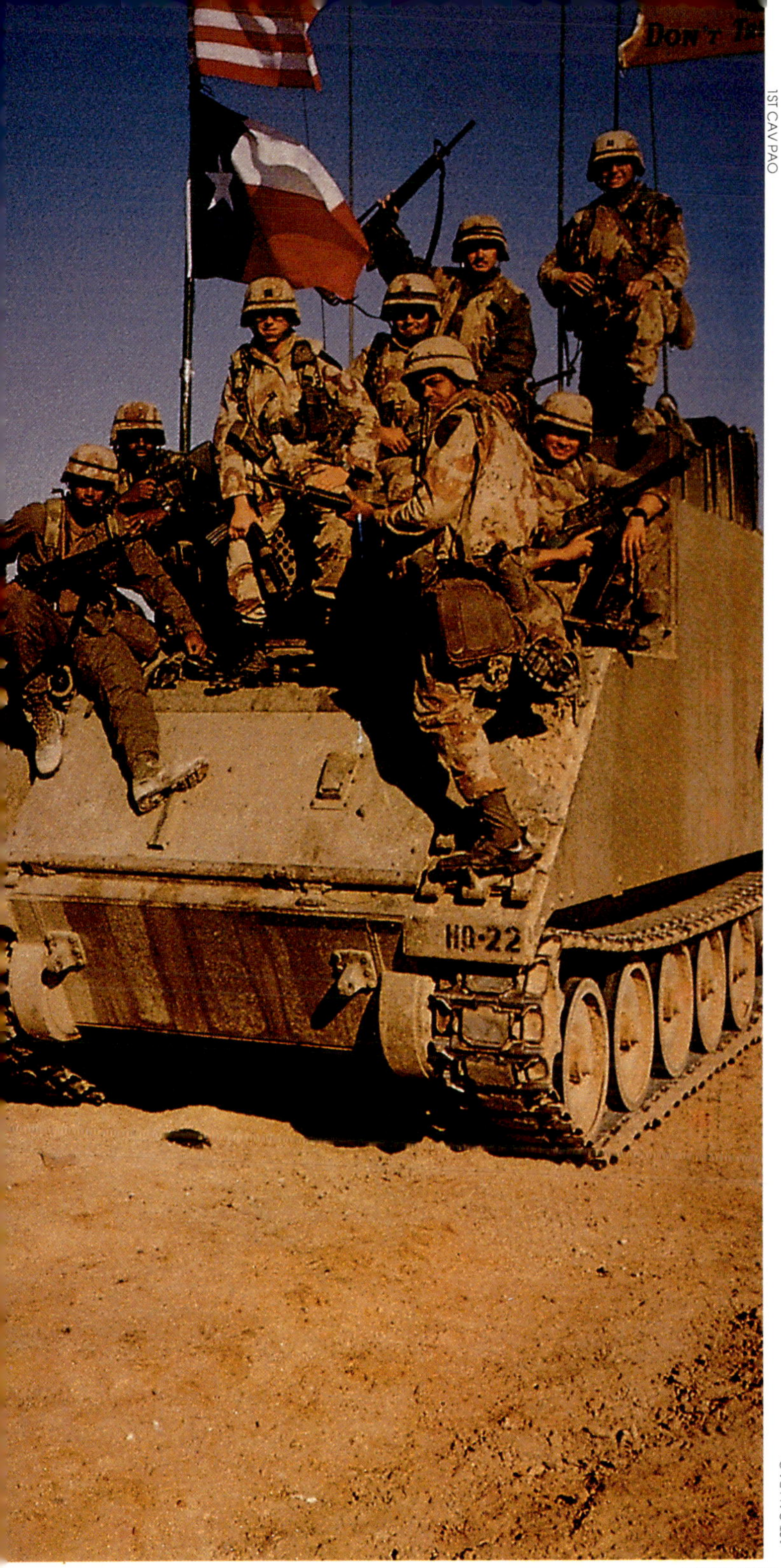

1ST CAV PAO

BRITT TOALSON

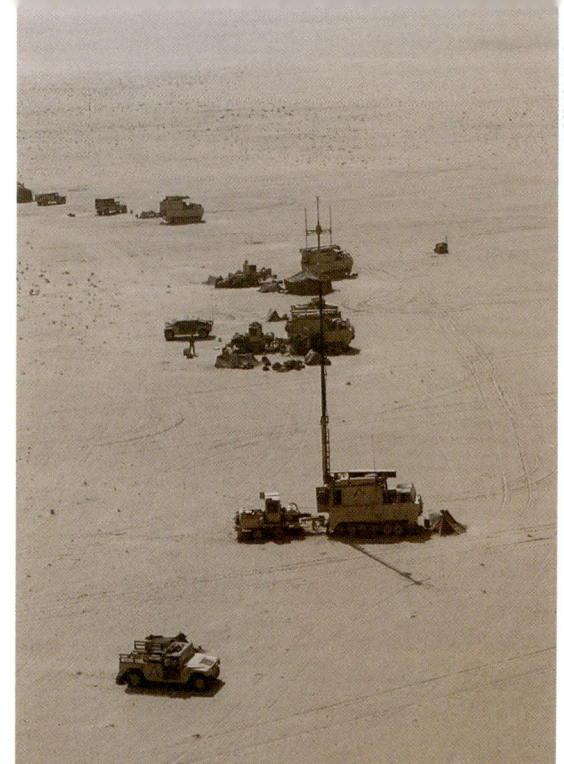

With the enemy in disarray, a 312th Military Intelligence Bn. "Trailblazer" listens in on Iraqi radio transmissions. Within seconds it could locate an enemy transmitter for friendly air or artillery strikes.

1ST CAV PAO

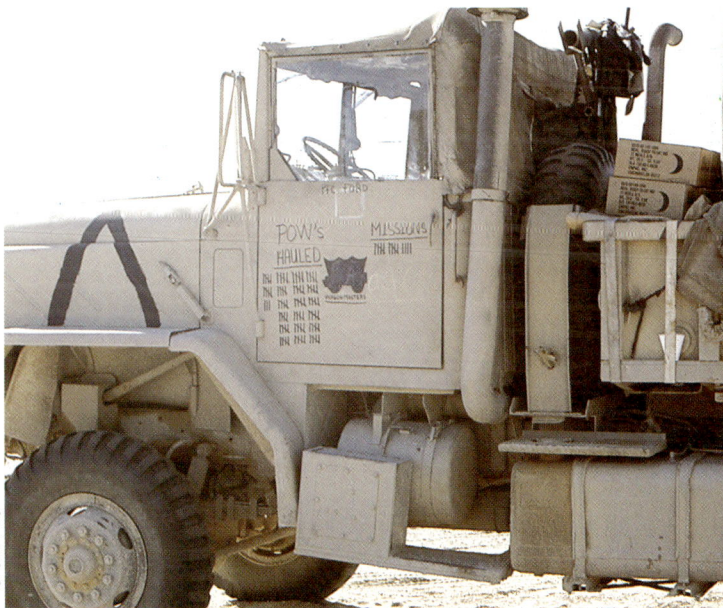

Transportation never left the short list of high priority requirements. The 43d Corps Support Group, attached to the division, supplemented the 1st Cav's trucks, one of which bears the tally of 104 prisoners hauled and 14 missions completed.

BRITT TOALSON

(Left) Each task force maintained small "combat trains," which provided immediate support to tank and Bradley units stripped to the essentials for the attack. These combat trains comprised a handful of fuel tankers and ammo trucks, mechanics, a medical aid station, and a command post.

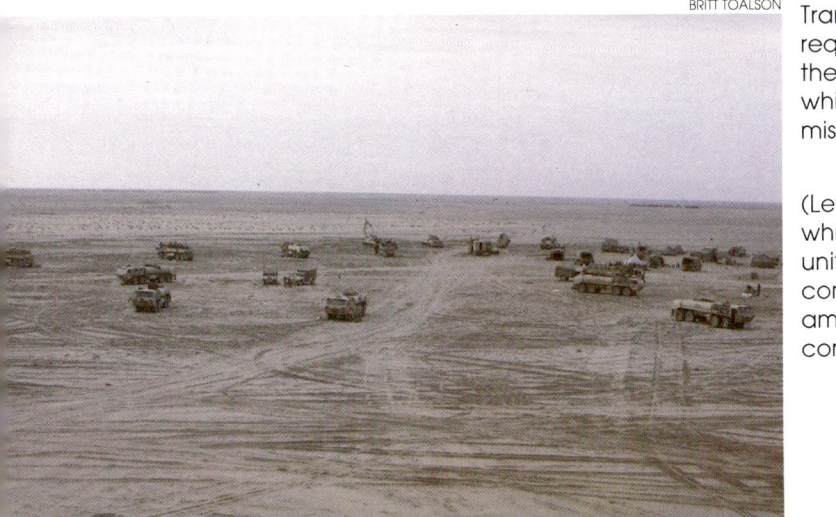

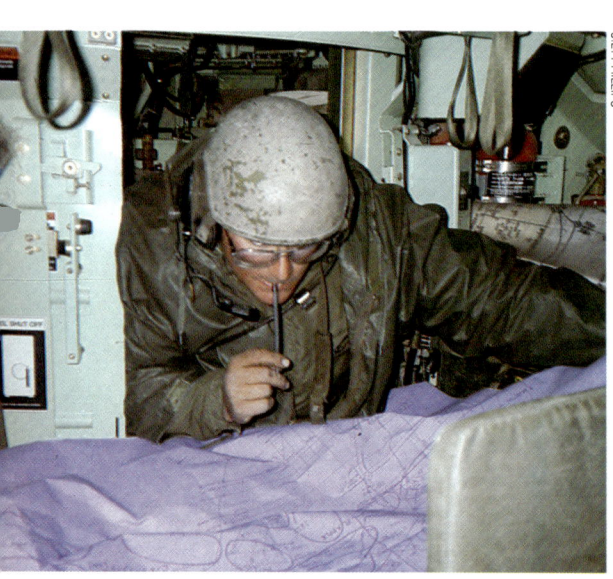

His Bradleys back from the fire trenches, Capt. David Francavilla, commander of Charlie Company, TF 1-5 Cav, pours over map graphics for the long-awaited attack through the breach.

Deep in Iraq, Associated Press reporter Mark Fritz pounds out a story from the belly of a TF 1-5 Cav Bradley. Yards away, an NBC-TV crew films the advance from another Bradley. After the division crossed the berm, most media stories were flown out on the division's helicopters.

Delta Company, TF 1-8 Cav, prepares to resume the drive north. Combat vehicles carried rolls of "concertina" barbed wire for local security, standard procedure in many units. In 2nd Brigade, each one also carried a stretcher.

BRITT TOALSON

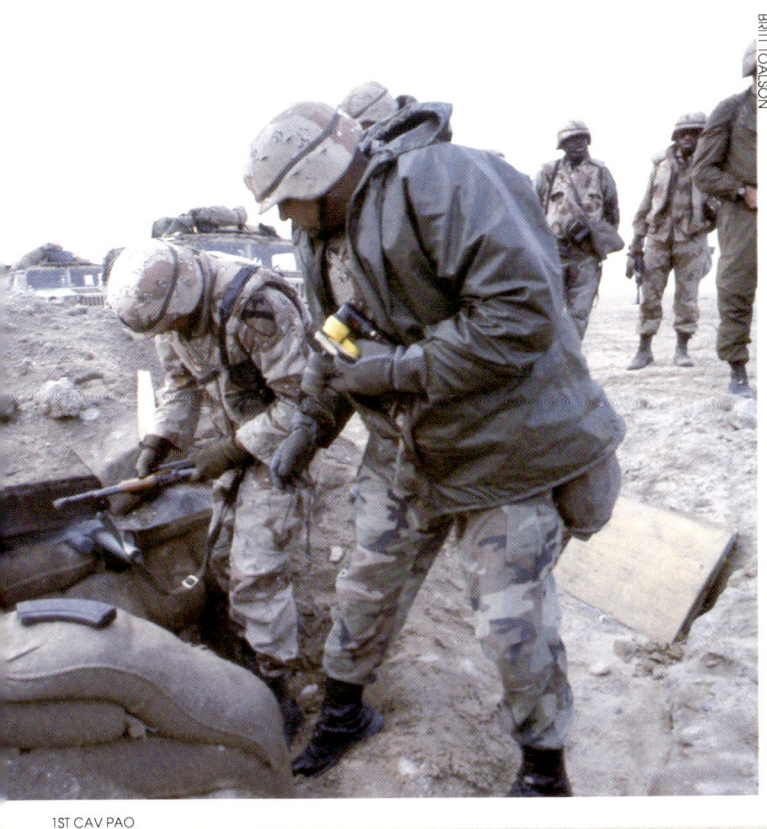

Clearing a bunker in their area, soldiers of TF 1-32 Armor cautiously collect an AK-74 rifle.

(Below) After fighting ended, Apache gun cameras recorded the wreckage of the Iraqi Army, helping chart the effectiveness of Allied weaponry. Here, Apaches overfly TF 1-5 Cav in Iraq.

1ST CAV PAO

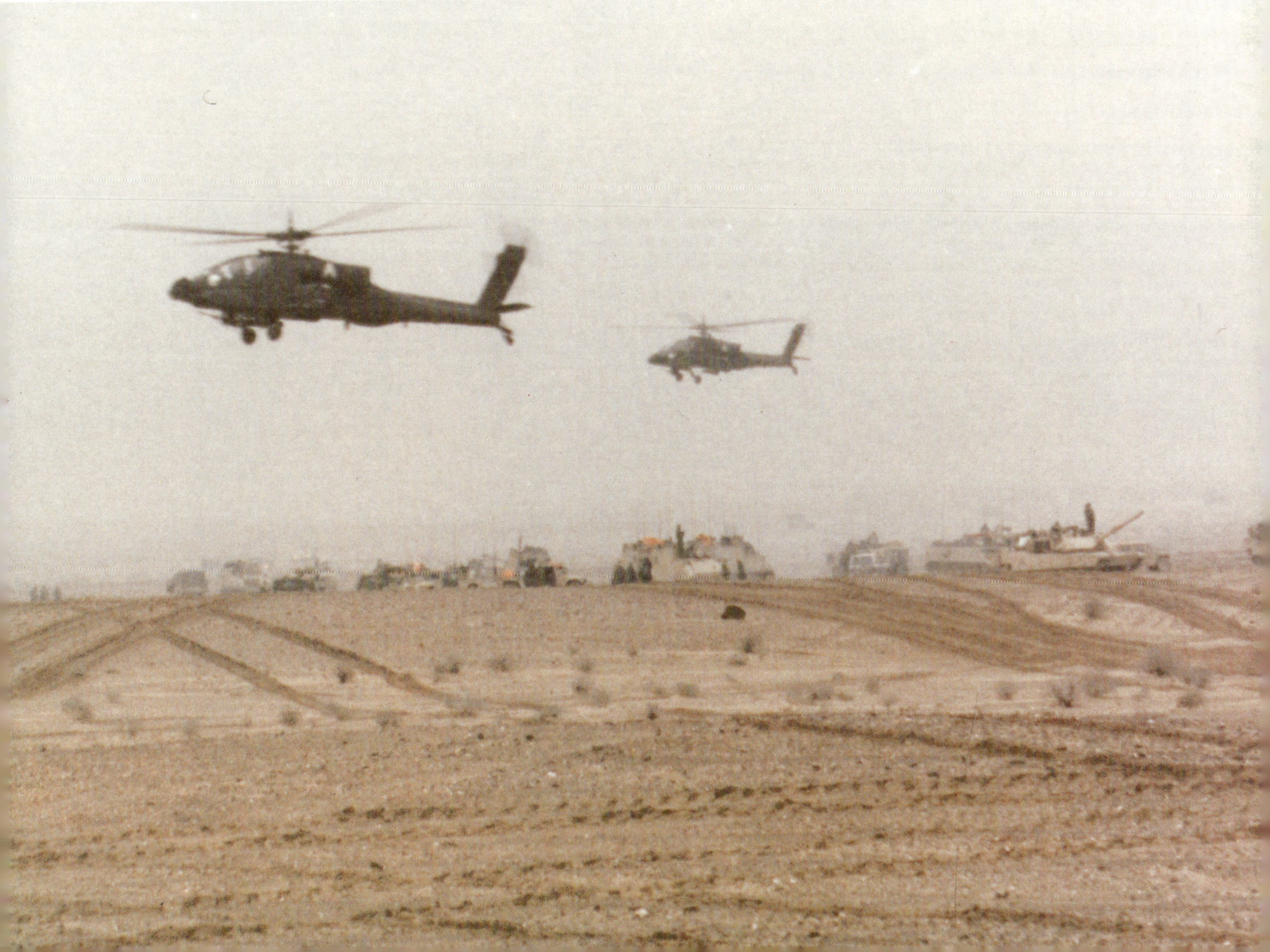

Returning from the Euphrates, a Bradley crew proudly fly the symbol of victory — and home.

Chemical suits peeled off, sleeping bags unrolled, an Abrams crew relaxes in the rare sunshine following the cease-fire and a 300 kilometer, 24-hour attack. A flak jacket, taped around the vulnerable bore evacuator (which prevented noxious powder fumes from entering the turret) protects it from shrapnel.

STEVE ELFERS

7
"And now ladies and gentlemen, the heroes of Desert Storm. Dismissed!"

— Release of soldiers to their families

Return of the champions, troops march into Fort Hood's Abrams Gym to a thunderous welcome, a roar no artillery raid could match. DUANE A. LAVERTY, *KILLEEN DAILY HERALD*

COMING TO AMERICA

No one really figured they would send folks home that quickly, but on March 9, a day after 1st Brigade went north to secure Highway 8, 901 First Team soldiers left the division for home. Called the "symbolic redeployment," it made good on President Bush's pledge to get troops home fast. It also assuaged Arab fears of a lingering American presence.

For nearly 17,000 envious troopers still in the desert, the symbolism was less than convincing. That changed quickly. On March 13, the last of the division, in a stately column of armor, passed through the berm, now an obstacle no more impressive than a snowplow's spoil. Iraq had changed. Where there had been only endless desert, wide roads were scraped out. Crude roadsigns almost casually referred to minefields off the road's shoulder. Vehicles of all sorts bounced to and fro as if on a phone run to the soldier's mall back in AA Horse. Veterans who had passed this lawless expanse in the black of an uncertain February night, relying solely on machine, buddies, and nerve, regarded all the gentrification with amazement — and thinly veiled contempt.

But simply to get out of Iraq was good enough, even if it meant stopping in Saudi Arabia. At least there one could walk around without fear of blowing up…

Ironhorse was headed south for the division's new home, called Assembly Area Killeen after the major town adjacent to Fort Hood. AA Killeen was located on the plain of the Wadi al Batin, just west of Hafar al Batin. "Haffer," as soldiers pronounced it, had returned from a limbo somewhere between peace and war. Its normal inhabitants — shopkeepers, shoppers, the Bedouin, children, sheep, even tourists — were out in strength and Haffer had returned to its customary chummy chaos.

Bedouin kids lined the trail, cheering weathered columns sliding around the outskirts of town and on to the assembly area. They clamored for handouts. A few succeeded in winning an MRE. The rains of January and February had brought up swaths of grass making the area distinctly un-warlike.

The first order of business — after getting a good count of sensitive items (weapons, classified material, expensive optics or electronics, etc.) and establishing the unit area (most units merely stopped parking-lot style; what minimum security was needed roving guards provided) — was a shower and a phone call. After the austerity of Iraq, AA Killeen, with the entire Aviation Brigade parked outside — complete with airstrip — looked a little like downtown. It took some searching to find the big shower tent and the familiar (but faded) Saudi phone tent. Everyone had the same idea: to call home and let someone know they'd made it. The line was long, but the wait worthwhile. With a little luck, the line at Chuck's Wagon would be bearable.

For those who hadn't managed to see any Iraqi equipment "up north," Maj. Gen. Tilelli (who had been promoted by Lt. Gen. Franks on Palm Sunday in AA Killeen) had directed the assemblage of trophies hauled out by the division. Destined for the division's museum at Fort Hood, there was one of almost every type, including the dreaded T-72M1. Now, looking vaguely embarrassed, they sat forlornly by the shower tent as curious cavalry troops climbed all over them.

Priority of effort was on maintenance — of body and equipment. The former suffered generally from neglect, the latter for want of decent facilities and time. Gear, filthy from campaigning, was cleaned up, inventoried, and packed away. Ammunition was hauled out of turrets and cargo bays, recrated and turned in. More than one soldier wished there had been more targets to shoot the stuff at in Iraq…

A soldier caught returning with contraband guns, ammo, etc., could count on misery: any unit "lucky" enough to have such a soldier would be pulled

Through the breach, 1st Brigade returns to Saudi Arabia on March 13 after an overnight stop in Iraq. Passing through the berm (its remnants visible at lower right) in single file, the brigade's column of more than 1,000 vehicles stretched past the northern horizon.

Angels in the wire, Bedouin children in the drab "thub" shirt worn by males of all ages, stand outside a unit perimeter near Hafar al Batin, visions of MREs dancing in their heads.

entirely from the deployment sequence and would "go to the end of the line." With that incentive, peer pressure took over.

Kevlar helmets gave way to "booney" caps and radio watch gave way to calendar watch. It was hard to believe that the time for westward flight was close. Some determined simply not to think about it… Yet.

One thing impossible not to think of — dwell on — was food. Since October, palates had been slowly wrecked by a siege of tedious, albeit nutritious… material. Meals, Operational, Ready to Eat (MORE) had begun supplementing the MRE and T-ration regimen in November, as the Army tried to conserve stocks of combat rations for the demands of VII Corps and a lengthy war.

The MORE was a commercial, off-the-shelf, single-serving item like ravioli. In November, as soldiers began to regard MREs with hostility, MOREs were welcome; but by March, picking one of the little cups for the hundredth time out of a container of lukewarm water meant to heat it, almost robbed one of an appetite. Almost.

In the nick of time, real food arrived and — after months of lifeless field rations — the first omelet to fill a soldier's paper plate was truly a thing of wonder, the pungent aroma of a sausage patty almost past imagining.

Things started moving faster, now. It was time to put the tracked vehicles aboard trucks for the trip south to the port (magic words, "the port") and that meant cleaning. They would be scrubbed in Dhahran, but had to be free of the "big stuff" before then. Sand leaves little substantial buildup, even four months of it, but it gets everywhere. The washrack proved a busy place.

Soon after the vehicles went, soldiers packed up. In convoys of busses, trucks, and Humvees, they left AA Killeen and the Wadi al Batin. Few, if any, looked back.

Mother of all displays, opposite the telephone center at the division's rear area, enemy combat vehicles captured deep in Iraq await shipment to Texas and a permanent home on a concrete slab outside the division's museum.

The convoys wound up at the sprawling, white concrete highrise apartment complex of al Khobar in Dhahran. Built for someone who had never decided to move in or rent out, the deserted buildings were perfect for a redeploying army. Al Khobar was at first a refreshing change, even miraculous — rooms with air conditioning, running water, and TOILETS. It sported a mall offering exotic draws like a photographer taking photos of soldiers on a camel. The food was catered and reasonably good. But, after the desert, it seemed closed in and tedious. Besides, home beckoned irresistibly now. Every day seemed a week.

The final washrack in Dhahran was wet hell. To meet U.S. Department of Agriculture requirements, it seemed the paint had to be washed off. A HMMWV took 7-10 hours, a tank all day and night. Nothing more contaminated than the underside of one's fingernails was going to get into the U.S.A. Even the little vials of sand (usually empty Tabasco sauce bottles from MREs) so carefully kept were contraband.

At last the day came — snuck up — when duffle bags were locked a last time and piled onto a stake and platform truck. When the last Saudi Pepsi went down. When the last farewell was said to buddies who had to spend another day or two in al Khobar. When the carry-on baggage was inspected and OK'd. When the steps up that beautiful white fuselage were underfoot and a smiling American flight attendant said "Welcome home." And when the door swung shut and the airplane moved, and then soared upward, and the whole thing became — a memory.

It was worth it.

As they had on the trip over, the flight crews made life seem even more wonderful to their visibly happier passengers. The cabins were bedecked with yellow ribbons and banners, the flight deck open. The atmosphere exuded welcome, relief, and reunion, all at once. Those flight crews were the first Americans most soldiers had seen, besides each other, in six months. They made first impressions count.

The cheer as wheels left King Fahd Airbase was matched only by the one that went up as the airplane crossed into U.S. airspace. By now passengers for nearly 18 hours, soldiers were a little groggy, but knew home when they crossed it at 40,000 feet.

And then a familiar sight of grey green, crisscrossed with trails and patches of caliche clay, swung into view, and the plane smoothed down to touch earth at Robert Gray Army Airfield, after so long.

The band was playing as soldiers walked down the steps, shook hands with the generals there to greet them, and walked into a small warehouse to turn in weapons and other sensitive items. The line moved fast, and they were soon on a bus, which took forever to get loaded and moving.

Lining the road, all the way from West Fort Hood, along the highway, through the main gate, along post, to the gym, hundreds of people stood, jumped, yelled, and waved. They carried banners, cards, flags, kids, and a greater good will and welcome than any soldier was prepared for.

Once in AA Killeen, crews turned in ammunition. Here the needle-like projectiles of 120mm "sabot" rounds are visible, encased in a collar. On firing, the collar, pronounced "sayboe" (French for shoe), falls away, leaving the ultra-hard depleted uranium round travelling at 1700 meters per second.

For most units, AA Killeen resembled a big parking lot, with vehicles in rows to ease maintenance and accessibility. A cot-side game of chess on a well-travelled board helped time pass.

Scrubbing away the war, gear was hosed down at AA Killeen, and scoured in Dhahran, until meticulous USDA inspectors gave the nod. Their chief concern was pests carried in dirt residue.

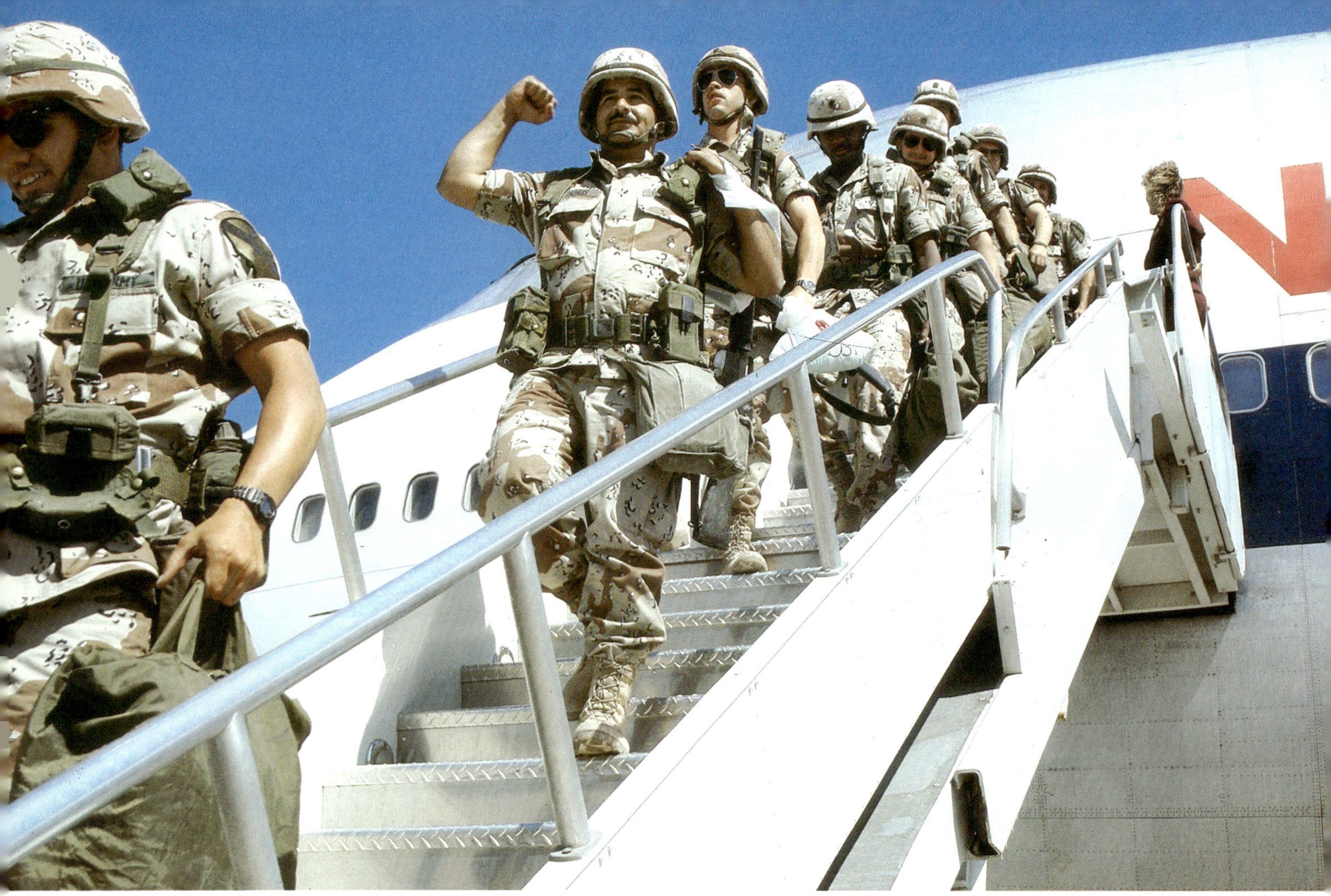

Triumphant return.

J.E. PHILLIPS

J.E. PHILLIPS

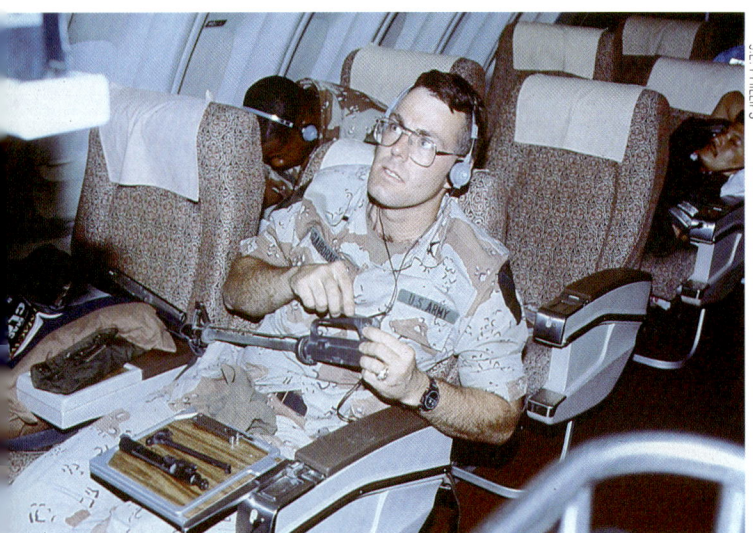

During the flight home, many soldiers relaxed for the first time in months. Some habits died hard: (above) 1st Lt. Ronald Claiborne, 545th MP Co. cleans his rifle while watching "Memphis Belle," a movie about a WWII bomber crew that finishes its combat tour — and goes home.

(Right) Few soldiers foresaw the welcome awaiting them. The way to the reunion site was packed with fans, many who returned flight after flight with a last, enduring message of support.

J.E. PHILLIPS

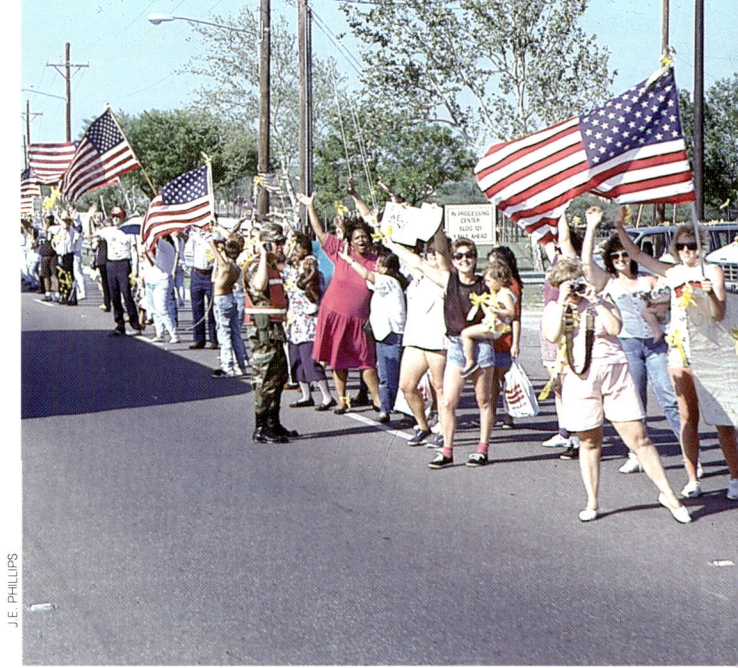

At the corner where the busses turned onto the highway towards the main gate, DJ "Big Joe" Lombardi staked out a spot for his radio van from which he broadcast arrival times to his (by now) huge audience. He gave updates from touchdown until the busses passed by him, accorded the rapt attention of families waiting at the gyms on post. He did so every day from the first flight in March to the last one in June. The corner is now called Victory Corner and has a little monument on it — to those who welcomed the disbelieving soldiers home.

Busses carrying First Team soldiers pulled up outside giant Abrams Gym. Packed inside, people spilled out, lining the entranceway. The horse cavalry platoon paraded outside, firing revolvers as the soldiers marched up in crisp formation, unit colors flying.

In marched the formation, 400 soldiers stopping and executing a left face to come eye to eye with the crowd, bigger by far, searching for a special face and thundering cheers in the echo chamber gym. A voice on the PA system announced, "And now, ladies and gentlemen… The heroes of Desert Storm. DISMISSED!"

Pandemonium. An explosion of joyous emotion, people running, catching, embracing, crying, screaming, whispering, laughing, and sobbing with the outflooding relief of a six-month eternal vigil finally ended.

It was impossible to remain calm and detached. People who knew no one on the flights came simply to welcome the soldiers and to be swept up in the pure emotion of the moment. Those reunions brought out the best in folks.

Reunion, and the best in America, seemed the theme for the spring and summer of 1991. To be a soldier and home was the finest of things. The First Team paraded down a dozen avenues — in Atlanta, Houston, and Dallas, in small town parades and big town parades. And in the biggest parades of them all: those breathtaking whirlwinds in Washington D.C. and New York.

To be a soldier in the Capital is a special feeling — on any day. To be a conquering hero there, even for just a fleeting moment, even if one knows he was just doing his job, is a lasting intoxication. To those who paraded down Constitution Avenue on June 8, it was like that.

If Washington D.C. was heady brew, New York City was a tumultuous revel. From the press of marchers, police, and media at Battery Park, the formation strode out to turn onto Broadway, a wide red carpet, and into the sunlit snowstorm of cascading paper so thick it was disorienting. But the wildly cheering crowds to the left and right guided the columns on. Where could all the paper come from? Who was going to clean it all up?

New York ended too soon, but the afterglow was nurtured at a party of mythic size aboard the U.S.S. Intrepid, a vintage aircraft carrier tied up on the west side. Symbolically, the warriors were being thrown a big welcome home party, while they were, privately to each other, saying farewell. This was the finale in the grand drama. The curtain was poised, the parts played through and the Heroes of Desert Storm prepared to leave the stage.

For Pfc. William Wagner, 1-7 Cav, a hero's family welcome awaits.

1ST CAV PAO

DUANE A. LAVERTY

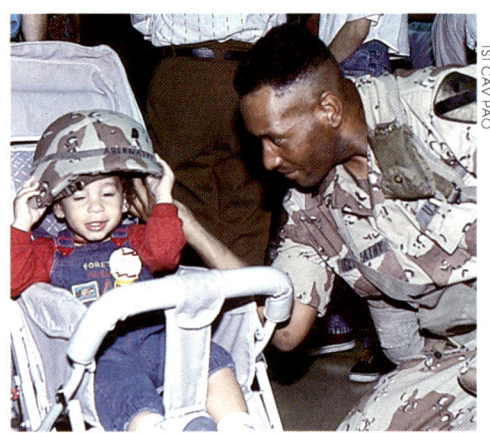

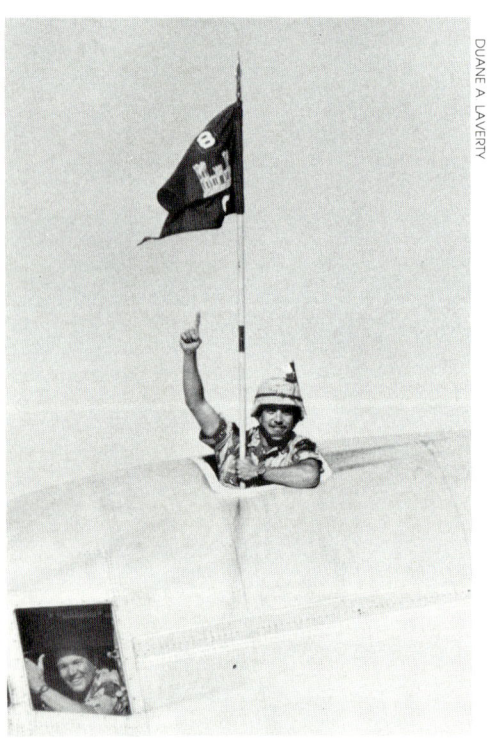

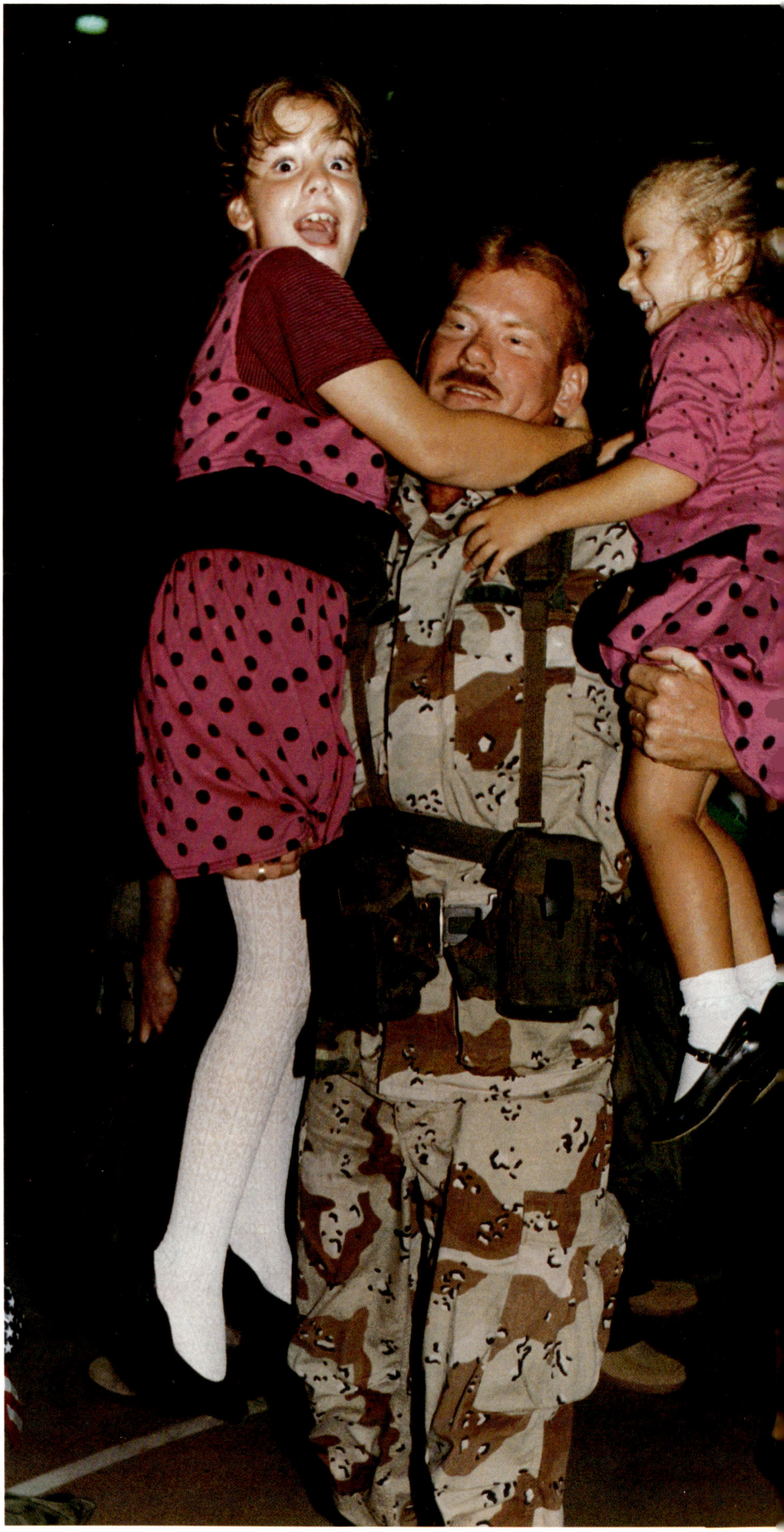

1ST CAV PAO

REUNION

Maj. Gen. John H. Tilelli Jr. leads the division in Washington D.C.'s "Victory Day" parade down Constitution Avenue and past the Lincoln Memorial on June 8.

On Broadway, New York, NY. The 1st Cav Band, led here by Sgt. First Class Gary Flake, Bandmaster, takes the Big Apple by storm, to the swaggering melody of the division song, "Garryowen."

Each under the boughs of a young Texas live oak, 12 plaques memorializing the 12 soldiers who made the highest sacrifice, were unveiled at the dedication of the 1st Cavalry Division Museum Desert Storm exhibit. Here, the family of Sgt. First Class Harold Witzke III, who fell in the fight for Kuwait.

8

"The Army must maintain a trained and ready force to meet ongoing commitments worldwide and for rapid action in unforeseeable contingencies."

— Army Focus, June 1991

Past as prologue, Army Chief of Staff Gen. Gordon Sullivan adds two campaign streamers commemorating the defense of Saudi Arabia and the liberation and defense of Kuwait to the 24 already crowning the division's colors, in a ceremony at Fort Bragg, N.C., in March 1991, as Division Commander Maj. Gen. John H. Tilelli Jr. proudly watches. Fluttering in the uncertain winds of a turbulent world, the streamers, which mark combat in four wars, affirm the wisdom of readiness. 22ND PUBLIC AFFAIRS TEAM

CONTINGENCY FORCE

"The essential foundations of the national military strategy are strategic deterrence, and defense, forward presence, crisis response, and reconstitution. These foundations of our strategy are supported by commitments to project overwhelming force to ensure decisive victory if required, maintain our technological superiority, [and] maintain a high degree of readiness to respond to regional contingencies..."

— Gen. Gordon Sullivan
Chief of Staff, United States Army

On August 6, 1990, the Army's 45-year focus on the defense of free Europe abruptly shifted 3,000 miles southeast to an entirely different continent. Prepared for the urban sprawl and the familiar plains and forests of Europe, the Army instead threw its weight onto the open, empty desert. Operation Desert Shield, like Just Cause in Panama, was a response to a regional crisis. It underscored a radically changing emphasis in U.S. defense planning, one that expanded the role of the Army.

Even as the Army's role actually increased, its most visible enemy, the Soviet-backed Warsaw Pact, collapsed. Fierce pressure was brought on U.S. lawmakers to reduce the armed forces; Americans revealed their historic dislike of large standing armies, intensified by the urgencies of a feeble economy and virulent deficits. The Republic demanded a smaller Army and, as it had for 215 years, the Army would support the Republic.

After every major conflict, the Army's reductions have left it unready for the next challenge. Post-WWI reductions led to WWII's frantic 9th hour build-up and early battlefield disasters. After 1945, the Army was dismantled, and five years later was nearly pushed into the sea in South Korea. The wreckage of Desert One in Iran symbolized the military's post-Vietnam crash.

The Soviet Union's fall invited the recurrence of disaster. By 1995, the active

The return from war meant a return to rigorous training. Pushing past pain, combat medics drag a "wounded" soldier to safety over an obstacle course designed to take them to the limits of endurance and skill as a team.

KEN HELLER

Army will be one third smaller than it was in 1991, smaller than at any time since the beginning of WWII. Yet with its Cold War victory, America enters a 21st Century threatened by the uncertainties of global arms proliferation and instability. The nation requires not a smaller Cold War Army, but an Army well-fitted to an evolving world.

This time, it will be different. The Army will enter the next century a versatile force, ready to operate in multiple environments worldwide. Vital interests most at risk will still be protected by forward stationed forces, in cooperation with host governments. Largely U.S.-based, the Army will respond to crises ranging from peacekeeping and humanitarian assistance, to war, with tailored "contingency forces," a fundamental change in focus from the extensive forward basing of the Cold War.

The 1st Cav, the Army's largest division, is at the heart of its contingency forces, equipped, poised, and ready to respond worldwide across the crisis "continuum." Indeed, the future of the First Team rides with the Army's deployable, mobile contingency forces.

The Army's deployability will be refined. Strategic lift, among Desert Shield's greatest challenges, will be enhanced through the improvement of naval and aerial lift capabilities. The expansion of materiel prepositioning, procurement of easily transportable equipment, and development of military-related infrastructures in conflict-prone areas will prove invaluable.

The Army will train jointly with sister services, and, combined with allied and friendly forces, develop and refine the skills and strengths which proved invaluable in the Gulf.

Drawing on the renewed partnership of active and reserve component elements, the reduced active Army will be able to expand quickly to fit its mission, progressing from early use of reserve component combat support elements through deployment of combat units.

And the Army will remain capable of decisive victory. Soldiers will continue to be equipped with world-class systems in sufficient quantity. Army doctrine calls for fast-paced, high-technology warfare that keeps the enemy reacting to friendly initiatives. U.S. soldiers will train under realistic conditions best exemplified by the National Training Center at Fort

Irwin, California. In the Gulf, 1st Cav troopers said repeatedly that when under fire they "simply did what [they] were taught at the NTC." U.S. soldiers — America's finest — well trained, cared for, and led, will guarantee the Army's utility to the nation.

In the end, it is the soldier who, serving selflessly as in wars and campaigns past, and in the deserts of Southwest Asia, will make the difference. As T.R. Fehrenbach so aptly wrote, "You may fly over a land forever; you may bomb it, and wipe it clean of life… but if you desire to defend it, protect it, and keep it for civilization, you must do this on the ground, the way the Roman Legions did… by putting your young men into the mud."

The troopers of the First Team will continue to be ready to make the difference. In a world bright with promise, the need for a strong Army will remain. When the nation calls, the First Team will be ready — wearing the Army's biggest patch, a big patch for big men and women who do big things.

A contingency force division, the 1st Cav is ready for crises from humanitarian assistance to war. In June 1992, 2-5 Cav soldiers trained in riot control and deployed to Guantanamo Bay, Cuba to perform security for the Haitian refugee camps. Two months later, First Team soldiers left for Kuwait to train with the Emirate's soldiers.

In June 1992, the 2nd Brigade deployed to Camp Shelby, Miss., to train National Guardsmen of the 155th Armored Brigade (the division's "round-up" brigade) during their annual training. An Army first, the program hiked readiness in the Guard, improved trainer skills in the 1st Cav.

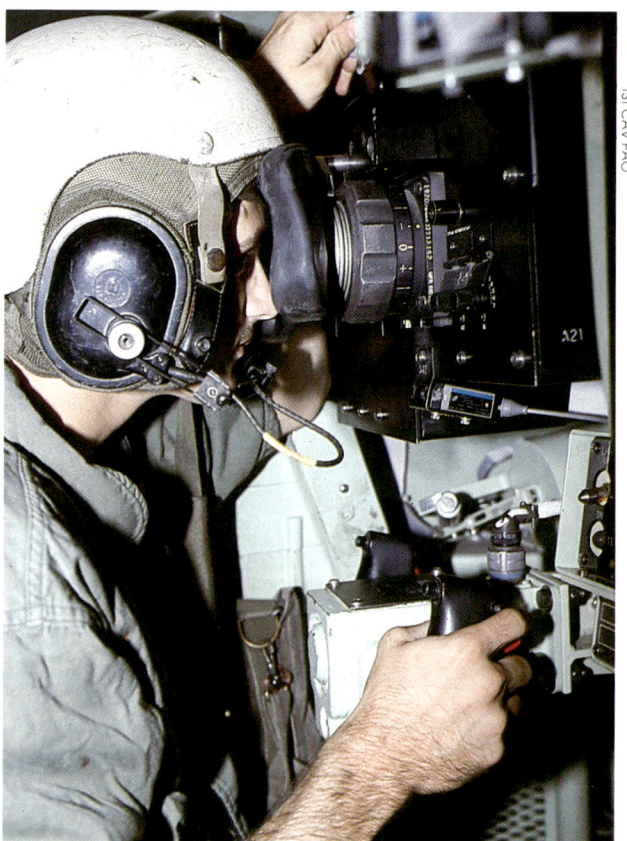

In a video gunnery "arcade," a Bradley gunner destroys his computer-image enemy. Computer simulation made extensive inroads into the domain of expensive "full-up" training. Simulators help train pilots, Abrams and Bradley crews, Stinger missile gunners, artillerymen, and even commanders and staffs, who maneuver "units" over computer-generated terrain, against electron enemies.

Under a laser-sensor halo, a Blackjack tanker returns from a laser-tag desert battle with the NTC's Opposing Force. In returning to the NTC, the division returned to the battlefield that prepared it for the Gulf and which has proven itself the Army's premium school of combat.

(Left) Like his Army, in mid-leap between the "solid" ground of the Cold War years and the uncertainty of Communism's free fall, this soldier is outward bound, with a firm grip on his direction and pace.

(Left) Training benefitted from the war's hard-won lessons. Leading a dirty mount, a 2-8 Cav "Mustang" tanker takes instructions from a chemical officer before guiding his "contaminated" tank to a decontamination site on the division's tactical gunnery training course.

(Below) On May 20, 1991, the Tiger Brigade was inactivated. The next day its soldiers reactivated the division's 3rd "Grey Wolf" Brigade. Growing further, the division added an engineer brigade in 1992. With their first shots since Kuwait, a Grey Wolf tank platoon fires simultaneously at an "enemy" company on a Fort Hood range.

9 "Faraway they battled the inner enemy of fear and won. And they set an embattled nation free. And they went to the Gulf not because it was the expedient way, but because it was the American way. Through their sacrifice as they caused brutal aggression to fall, they renewed our faith in ourselves."

— President George Bush

Each evening the ritual of "Retreat" is carried out at Army headquarters the world over. To the clear notes of a stirring bugle call, Old Glory is slowly lowered and folded, to rise again on the morrow's dawn. J.E. PHILLIPS

COMMANDERS AND COMMAND SERGEANTS MAJOR

DIVISION COMMAND GROUP
Maj. Gen. John H. Tilelli Jr., Commanding General
Brig. Gen. Josue Robles Jr., Asst. Div. Cdr., Support
Brig. Gen. Tommy R. Franks, Asst. Div. Cdr, Maneuver
Col. Leon J. LaPorte, Chief of Staff
Command Sgt. Maj. Robert Wilson, Div. Command Sgt. Maj. (Desert Shield)
Command Sgt. Maj. Gilbert Paez, Div. Command Sgt. Maj. (Desert Storm)

1ST "IRONHORSE" BRIGADE
Col. George H. Harmeyer
CSM Keyron J. Parker
2ND BATTALION, 5TH CAVALRY
Lt. Col. Thomas W. Suitt
CSM Grover F. Lehman
2ND BATTALION, 8TH CAVALRY
Lt. Col. Daniel Peterjohn
CSM Marvin W. Loris
3RD BATTALION, 32ND ARMOR
Lt. Col. Steven C. Main
CSM James A. Walker

2ND "BLACKJACK" BRIGADE
Col. Randolph W. House
CSM Ronald A. Parrett
1ST BATTALION, 5TH CAVALRY
Lt. Col. Michael W. Parker
CSM Jackson F. Palmer
1ST BATTALION, 8TH CAVALRY
Lt. Col. John C. Burch
CSM James E. Curtis
1ST BATTALION, 32ND ARMOR
Lt. Col. James R. Methered
CSM Charles M. Gee

1ST "TIGER" BRIGADE
Col. John B. Sylvester
CSM Thomas J. Calkins
3RD BATTALION, 41ST INFANTRY
Lt. Col. Walter Wojdakowski
CSM Arthur Harvey
1ST BATTALION, 67TH ARMOR
Lt. Col. Michael T. Johnson
CSM William E. McCune
3RD BATTALION, 67TH ARMOR
Lt. Col. Douglas L. Tystad
CSM Ralph Salas

4TH BATTALION, 5TH AIR DEFENSE
Lt. Col. Randall D. Harris
CSM V. Carl Strebe

8TH ENGINEER BATTALION
Lt. Col. Hans A. Van Winkle
CSM Wayne H. Hackman

DIVISION ARTILLERY
Col. James M. Gass
CSM David L. Cates
1ST BATTALION, 82ND FIELD ARTILLERY
Lt. Col. John K. Anderson
CSM Michael D. Tavares
3RD BATTALION, 82ND FIELD ARTILLERY
Lt. Col. Kenneth R. Knight
CSM Gordon C. Tolleson III
1ST BATTALION, 3RD FIELD ARTILLERY
Lt. Col. James R. Kerin, Jr.
CSM Albert J. Brodeur

AVIATION "WARRIORS" BRIGADE
Col. William D. McGill
CSM Nicholas M. Vullo
1ST SQUADRON, 7TH CAVALRY
Lt. Col. Walter L. Sharp
CSM Guillermo C. Ortiz
1ST BATTALION, 227TH AVIATION
Lt. Col. Craig D. Hackett
CSM Sam W. Starr

DIVISION "WAGONMASTERS" SUPPORT COMMAND
Col. Richard J. Fousek
CSM Albert Mallet
27TH MAIN SUPPORT BATTALION
Lt. Col. John E. Firth
CSM James A. Washington
115TH FORWARD SUPPORT BATTALION
Lt. Col. Timothy J. Wilcox
CSM Danny D. Matlock
15TH FORWARD SUPPORT BATTALION
Lt. Col. Richard A. Kaye
CSM Lincoln H. Ellis
502ND FORWARD SUPPORT BATTALION
Lt. Col. Coy R. Scroggins
CSM Ivan L. Andrus

13TH SIGNAL
Lt. Col. Edgar W. Steele
CSM Donald L. Tolbert

312TH MILITARY INTELLIGENCE BATTALION
Lt. Col. Richard N. Armstrong
CSM Lawrence W. Coonrod

1ST CAVALRY DIVISION UNITS IN DESERT SHIELD AND DESERT STORM

1ST "IRONHORSE" BRIGADE
2nd Battalion, 5th Cavalry Regiment
2nd Battalion, 8th Cavalry Regiment
3rd Battalion, 32nd Armor Regiment
Headquarters and Headquarters Company

1ST "TIGER" BRIGADE
3rd Battalion, 41st Infantry Regiment
1st Battalion, 67th Armor Regiment
3rd Battalion, 67th Armor Regiment
Headquarters and Headquarters Company

DIVISION "RED TEAM" ARTILLERY (DIVARTY)
1st Battalion, 3rd Field Artillery Regiment
1st Battalion, 82nd Field Artillery Regiment
3rd Battalion, 82nd Field Artillery Regiment
Battery A, 333rd Field Artillery Regiment
Battery A, 21st Field Artillery Regiment
Battery A, 92nd Field Artillery Regiment
Headquarters and Headquarters Battery

2ND "BLACKJACK" BRIGADE
1st Battalion, 5th Cavalry Regiment
1st Battalion, 8th Cavalry Regiment
1st Battalion, 32nd Armor Regiment
Headquarters and Headquarters Company

AVIATION "WARRIORS" BRIGADE
1st Battalion, 3rd Aviation Regiment
1st Battalion, 227th Aviation Regiment
Company D, 227th Aviation Regiment
Company E, 227th Aviation Regiment
Headquarters and Headquarters Company

DIVISION "WAGONMASTERS" SUPPORT COMMAND (DISCOM)
27th Main Support Battalion
115th Forward Support Battalion
15th Forward Support Battalion
502nd Forward Support Battalion
Company F, 227th Aviation Regiment
Headquarters and Headquarters Company

43RD CORPS SUPPORT GROUP

DIVISION "MAVERICK" TROOPS
1st Squadron, 7th Cavalry Regiment
4th Battalion, 5th Air Defense Artillery
13th Signal Battalion
312th Military Intelligence Battalion
8th Engineer Battalion
A Company, 17th Engineer Battalion
U.S. Air Force Teams 1 and 2
123/577 Engineer Detachments

545th Military Police Company
68th Chemical Company
44th Chemical Company
15th Finance Support Company
15th Personnel Service Company
1st Platoon, 502nd Military Police Company
Hqs and Hqs Company, 1st Cavalry Division
Trial Defense Service

NON-DIVISIONAL UNITS WORKING WITH THE FIRST TEAM
212th Field Artillery Brigade
75th Field Artillery Brigade
42nd Field Artillery Brigade
59th Military Police Company
413th Civil Affairs Company
159th Mobile Army Surgical Hospital

4th and 13th Public Affairs Teams
Battery C, 26th Field Artillery
300th Adjutant General Postal Company
Ground Surveillance Radar Section, 522nd Military Intelligence
Air Traffic Control Section, 2-58th Aviation
Arcent Liaison Team

(Note: Units are listed here with complete unit designation, in "pure" form. In practice, maneuver units cross attached elements, giving them a mix of infantry and armor. Further, depending on the mission requirements, they were supplemented with combat support and service support elements. Called "task organizing," a unit so altered was called a "task force." Thus, 2nd Battalion, 5th Cavalry (2-5 Cav, a mechanized infantry battalion), exchanging a company of Bradleys with 3rd Battalion, 32nd Armor (a tank battalion), for an element of tanks, was then referred to as Task Force 2-5 Cav. Maneuver brigades were routinely supplemented with elements from DIVARTY, DISCOM, Division Troops, and even non-divisional units.

SILVER STAR

The Silver Star is the nation's third highest military award for valor, given for gallantry under fire. The following 1st Cavalry Division and Tiger Brigade soldiers received the Silver Star:

Spec. Jonathan Ray Alston
Capt. Roy Bierwirth
Capt. Matthew Brand
Staff Sgt. Jesse Brown
Pfc. Craig Burton
Capt. James Burton
Staff Sgt. Christopher Cichon
Cpl. Calvin Clark
Pfc. Ardon Cooper
Staff Sgt. Michael Duda
2nd Lt. Matthew Elledge
2nd Lt. Allan Fraser
1st Lt. Frederick Hager
Capt. Timothy Harnois
Col. Randolph House
Capt. Michael Kershaw
Maj. Matthew Klimow
1st Lt. Joseph Layton
Staff Sgt. Rafael Martinez
1st Lt. Dale Ringler
1st Lt. Todd Rodeheaver
Pvt. II Steven Lee Shafer
Pfc. Daniel Sheets
1st Lt. Daniel Stempniak
Col. John Sylvester
Lt. Col. Douglas Tystad
Capt. Gary Walters
Maj. Volney Warner
Sgt. Ronald Williams
Sgt. First Class Harold Witzke III
Lt. Col. Walter Wojdakowski

DISTINGUISHED FLYING CROSS

The Distinguished flying cross is the highest aviation award earned for bravery while flying aircraft while in conflict with the enemy. First Team soldiers who earned the DFC are:

1st Lt. Robert Johnston
CW2 Edward Sanderlin

CHRONOLOGY

AUGUST 2
Iraq invades Kuwait
AUGUST 6
United States embarks on Operation Desert Shield
SEPTEMBER 16
1st Cavalry Division airlift to Saudi Arabia begins
OCTOBER 17
Last main body planeload lands.
29 NOVEMBER
U.N. Security Council Resolution 678 authorizes use of force if Iraq not out by January 15
12 JANUARY
Congress grants President Bush authority to use U.S. military force
JANUARY 13-17
1st Cavalry Division defends Wadi al Batin: First U.S. defense along Saudi/Iraq border.
JANUARY 16 (JANUARY 17 IN THE GULF)
Air campaign begins

FEBRUARY 7-25
1st Cavalry conducts Theater deception, covering movement of VII Corps and deceiving Iraq into believing main attack planned for Wadi al Batin

1st Cavalry Division fires first Copperhead laser-guided munition and multiple launched rockets of war
1st Cavalry Division conducts first artillery raids of war
1st Cavalry Division conducts first mobile ground combat of war

FEBRUARY 24
Ground campaign begins
1st "Tiger" Bde attacks
FEBRUARY 26-27
1st Cav attacks to join VII Corps
FEBRUARY 28
After 100 hours, a cease-fire halts the ground war
MARCH 9
1st Cavalry Division begins redeployment to the United States.
APRIL 7
Iraq accepts permanent cease-fire conditions.

IN APPRECIATION

At the risk of committing the unforgivable and neglecting a name, the authors deeply thank the following people for their great assistance in recording this story:

Brig. Gen. Randolph House, Col. George Casey Jr., Col. Richard Fousek, Col. Lawrence Schneider, Lt. Col. Clint Anderson, Lt. Col. Robert Bryant, Lt. Col. Norman Greczyn, Lt. Col. Pat Hanley, Lt. Col. Michael Starry, Lt. Col. Timothy J. Wilcox, Maj. Charles Aycock, Maj. Linda Christ, Maj. Alan Dunavan, Maj. Marline Johnson, Maj. Paul Loveless, Maj. Mike Masterson, Maj. Susan Roma, Maj. Gil Steinke, Maj. Marshall Townsend, Capt. Allen Batschelet, Capt. Hampton Hite, Capt. Michael Klingele, Capt. David Lemelin, Capt. Charles Watts, 1st Lt. Kenneth Cary, 1st Lt. Daniel Corey, 1st Lt. Kent Kildow, 1st Lt. Mark Soloman, Chief Warrant Officer Carlos Keith, Chief Warrant Officer John Kelsey, Chief Warrant Officer Stan Pauley, Chief Warrant Officer Gerald Walters, Sergeant Major Charles Hatten, 1st Sgt. Terry Tolar, Sgt. First Class Dennis Heim, Sgt. First Class Jose Luciano, Sgt. First Class Steven Wojciechowski, Sgt. Gordon Ziegler, Steve Elfers, Joseph Galloway, Duane Laverty, *Killeen Daily Herald*, Killeen Chamber of Commerce, Dave Martin, Steve Raymer, Rick and Geri Shelp, the Center for Military History, the Fort Hood Training Support Center, the staffs of the Hallmark and Office restaurants, and our families.

Special Appreciation to:

Maj. Gen. and Mrs. John H. Tilelli, Jr.

Brig. Gen. Arthur Junot and the 1st Cavalry Division Association

Col. Leon J. LaPorte, advisor

Maj. Randy Brown, editor, *1st Cavalry Division Command Report* on the Southwest Asia Campaign

Don Moore, Illustrator, for the maps, (817) 554-8008

The First Team Public Affairs Office; members serving in Southwest Asia: Capt. Pamela Keeton, Capt. Reginald Smith, Master Sgt. Thomas Fuller, Sgt. Rob Tankersley, Sgt. Britt Toalson, Sgt. Dean Welch, Spec. Mark Bookout, Spec. Janie DeLaCruz, Spec. Curtis "Zak" Hocom, Spec. Daniel Maloney, Spec. Jose Zuniga.

Joining since SWA: Capt. Douglas Hinckley, Capt. Reginald Williams, Sgt. Kenneth Heller, Spec. Lisa Prentiss, Spec. Brian Le Vassaur and Pfc. Larry Butterfas.

And especially, the soldiers and families of the 1st Cavalry Division, who, as always, *are* the story...